THE EARLY YEARS OF
PEACE CORPS
IN
AFGHANISTAN

THE EARLY YEARS OF PEACE CORPS IN AFGHANISTAN

A Promising Time

FRANCES HOPKINS IRWIN

AND

WILL A. IRWIN

A PEACE CORPS WRITERS BOOK

The Early Years of Peace Corps in Afghanistan
A Promising Time

A Peace Corps Writers Book
An Imprint of Peace Corps Worldwide

Printed in the United States of America
by Peace Corps Writers of Oakland, California.

Front Cover: Hazrat Ali Shrine in Mazar-i-Sharif, photo by Bob Steiner; Back Cover: An irrigation canal in Logar, photo by Frances Hopkins.

For more information, contact peacecorpsworldwide@gmail.com.

Peace Corps Writers and the Peace Corps Writers colophon are trademarks of PeaceCorpsWorldWide.org.

ISBN: 1935925369

ISBN-13:   978-1-935925-36-1

Library of Congress Control Number: 2013956993

Peace Corps Writers Oakland, CA

First Peace Corps Writers Edition, February 2014

For all those working to build
another promising time in Afghanistan

CONTENTS

Part II Voices of Volunteers

FOREWORD

In my official capacity in the Afghan Ministry of Education, responsible for technical and vocational education and teacher training in the 1960s, I had the privilege of cooperating with the American Peace Corps. The volunteers were largely young idealistic Americans, who had embarked on a journey of adventure and service. They were enthusiastic, learned the local language, tried to understand the culture of the host country, and coped with sometimes difficult living and working conditions in Afghanistan. The volunteers were guided by an able and wise man of culture, Robert Steiner, who spoke fluent Dari and maintained excellent relations with the ministry. Eventually he became a life-time friend of Afghanistan.

Fran and Will Irwin were among the volunteers who served there, and now they have written this fascinating success story of early years of Peace Corps in Afghanistan. The authors have interviewed Robert Steiner and some of the volunteers, researched and collected an enormous amount of testimonies and documents related to Peace Corps activities in the country. They have described the social and political changes in Afghanistan in the 1960s and the changing political climate in the United States during that period. The Peace Corps started with only nine volunteers in 1962 in Kabul and this number reached 200 in 1966, with half of the volunteers working in the Provinces. While many worked as teachers, they also served in the medical field and administration. A total of 1650 volunteers had served in Afghanistan by 1979, when the volunteers left Afghanistan, under unfortunate circumstances.

The authors have reflected the overall positive experiences of the volunteers. In spite of the challenges in performing their duties, the volunteers served well and returned to the United States with valuable experiences. During their service, they also tried to interact with a conservative Afghan community. Many continued to follow the developments in Afghanistan. The Friends of Afghanistan in the USA currently has about 450 members. The credit for the success of Peace Corps goes to the idealism and commitment of the volunteers but also to the philosophy and leadership of the Director of Peace Corps, who advised the volunteers to work within the Afghanistan system and culture.

The authors have prepared a book of historic significance for the Peace Corps. I might say that throughout my career in Afghanistan and at UNESCO, I had the fortune to collaborate with many academics and professionals. Working with young American Peace Corps volunteers has been a very special and unique experience for me. I believe the inspiration of creating the Peace Corps by President John F. Kennedy was imaginative and important for international cooperation because it mobilized the energy and enthusiasm of young Americans on a voluntary basis to participate in the development of other countries. They helped the host countries, acquired invaluable experience and enriched their lives. This experience also benefited the United States international relations. The Peace Corps service reflected the idealism and hopes of humanity for peace and solidarity around the world.

Saif R. Samady, Ph.D.
Former Deputy Minister of Education in Afghanistan
London October 2013

PREFACE

As Volunteers who served in Afghanistan (Fran in Group IV from mid-1964 to mid-1967 and Will in Group VIII in 1966 and 1967), we were intrigued with the stories that Robert L. (Bob) Steiner, the first director, told about the early days at a session organized by Friends of Afghanistan during the 50th Anniversary of Peace Corps in September 2011. We learned that the Steiners had not recorded their memories of Peace Corps in Afghanistan between 1962 and 1966, and we offered to do that.

At Bob's request, the next step was to prepare a list of questions. To help us develop that list, Rosalind Pace shared her memories as a member of Group I. We reviewed our letters to our families and also three years of the *Kabul Times* newspaper where Fran served as a Volunteer and Will, after teaching English at the Afghan Air Authority, also worked. In December 2011, we took our questions and a digital recorder to Lancaster, Pennsylvania, for conversation over two days with Bob and Sherry (Margaret) Steiner at their home. We found that Bob had already contacted early Afghan staff member Sami Noor, who had emailed his answers to several questions from Germany. We were encouraged by his enthusiasm for the project and his positive memories of working with Bob and with Peace Corps Volunteers: "The time, though short, with Peace Corps had a very deep influence throughout my life – until today." The extensively edited (by us and the Steiners) and reorganized transcript of our conversation became the starting point for this book.

We also got encouragement from Steiner sons Chip and John. We drew from comments by Chip on the transcript of the conversation with his parents and some of his own writing and from an article John wrote about his father's life for the Friends of Afghanistan newsletter. John also provided digital copies of photographs taken by Bob and Sherry in Afghanistan. We have enjoyed the continuing conversation with the Steiners and appreciated their patience as they dealt with further questions over the next two years.

Once we had the framework, we looked for ways to check the facts and provide more detail. We searched our own boxes of materials from Afghanistan for documents such as the handbook and newsletters and encouraged others to do so. Linda Abrams (Group V) located additional Peace Corps Afghanistan newsletters from 1965 and 1966. Will made several trips to the National Archives in College Park, Maryland, to explore the far from complete but sometimes surprising records. Stephen Nadler (Group VI) provided documents from an earlier foray into the Archives. Stanley Meisler, who was deputy director of the Peace Corps Office of Evaluation and Research in the mid-1960s and wrote *When the World Calls: The Inside Story of the Peace Corps and its First Fifty Years*, gave us insight into the evaluation process as well as his experience with material in the National Archives. We found that the Peace Corps Digital Library has continued to grow and now serves as an accessible source for some Peace Corps documents including annual budget presentations as well as stories and photographs searchable by country.

Our contacts with other returned Volunteers and staff multiplied as we looked for ways to include a range of perspectives.

Bob Pearson, an English teacher in Group I and later Afghan desk officer and a training officer, read the transcribed conversation. He clarified several confusions and shared his own stories. In a number of cases, we drew on the publications and presentations of others. David Fleishhacker encouraged us in using quotations from his memoir *Lessons from Afghanistan,* in which he describes the country he got to know as a teacher in Group I. He suggested an additional key source after reading an early draft of the manuscript. Dennis Aronson (Group III) provided a presentation which describes the experience he and his wife Susan had in Ghazni. David and Elizabeth McGaffey (Group IV) gave us permission to use excerpts from their letters home from Farah. Leonard Oppenheim (Group IV) encouraged us by digging out paper records, sharing letters of his experience in Kandahar, and reviewing the manuscript. Betsy Thomas Amin-Arsala (Group VI) contributed memories from serving in Herat and also made editorial and substantive suggestions on several drafts of the manuscript. We sparred with Saul Helfenbein (Group VIII) about the relation of Peace Corps to development as he wrote memoir about the health development business and also read a late version of our manuscript.

We reconnected with Robert S. McClusky, who served as deputy director from 1963 to 1966, and shared memories—and the present—over several lunches with him and Nancy on our trips to Ohio to see family. We drew the story of the reception for Volunteers held by the Royal Family in 1964 from a presentation he made in Oberlin. He provided the photographs of the reception. He also commented on and contributed to a late draft and put us in touch with Pat Sullivan Meyers, an early desk officer in Peace Corps Washington, who told us about working in Peace Corps Washington in the first years.

The ideas for what pieces to include in the section on Voices of Volunteers emerged gradually. Janet (Walback)

Butler (Group VIII), co-editor of *Mister, where you go?*, welcomed our suggestion to include copies of contributions to this booklet. She and Stuart Schmidt (Group V) also provided photographs. Jon Wicklund (Group II) shared memories from serving as a Volunteer and staff member. As we completed the manuscript, he forwarded the 1964 collection of stories on Afghanistan that a friend looking for stories on Peace Corps in Colombia had found. He had forgotten that he had compiled it 50 years ago.

We are grateful to Dr. Saif R. Samady, who as a director and then deputy minister in the Afghan Ministry of Education played an important role in enabling Peace Corps Volunteers to serve effectively in Afghanistan. He responded immediately to Bob Steiner's inquiry about writing the Foreword and also provided the link to his history of education in Afghanistan written while working with UNESCO. We especially thank our one-time colleague and long-time friend Nour Rahimi for reviewing the manuscript, drawing on his experience as a reporter and editor in Afghanistan (including editor-in-chief of *Anis* and *Islah,* Dec. 1972-July 1973, and editor of the *Kabul Times,* 1973-1978) and later an international broadcaster at the Voice of America. He served as a valuable sounding board and saved us from several errors. He also suggested an additional piece to include in Voices of Volunteers.

The benefit for us in writing this story has been in getting in touch with so many people associated with Peace Corps—some of whom we knew and others we did not. We are grateful to them all for their contributions. We know there are still many other stories. We hope this one, told from the view of the early staff and Volunteers, will inspire others to share their own perspectives on the encounters of Afghans and Americans that came out of the Peace Corps. We thank John Coyne and Marian Haley Beil, who have encouraged Peace Corps writers for more than four decades, an effort that now includes the series Peace Corps Writers of which this book is a part.

Telling the tale has also resulted in rewarding conversations with other friends. For instance, a visit with his daughter Sarah (our daughter's college roommate) on the weekend of the 2012 inauguration turned into an opportunity to exchange experiences in writing and publishing family history and other stories with Dan Crofts, a professor of history at The College of New Jersey, and his subsequent review of the manuscript.

We have been extremely fortunate in the support from all members of our families over the years. They have provided the roots that enabled our wings. We especially thank Angene and Jack Wilson, Fran's sister and brother-in-law, with whom we share the Peace Corps experience. They have inspired us with their own writing about Peace Corps: first, letters home as Volunteers in Liberia; later, letters from Sierra Leone, where Jack was associate director in Bo, and then from Fiji, where Jack was director. More recently, we have learned from serving as early readers as they wrote *Voices from the Peace Corps: 50 Years of Kentucky Volunteers* and Angene put together *Africa on My Mind: Educating Americans for Fifty Years Living Peace Corps' Third Goal*. We improved our computer skills thanks to patient help from Fran's brother Giles as he disentangled us from many snags. Our daughter Amanda Irwin Wilkins demonstrated her personal and professional skills in helping writers say what they mean and revise relentlessly.

Fran and Will Irwin
Bethesda, Maryland, September 2013

INTRODUCTION: A PROMISING TIME

In 1962, the first nine American Peace Corps Volunteers arrived in Kabul. Before Peace Corps left in 1979, about 1650 Volunteers had served in Afghanistan. This is the story of the first four years and how Peace Corps found a way to work and live within the Afghan culture and economy in a promising time.

We wanted to know more about the period between the summer of 1962 and mid-1966 during which Peace Corps Afghanistan grew from the first small group, all living in Kabul, to 200 Volunteers, with close to half living in the provinces. How had a program initially viewed so skeptically by Afghans and the international community in Kabul found its way? How had this fledgling U.S. government program succeeded in Afghanistan?

Why tell the story of Peace Corps Afghanistan's early years now, after the Soviets and the mujahideen, after a civil war, after Taliban rule, after more than ten years of U.S. and NATO presence? For us, and even more for our Afghan teachers, colleagues, students, and friends, the violence of the recent decades and the challenges of the present can overwhelm. Why tell the story fifty years later in a time when many Americans feel the U.S. must focus on needs at home? Besides, the Peace Corps was just a small group in Afghanistan for what was one short moment in the thousands of years of people coming and going at this crossroads in Asia.

Our answer to the question of "why now?" is that we want to contribute to the record of engaging peacefully across cultures. We want to document what Peace Corps Volunteers learned in Afghanistan about how diversity among people can be used to enrich cultures, rather than homogenize or destroy them (as Steiner once wrote). How a small number of Americans came as guests, lived as foreigners, taught and nursed (and did many other jobs), made friends, and made a difference in the lives of some Afghans—as they made a difference in ours. Recognizing this is a very different time, we want to encourage reflection on and use of that experience.

We arrived at what seemed a promising time in both Afghanistan and the United States. Both countries were reaching out while trying to broaden freedoms at home. For some Afghans in Kabul, especially looking back, the 1960s were a golden age; for many more around the country it was a time of change and mostly peace. In the United States, promise was manifold—if not manifest—from developments in science and health to demands for civil rights and economic opportunities. A new generation of leaders was introducing initiatives in foreign policy like the Peace Corps, which provided an opportunity, especially for the increasing number of college-educated youth, to experience the "real world," to combine adventure with using skills gained in their prosperous country to work with people of other cultures to overcome—as President Kennedy put it in his inaugural address—"the common enemies of man: tyranny, poverty, disease, and war itself."

Political competition, both within countries and among them, both overt and more submerged, continued. Yes, the U.S. was competing in the Cold War. Yes, Afghanistan was using its stance as a non-aligned country to obtain as much technical assistance as possible. But other motives were also at work. Might there be ways to engage besides practicing traditional diplomacy, seeking intelligence, and bearing arms? Development assistance was growing. Could it be more than new buildings and equipment that were unlikely to be maintained? Might citizens of different countries, working with each other every day, experience an inkling of what it might mean to become citizens of the world?

Peace Corps stories reflect who we were when we arrived, our experiences in the country, and the particular times. Working on this project, we were reminded how important it is to keep in mind that social and political changes in Afghanistan and in the United States, even within just this four-year span of 1962-66, were dramatic, and they were followed by many more changes in the 13 additional years that Peace Corps remained.

Change was coming to Kabul in 1962. Women were teaching in the schools. About ten percent of students at the university were women. Some streets had been paved, though traffic was as likely to be camels and donkeys as cars and trucks. Access to electricity was increasing. Radio was the important means of communication; there was no television. The government monitored contact of Afghans with foreigners and required foreigners traveling outside the capital to get its permission. The independence of India—and the partition creating Pakistan—still seemed recent. Tourists numbered in the hundreds annually rather than the tens of thousands, including world travelers and Pakistani shoppers, who were coming by the end of the decade. Kabul was not yet the lively international city it was to become, at least on the surface, for many urban Afghans and for foreigners, in the later 1960s and early 1970s.

In the United States, the civil rights movement reached its peak as the first eight groups of Volunteers came to Afghanistan. The decisions of young American men were beginning to be influenced by the military draft, but the major escalation in Vietnam, protests against the war, and the killing of Martin Luther King and Robert F. Kennedy were in the future. Socially what was later called "paternalism" was still common in American colleges and was reflected in the Peace Corps as it began. Some early documents referred to the Volunteers as "boys" and "girls" and older supervisors might still be addressed as "Mr." Although President Kennedy established a Commission on the Status of Women in 1961, *The Feminine Mystique* wasn't published until 1963. The Foreign Service was not yet accepting "married ladies" and news magazines did not hire women as writers, only as researchers. Drug use did not even come up in the first group's training.

The early Volunteers served in Afghanistan during a constitutional monarchy and as a new parliament was elected and convened. What had seemed a promising turn toward a "new democracy" and more balanced development across the country soon ran into headwinds. Volunteers in the later 1960s served as discontent with the Afghan government grew and those who came in the early 1970s in a time of famine in some sections of the country. Volunteers served in the Republic after former Prime Minister Daoud exiled his cousin King Mohammed Zahir in July 1973 and tried to establish one-party rule as several communist and Islamist groups contended for power. Daoud and his family were killed during the April 1978 communist coup. The last Volunteers departed after the killing of the U.S. Ambassador in February 1979. The Soviet invasion came in December of that year.

We tell the story of the early years of Peace Corps in Afghanistan in two parts. The first presents the story chronologically based on our conversation with the Steiners, along with contributions from a dozen other staff and Volunteers. The second part provides voices of the Volunteers as they got to know the people of Afghanistan. These voices are presented in three collections of pieces, mostly written by Volunteers at the time they were serving in Afghanistan. They are followed by a discussion of the sources we used and also a list of the growing number of Peace Corps Afghanistan stories.

PART I

Our conversation with Bob and Sherry Steiner frames the story of the first four years of Peace Corps in Afghanistan. Woven into the conversation are contributions from other staff and Volunteers and material drawn from newsletters and documents.

After setting the scene in Afghanistan and the United States, we focus primarily on how it was that the initial program of nine Volunteers all in Kabul grew to over 200 in all areas of the country between 1962 and 1966. What were the early decisions about how the Volunteers would live and work in ways that enabled them get to know Afghans and support the local economy? What activities helped Volunteers move beyond the status of "guests"? What were the indications of change in the relationship among Afghans and Volunteers? What issues arose in the second two years as the politics in both countries shifted? What did Volunteers learn about being the personal link between cultures—in the ambiguous position of being influenced by another culture even as they influenced it?

Not able to find the information elsewhere, we used the Peace Corps Afghanistan newsletters and the handbook to compile two lists as markers for the conversation. The first describes the eight groups of Volunteers that arrived between 1962 and 1966—where they trained, when they arrived and departed, types of jobs in which they worked, and locations of service in Afghanistan. The second lists staff members. These lists and a copy of a 1964 brochure describing Peace Corps Afghanistan appear following the conversation along with the References.

CHAPTER 1 A MOMENT OF OPENNESS

The Peace Corps arrived in Afghanistan in 1962 at a moment of openness in each of two very different countries on opposite sides of the earth. In Central Asia, just south of what was then the Soviet Union, King Mohammed Zahir was about to introduce an experiment with democracy as Afghanistan explored ways to modernize and reclaim its historic role as a continental crossroads. Across the globe, John F. Kennedy had won the presidency of the United States in 1960, describing a New Frontier and encouraging citizens to prove that their country could compete with the Communist system around the world. At the same time a civil rights struggle was growing at home.

Afghanistan had declared itself a non-aligned nation. Its leaders were seeking technical assistance in building their country from both sides in the Cold War.[1] The U.S. had reexamined its policy toward Afghanistan in 1956. A cable at that time explained that the goal of the U.S. was to keep the country independent, forestalling its absorption into the Soviet orbit and deterring the Soviets from using Afghanistan as a way to extend their influence into South Asia. To achieve this goal, the cable listed activities ranging from building air transportation, road links to Pakistan, and vehicle maintenance facilities to sending university education teams to teach English and agriculture and continuing work on the irrigation project in the Helmand Valley.[2] Kennedy had introduced a new element into relations with countries like Afghanistan when he pledged in his inaugural address the best efforts of the U.S. to help people help themselves to fight poverty across the globe and established the Peace Corps as one way to fulfill that pledge.

When Sherry Steiner and the three Steiner sons landed at the Kabul airport, they immediately experienced one indication of both the competition fueled by the Cold War and the need for technical training. They saw a modern structure built by the Soviet Union but were steered to a small mud-walled building where soldiers searched their bags before letting them enter the capital city. As Chip Steiner, then 14, recalls: "The new airport in Kabul was built when we got there in 1962 but it wasn't being used. I can remember this distinctly because the situation was exactly the same in Kandahar where we had stopped for repairs on the way. There was the new American-built airport and right next to it the Quonset hut that actually served as the terminal building." Afghanistan was carefully balancing American and Soviet assistance, but it was easier to get modern equipment and construct new facilities than to develop the skills to operate and maintain them.

Bob Steiner had arrived in Afghanistan a few weeks before his family to lay the groundwork for Peace Corps. Kabul was simmering with social, economic, and political change that fall of 1962. More Afghans were graduating from university faculties in Kabul and returning from education abroad.[3] They sometimes collided with the increasing number of technical advisors from around the world. Some women were studying at the university, teaching, working in government offices and as radio announcers and flight attendants. Led by the royal family and wives of government officials, they had

had the choice to appear in public without the veil since 1959.[4] The Women's Welfare Society held a first gathering of leading women from all over the country in 1962.[5] Prime Minister Daoud had announced a Second Five-Year Plan focused on mining and manufacturing (the Soviets had found gas in the north), agriculture, irrigation, communications, and transportation. At the same time, efforts were underway to mediate disagreement that had once more flared between Afghanistan and Pakistan over the future of the Pashtun tribes that lived on both sides of the border, called the Durand line and drawn in 1893 in the time of British India.

In the spring of 1963, King Mohammed Zahir edged aside his first cousin Daoud, who had served as prime minister for a decade, and named the first commoner to serve as prime minister. The drafting of a new constitution got underway. Adopted the next year, it provided for separation of powers, formation of political parties, equal rights for men and women, and secret and direct ballot for parliamentary elections.[6] An agreement with Pakistan stopped fighting on the border—for the moment—and reopened important trade routes that summer.

In the United States, as the Peace Corps was getting started, demands for civil rights were growing at restaurants, hotels, stores, theatres, schools and universities, and at the ballot box. Activists and college students boarded buses as freedom riders to desegregate interstate transportation in southern states in the spring and summer of 1961. President Kennedy used the National Guard to enable black students to enter state universities, first in Mississippi in 1962 and then in Alabama in 1963. In August 1963, Martin Luther King inspired not only the 250,000 participating in the March on Washington for Jobs and Freedom but millions more listening on the radio or watching on television with his "I Have a

Dream" speech. At the same time, U.S. competition with the Soviet Union was taking many forms—deciding in May 1961 to go to the moon before the end of the decade, responding to the building of the Berlin Wall in August 1961 and then to the placement of missiles in Cuba in October 1962, and signing of the ban on nuclear testing in October 1963.

The Peace Corps was established with unusual rapidity for a U.S. government institution. In the last weeks of his 1960 campaign, Kennedy drew on his own experience in other countries and long-discussed ideas of many others to suggest a fresh approach to Cold War competition. On October 14, he challenged waiting students at an after-midnight rally at the University of Michigan to show that their country could compete by contributing their skills around the world: "How many of you who are going to be doctors are willing to spend your days in Ghana? Technicians or engineers, how many of you are willing to work in the Foreign Service and spend your lives traveling around the world? On your willingness to do that, not merely to serve one year or two years in the service, but on your willingness to contribute part of your life to this country, I think will depend the answer whether a free society can compete."[7]

Kennedy was drawing not only on the current interest in the idea of a program like the Peace Corps—the name was first used in proposed legislation offered by Senator Hubert Humphrey and Representative Henry Reuss earlier that year—but on the long history of young people serving others. In their report on the feasibility of a Youth Corps prepared for Congress, a Colorado State University group found dozens of organizations with such programs including the International Voluntary Service, the American Friends Service Committee, the Experiment in International Living, and the Thomasites, who had taught

English in the Philippines.[8] The history went back through many private organizations to William James' 1910 pamphlet, "The Moral Equivalent of War," and to the experience of missionaries.[9]

After receiving an enthusiastic "yes" in the form of a deluge of letters in response to his question at the Michigan rally, Kennedy used an address in San Francisco a few weeks later to propose that U.S. foreign policy activities

> . . . be supplemented by a peace corps of talented young men and women, willing and able to serve their country in this fashion for 3 years as an alternative or as a supplement to peacetime selective service [applause], well qualified through rigorous standards, well trained in the languages, skills, and customs they will need to know. . . . I am convinced that the pool of people in this country of ours anxious to respond to the public service is greater than it has ever been in our history. I am convinced that our men and women, dedicated to freedom, are able to be missionaries, not only for freedom and peace, but join in a worldwide struggle against poverty and disease and ignorance. . . . I think this country in the 1960's can start to move forward again, can demonstrate what a free society, freely moving and working can do. [Applause.][10]

In his inaugural address, after the now familiar exhortation—"My fellow Americans, ask not what your country can do for you—ask what you can do for your country"—Kennedy placed the idea of a U.S. peace corps in a larger context: "My fellow citizens of the world, ask not what America will do for you, but what together we can do for the freedom of man."[11] Within the first months of 1961, he asked his brother-in-law Sargent Shriver to take the lead in starting the Peace Corps, and on March 1 it was established as an independent agency by an executive order.[12] In September, after intensive lobbying by Shriver, Congress adopted the Peace Corps Act to promote world peace and friendship with three broad purposes:

- To help people of interested countries meet their need for trained men and women;
- To promote better understanding of Americans on the part of the peoples served;
- To promote better understanding of other peoples on the part of Americans.[13]

Congress appropriated $30 million dollars for Peace Corps' first year. By October of 1961, 400 Volunteers were already serving in countries including Colombia, Chile, Ghana, Nigeria, Pakistan, the Philippines, Tanganyika, and the West Indies.[14] The program in Afghanistan would start the following year.

CHAPTER 2 A PERSIAN-SPEAKING CHICKEN FARMER IN VERMONT

In the summer of 1962, Bob Steiner was raising chickens in Vershire, Vermont, a village of about 235 people. He and Sherry had moved there with their family four years before. He was ready for a break from day-to-day grappling with the bureaucracy during the 1950s, first as a cultural officer at the U.S. Embassy in Iran and then with several organizations including American Friends of the Middle East. A friend from Steiner's embassy service in Iran was in Vershire, raising chickens. He knew Bob wasn't going back to Iran because his father was ill and encouraged him to move to Vermont.

Steiner had never farmed before, and he had to learn how to raise chickens and sell eggs. The Steiners' three sons attended elementary grades in a two-room schoolhouse in Vershire, their daughter attended high school in Bradford. To help make ends meet, and to allay the boredom of raising chickens, Steiner served as a tax assessor and taught a math course and a history course at the high school, introducing the students to *The New York Times*. The Steiners also built cottages on their farm to rent and a little ski slope as other sources of income.

Steiner had been born in Iran (then Persia) and lived the first 16 years of his life there. His father taught math and economics at Alborz College in Tehran. Steiner had learned to speak Persian (Farsi) and experienced the culture. On landing in Boston for his first visit to the United States at age five, he had observed to his father his surprise that everyone talked in English. He had served as a Navy fighter pilot in the Pacific during World War II, and then earned a Master of International Affairs degree from Columbia University. He had studied math and physics in getting his undergraduate degree at the College of Wooster (in Ohio) in 1942, but the Columbia admissions officer spotted his promise and Steiner worked hard to get through the program, taking courses in history, sociology and international law.

When anyone from the outside world appeared in Vershire, word traveled fast among Steiner and his friends. In the summer of 1962, Roy Hoopes, who had written a guide to Peace Corps, came to visit.

Bob Steiner *Hoopes, who knew Sargent Shriver, returned to Washington and told Sarge there was a Persian-speaking chicken farmer in Vermont. Sarge had an ear for the unusual, and, within days, I got a call from the Peace Corps saying that Shriver would like to meet me. I gladly and readily accepted the invitation because the idea of the Peace Corps had great appeal. It was an opportunity to respond to the Kennedy allure while, quite frankly, escaping the oppression of chickens. Within the week, Peace Corps staff had scheduled a luncheon meeting for me with Shriver. After I took a shower to remove the barnyard odors, I was off to D.C. for the meeting—it was at a street-level restaurant near the Peace Corps office.*

Frankly, I was not entirely pleased with Shriver. He and I were different personalities. He was a salesman, and I'm not. But apparently I met with his approval because within a few days a telephone call advised me that Shriver would like me to go either to Iran as part of the

*staff there or to Afghanistan, to start a program there. I
immediately said I wanted to go to Afghanistan, because
I'd never been there and the challenge of starting a new
program in a country I'd never seen was irresistible.*

That was how Bob Steiner became the person to build a
bridge between Afghanistan and the United States at this moment of openness to the world in both countries. To establish
and serve as director of Peace Corps Afghanistan, he brought
his knowledge of the culture and language from growing up in
Iran, academic training in international affairs, much of a decade working in cultural affairs with countries in the region,
plus the years making a life in Vermont.

**Peace Corps Director Sargent Shriver (left) arrives in Kabul
with Bob Steiner (right) in January 1964 to visit the program in
Afghanistan. Charles McClure, director of the U.S. AID mission
in Afghanistan, is in the middle. Ambassador John Steeves is
partially obscured to Shriver's left.** (*Credit: Sherry Steiner*)

When he arrived in Washington, Steiner learned that his first task was to push the U.S. Embassy in Afghanistan to get the formal agreement between the two countries completed. Thus the timing for Bob and his family's trip to Kabul was uncertain. Their departure became an adventure of its own with two false starts.

Bob Steiner *I was in D.C. in response to Peace Corps' urgent calls to come on down as soon as I could. I arrived only to learn that there was no Afghan-U.S. agreement for the Peace Corps program in Afghanistan! So, what to do about this, I asked, and was told that the U.S. Ambassador in Kabul was being urged to get this done.*

I found Peace Corps Washington to be a heady place. With Shriver as the brother-in-law of President Kennedy, all sorts of luminaries were coming in and going out, while the press was pushing for news. The result seemed like absolute chaos, very exciting, but a sharp contrast to the serenity of Vermont. We would cable the ambassador and ask when the program was starting. And the Embassy would say: "Well, we don't have an agreement with Afghanistan yet." I knew enough about bureaucracy to know how to put a little fire in people. So, I said to the Peace Corps: "Just wire—cable him—and tell him I'm on such-and-such a plane and will be there at such-and-such a time."

This was tried, generating frantic cabled replies—"not yet, don't send him, it's not ready." I think this happened about three times. Meanwhile, Sherry in Pennsylvania—Huntingdon, Pennsylvania—was waiting for me to get the approval from Afghanistan. I would call her after we would send these cables to the field and say, "Sherry, we're leaving on Monday." She would hustle and get her parents—who were frantic, thinking I was mad to be on this wild endeavor—to load her and the three boys into the car and take off on the Pennsylvania Turnpike.

Her father was a law-abiding man who would never break a single rule. Meanwhile, at Peace Corps in Washington, we would get a negative from Kabul. Then the Peace Corps would call the state police in Pennsylvania asking them "Please find her car and stop it." In those days, when anybody in Washington related to Kennedy would call state officials, there was immediate action. All rules were broken, and in our case the Pennsylvania state police chased her father's car with sirens and flashing lights. Having never been stopped by police, he stopped—annoyed and greatly puzzled. This happened the first time in Harrisburg, Pennsylvania. And so he pulled over and the policeman came and said: "There's been a cable, and you're to return to Huntingdon. You are not going to Kabul right now." So, they turned around and went home. There were no cell phones, of course.

Sherry Steiner This happened again and this time we were in New Jersey—we'd gotten quite a bit farther—but this time we weren't so upset when we were stopped by the police. Again, we did not get on the plane and leave.

Bob Steiner *Yes, I was going to meet you at the plane in New York that time. So once more we cabled the embassy and said that I was coming, but this time I didn't call Pennsylvania. I went by myself in August. I got to Kabul to find the agreement had been reached. But I found no program planning had been done—or at least no one had told me that any had been done.*

Sherry Steiner *Well, after he got there I waited until he cabled me and said, okay, come. So, then the three boys—9, 10, and 14—and I got on a plane and went. We got there just about the time school started in early September.*

When we lived in Iran in the 1950s, we had taken a ship to Beirut and then driven to Tehran. Crossing the Arabian Desert, we could see 360 degrees; I thought that was fantastic. But flying over this desolate, desolate, desolate land—I thought, I can't stand this.

Louis Dupree, an American anthropologist living in Kabul, described Afghanistan as a "harsh, brutal, beautiful land, dominated by the disembodied mountainous core of the Hindu Kush. . . . Anyone flying over Afghanistan will be struck by the nakedness of the terrain. Bare rock dominates dramatically everywhere above 14,000 feet. . . ."[1] In winter, the drama of the panorama was heightened by a blanket of snow.

Looking back, Chip Steiner recalls the flight from Tehran to Kabul. The first two trips down the runway, the Ariana Afghan Airlines DC-4 had failed to take off. The third time they boarded, the plane got into the air and, staying close to the land, made it as far as Kandahar before engine trouble grounded it again.

Chip Steiner *A modern new terminal, built with millions of American dollars, sits empty, unused, upon the* parched earth. It rises up to taunt us with false promises of soaring, air conditioned hallways, iced drinks, ice cream. Mercifully, the pilot sets the staggering plane and its cargo down upon the concrete runway. We taxi past the archy new terminal to park before a metal Quonset hut squatted low to the ground. Eight dazed and frightened passengers wobble across the hot concrete into the hut. A few rickety tables and chairs give some relief to the grayness of the floor. We drink hot tea and intermittently peer out through the open door to check the repair progress on our aircraft. Men in pajamas and long cloth streamers wound round their heads tinker and fiddle with this broken mechanical beast from the far west which must still hoist us another 250 miles to Kabul, capital of the Kingdom of Afghanistan.

But they did fix it.

Sherry Steiner So when we got to Kabul, there was this little mud building serving as the airport terminal. I just could not <u>believe</u> that this was the airport of the capital of the country.

David Fleishhacker [Volunteer in Group 1] Kabul in September of 1962 was a city unlike I had ever seen or have seen since. A few square blocks reflected the 20th century, but most seemed to belong to the world of one hundred years earlier, and large sections would not have been out of place in the Middle Ages . . . . The widest streets had been paved, but only recently. Behind the main streets there were narrow unpaved alleys. Along the main streets there were sidewalks, some of them paved, many not. Usually there were deep ditches on both sides of these streets, serving as gutters and to some extent as open *sewers . . . . There was one stoplight in the city, near the Kabul Hotel. There were streetlights in some areas. Traffic consisted of bicycles, donkeys, or donkey [or horse] carts, camels, sheep, and pedestrians, all mixed together, and a few cars, mostly Russian ones.*

Carpets dry along the Kabul River. *(Credit: Dennis Aronson)*

There was one modern hotel. There was one modern restaurant. There were perhaps a dozen or so buildings of more than two stories. There were, of course, no department stores; there were really no stores at all that would resemble what one would expect to find in a major city. There were shops of varying types, but these were always one-room affairs. One could find, for example, a shop near the Kabul Hotel which had a dozen or so appliances on display, small refrigerators and radios, mostly German.[2]

Once on the ground in Kabul, Volunteers found the setting on the plain formed by the Kabul River at about 5800
feet spectacular. From the flat roofs of their houses they could
see the mountains including the Paghman range to the west
and northwest and the Sulaiman to the east that provided a
horizon of white from November through April, until the dry
summer winds filled the air with dust. Within the city, the
Kabul River (now usually dry) then still flowed through the
pass between Sher-Darwaza (the Lion's Gate) on the south
and Asmai to the north.

In their early explorations of the city, Volunteers often
climbed Sher-Darwaza as far as the old cannon that was still
being discharged every day to signal that it was noon. The
cannon was the only visible weapon besides equipment sometimes displayed at Independence Day celebrations and the
rifles from the wars with Britain sold in the bazaar as antiques
or occasionally shot off at weddings or seen in rural areas. A
first trip out of the city – especially during the summer – was
likely to be for a picnic in Paghman, less than an hour into the
mountains or over the Khair Khana Pass and to the Kohdaman
Valley, often stopping in Istalif, famous for its turquoise pottery. A later trip might be by the Afghan Post bus to Peshawar
in Pakistan via the Tangi Gharu Gorge cut by the Kabul River
and the Khyber Pass. As storied as the pass is, "[i]n its rugged-
ness the Tangi Gharu is far more spectacular than anything to
be seen in the Khyber Pass."[3]

A view from an old sentry post shows the drop through the Tangi Gharu Gorge. (*Credit: Will A. Irwin*)

CHAPTER 4   A CAUTIOUS START

The Afghans were cautious. They had invited a few Americans to teach English and technical subjects at least a decade earlier. Then they had welcomed U.S. government funding of university teams of educators in the mid-1950s. But the Peace Corps was a new concept. The Afghans set the initial scale and pace of the program. Start small and in Kabul were their conditions. They were not ready for hundreds of young Americans to roam their country. They were not sure they could guarantee their safety outside of Kabul. Besides, the capital city could use their skills.

The official agreement between Afghanistan and the United States was an exchange of notes negotiated by the U.S. embassy and the Afghan foreign ministry and signed in early September 1962, just before the Volunteers arrived. It referred to recent conversations between representatives of the two governments about "the men and women of the United States of America who volunteer to serve in the Peace Corps, and who at the request of the Afghan Government would live and work in Afghanistan for such periods of time and in places as may be mutually agreed upon between the two governments."[1]

Bob Steiner *After I arrived in Kabul, I began by meeting people, and defining my role, and looking for an office. I still didn't know what the program was going to be.*

Fran Irwin *Who was supposed to be deciding?*

Bob Steiner *I thought I was supposed to be. And I thought I was to talk to the Afghan government and find out what skills they wanted. However, within weeks a cable came from Washington. It said we have a dozen Volunteers for Afghanistan, and they're in these fields— teaching, nursing, mechanics. They had already started training at Georgetown University in Washington, D.C. So much for my role! I was to get jobs for them. I didn't know how they chose the number, or the skills. I just knew that's what they were.*

Our search of the National Archives yielded one piece of evidence of the origin of the initial request for Volunteers in Afghanistan. The minutes of the Peace Corps Director's staff meeting in Washington on February 15, 1962, include a report of a recent trip to discuss a program in Afghanistan by Cleo Shook.[2] He had taught at the Afghan Institute of Technology and worked with U.S. technical assistance programs in Afghanistan in the 1950s and was in 1961 and early 1962 working in the Peace Corps Washington office helping develop country programs.[3]

During his visit to Kabul, Shook reported finding much interest in having Volunteers among Afghan ministries, but also learned that Prime Minister Daoud had political concerns, given Afghanistan's policy of non-alignment. Foreign policy followed that of Arab countries such as what was then the United Arab Republic, and no Arab country had a Peace Corps program. For Daoud, who was at odds with Pakistan about Pashtunistan, Pakistan's having agreed to host a Peace Corps program was a negative even though it was Moslem country. In addition, Afghans were concerned that the Soviet Union

might insist on bringing in an equal number of Soviet technicians. Through its UN representative the Afghan government
learned that the smallest Peace Corps program was in Saint
Lucia and used it as a model to suggest a 12-member contingent for their country.

The minutes of the Peace Corps Director's meeting record a plan to recruit a dozen Volunteers (six English teachers, four nurses, and two mechanics) and to work through the
Afghan ambassador in Washington to get a specific agreement signed. The Peace Corps budget presentation for fiscal
year 1963 (starting July 1962), probably a draft prepared early
in the spring, lists the same job categories and describes the
program as "experimental." Afghanistan is listed as one of 32
countries in which projects were then under way or firmly
scheduled.[4]

Shriver was intent on getting a significant number of
Volunteers on the ground in a significant number of countries around the world within the first year. More than
30,000 Americans applied to the Peace Corps in 1961 and
1962. He pushed hard to take advantage of and sustain the
political momentum at home and to meet the requests for
Volunteers from countries such as Ghana and India which he
had received on a trip in the spring of 1961. After describing
his three-month push to get the agreement and start training for the program in Nigeria, Brent Ashabranner, who later
directed the program in India and served as deputy director
of the Peace Corps, writes: "No one seriously questioned that
a fast and dramatic start with all its loose ends and frantic midnight planning was worth the problems it would create. Everyone simply assumed that it was essential to have
the Peace Corps in action in the field before the end of the
President's first year in office."[5] Shriver inspired enormous

effort from the staff, Charlie Peters, who directed the evaluation division, wrote in his memoir. He also observed: "It was exciting to work for the United States government in the early sixties."[6]

Pat Sullivan Meyers, who became the desk officer for Afghanistan, remembers the 12-hour days that the staff spent figuring out how to meet the challenges of launching a program so rapidly. She had graduated from Bennington College, worked for the Democratic National Committee, and almost completed a master's program in Middle Eastern studies before going to work at the Peace Corps. She recalls that she and others thought it was normal for recent college graduates to be given major responsibilities that included flying around the world – in her case to Tunisia, Morocco, and Cyprus and later Afghanistan. "We were young – we didn't know 'it couldn't be done.'" Her appointment calendar first mentions Afghanistan in March 1963.[7]

The eagerness to get country programs started continued into the second year of Peace Corps. One indication is that recruiting and training of Volunteers and hiring of a Representative (later called director) for the program in Afghanistan both went ahead, apparently on separate tracks, months before the formal diplomatic agreement with Afghanistan was actually signed. Turnover at the embassy in Kabul and at Peace Corps may have been a factor in the delay in negotiating the agreement and in Steiner's not learning that Volunteers were already in training at Georgetown in his few weeks in Washington. John Milton Steeves presented his credentials as the new American ambassador in March of 1962; the previous ambassador had left in January, probably just as Shook did his reconnaissance. Shook himself left Peace Corps Washington that summer.

Bob Steiner *So I had to hustle around and find jobs for the Volunteers through the various ministries and schools, asking "Do you want an English teacher?" I'd go to the girls' schools and simply ask them that question. This was a new approach for the ministries of education, health, and, of course, for the automotive section of the Afghan government. I went around and tried to describe our approach. Of course, government officials and school principals wanted to know who these people were, their qualifications, what they were expected to do, and how they fit into the system, theirs and ours. They knew* <u>nothing</u> *about it. And I wasn't sure* <u>I</u> *knew much about it either.*

Fran Irwin *Did you find some Afghans who were particularly interested?*

Bob Steiner *Oh, yes, some were very interested, and others were very skeptical. The Ministry of Health was particularly skeptical. The Ministry of Education knew the AID* [Agency for International Development] *program. There had been Americans teaching in Afghanistan. The education team from Columbia University helped in terms of jobs and where the possible openings for Volunteers might be found. The teaching jobs were easily identified, but the nursing positions were more difficult. The sex of nurses was a problem. The Afghan nurses were women, but the Volunteers would be foreign women working for male doctors.*

Meanwhile, the Volunteers were completing their training. The group going to Afghanistan (of the fourteen who started training, nine became Volunteers in Kabul) seemed

tiny compared to the 300 Volunteers training at Georgetown
University at the same time to go to Ethiopia.

The National Archives has an undated draft of what apparently became the announcement to recruit Volunteers for
Afghanistan. It called the program "one of the most fascinating
and challenging Peace Corps programs yet to be announced"
and said the details of the training program were in the last
stages of development. It described this group as "a pioneer
effort" and noted that "acceptance by Afghanistan of larger
projects in the future will depend in part on how the members of the first contingent conduct themselves." It described
Peace Corps practice: "Both nurses and mechanics—as well as
teachers—will be expected to teach either formally or through
demonstrations. This is because one of the basic elements of
this project (as in other Peace Corps programs) is to train local citizens to the point where they in turn can train others.
In this way, the project has a lasting value; instead of ceasing
when the Volunteers leave the country, it continues under local management."

The announcement outlined living conditions—the city's
electrical system is still being developed, teachers ride bicycles,
fruits and vegetables may be in short supply in winter months.
It suggested the Peace Corps experience might result in later
job opportunities with companies working in Afghanistan, the
U.S. Foreign Service, or academia, but that in any case, the
Volunteers would find their horizons vastly widened by coming to know another culture and understand their own better,
thus becoming better citizens. It also appealed to adventure
and idealism.[8]

Bob Pearson [Volunteer in Group I] *The Peace Corps
did the best it could with training. There was little time
between the decision to have a program in Afghanistan*

and then recruit and train our first group. Except for the person teaching us Persian, all the rest of our key instructors had been to Afghanistan and their wisdom was greatly appreciated. But the methodology was almost all lecturing, and the cross-cultural aspects of adjusting to the Afghan culture were only theoretically mentioned at best. We did have one excellent role play. I believe a guy from USIS [U.S. Information Service] played a Russian challenging what we were doing in Afghanistan. It brought home to us the reality 'on the ground' that we would face interacting with Afghans and Russians who might take us as innocents.

" "The Afghans viewed the Volunteers with curiosity, not unmixed with a healthy dose of skepticism," a Peace Corps Washington report quotes Steiner as commenting. "They assumed these young Americans were just one more breed of foreign technical assistance—and a pretty inexperienced breed at that."[1]

In writing about the beginning of Peace Corps in Afghanistan, Louis Dupree observed that the Volunteers were "greeted by Afghans who viewed them with suspicious concern. The Soviet personnel in Kabul continued to consider the Peace Corps as an adjunct of the Central Intelligence Agency. The reaction of other foreigners in the capital ranged from incredulity to contempt. Some members of the American colony in Kabul coddled the 'poor dears,' while other Americans remained aloof and even disparaged the PCVs' initial efforts to be effective. Among these latter were a number of 'experienced' AID and embassy personnel who doubted that the young, raw PCVs could avoid making mistakes."[2]

Bob Pearson *When we first arrived in September 1962 the Russians had been putting out propaganda about us Volunteers being in reality CIA agents. On our several-day layover in Tehran on the way over, we were* *"accidentally" joined by an Afghan who just happened to be there. We knew who had sent him—the Afghan government to start seeing if we were in fact CIA. In any case, when we got to Afghanistan, this guy kept showing up. One day he asked me very forthrightly: "Bob, so what do you REALLY think about Afghanistan?" I told him, "I love it," which was the truth.*

As they encountered the expectations of others, the Volunteers were clarifying their own understanding of why they had joined the Peace Corps. One of the fundamental issues Volunteers recall was the importance of balancing their own interests in being in the country and their idealism.

David Fleishhacker . . . *[N]ot long after we had arrived in Kabul and met our on-site director, Bob Steiner, I heard him tell us all that we were there for the best possible reasons: what he called "enlightened self-interest." All of us felt we would benefit in various ways from the experience, and that was much better than if we were a bunch of starry-eyed idealists who thought we were sacrificing ourselves. He was right, of course; people who are working in their own self-interest are less likely to abandon their work when the going gets rough.[3]*

And all nine of the first group did stay. At his departure in 1966, Steiner said in a newspaper interview that the early-termination rate of Volunteers in Afghanistan was about four percent during his time as director [See Chapter 18].

David Fleishhacker *And on a much deeper level, we had already been made to understand during training that Peace Corps itself was an example of enlightened* *self-interest on the part of our country. Whether or not we could accomplish something of value for the countries we served was problematic at best. But there was a less-advertised purpose behind the creation of the Peace Corps. Ten years later, twenty years later, and even later still, there would be thousands and thousands of Americans of all ages who had lived and worked in far distant countries with far different cultures and whose perception of the world would be altered by that experience. That core of Americans, educated by an experience like no other, would change how America viewed the world. It was a huge experiment in national adult education, and to a large extent it has worked. I have met many former Peace Corps volunteers, but I have met none who were not profoundly changed by their two years of life in a developing country.[4]*

Rosalind Pace [Volunteer in Group I] *We first heard about the Peace Corps when we were at the University of Michigan during the academic year 1961-62. Bob* [Pearson, her husband at that time] *had decided he didn't want to continue on his PhD, and he definitely didn't want to go to Viet Nam. . . . The best part of our training was that I think none of us came to Afghanistan thinking we could change anything. We were going there to do the jobs that were assigned us as best we could. So we were completely open to taking in all the frustrations and wonder and excitement, and discovered that Afghanistan was an easy country to love.*

Although Steiner was not involved in training the first group of Volunteers, once they arrived in Kabul he inculcated in them—as in later Volunteers—that they needed to understand why their Afghan co-workers did what they did. The Volunteers were to work within the Afghan system.

Bob Steiner *I think the thing I stressed most when they arrived was that they were to find out why the Afghans did the job the way they did. Otherwise, they would never know how to improve what the Afghans did; they wouldn't know what assumptions Afghans were making. The Afghans were just as smart as they were, and so if the Volunteer didn't figure out what the Afghans knew—why they did what they did—they would never be aware of the Afghans' wisdom and why they were performing as they did.*

Overall, Steiner remembers that the Volunteers quickly showed that they were competent to perform their jobs, but, of course, there were issues.

Bob Steiner *One of the biggest and earliest problems for the teachers was the lack of integrity in the school system. For example, exams were scheduled at such and such a time but they wouldn't materialize. They might not even hold the exams until three weeks later. Then Volunteers also all had trouble adjusting to reporting to their supervisors.*

Bob Pearson *When we teachers first got there we were told we would be "supervised" by members of the Columbia team. By chance my "supervisor" was a college classmate of mine, and I remember telling him that I couldn't prevent him from entering my class, but that I would not take orders from him. As I remember, all of us teachers complained to Steiner, and in his smooth and clever way he solved the problem by telling the Columbia*

*team that they would not be allowed to supervise us be-
cause the Peace Corps required that we be supervised by
Afghans only. So that responsibility fell to our principals.*

A brochure distributed two years later in Dari and English describing the Peace Corps in Afghanistan (see pages 189-195) explained: "While in this country, a Volunteer is responsible for his
over-all performance to the Peace Corps Director in Afghanistan;
however, in his job he is *directly responsible* to his *Afghan supervisor.* [Emphasis in original.] The Volunteer is basically in
Afghanistan to work for Afghans, under Afghan supervision on
projects selected by the Royal Government of Afghanistan."

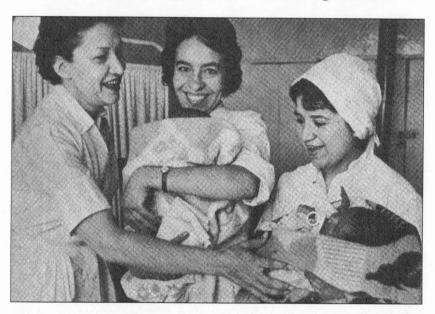

**Dorothy Luketich (left), a nurse in Group I, with nurse colleagues
and newborns at Masturat Hospital, Kabul.** *(Credit: January 1964
Peace Corps Volunteer)*

Bob Steiner *Now, with the nurses it was a little different from the teachers. The nurses had a particularly*

tough time with doctors who often knew less than they did and still they had to maintain the inferior position. It was very ticklish for them. Really tough. They handled it well. They handled it well.

Later with the secretaries, I always worried about this. They, of course, ran into the problem of the boss making advances. One was even given a coat, a fur coat, and I said you better give that back to him right away, which she did, but reluctantly. It was a beautiful coat. That kind of relationship with a supervisor—teacher or nurse or whatever—was ticklish. Refusing a gift in Afghanistan could be considered an insult—usually the Afghans would consider the refusal to be a peculiar foreign custom.

As the Volunteers got into their jobs, they were confronted with what it meant to be working in the Afghan culture, as David Fleishhacker describes in detail in *Lessons from Afghanistan*. The teachers learned that they were often teaching students a third foreign language, in a culture of rote learning, in a country where classroom order was kept through fear. Teachers, nurses, and the mechanic all struggled with locked-up supplies—books, medical instruments, towels and soap, or tools and parts for trucks and buses — watched over by the people in charge of storerooms who were personally responsible to pay for any items lost and thus had every incentive to keep all items locked up rather than have them used.[4] Volunteer Frank Brechin worked as a mechanic at Zenda-ba-Non, a large automotive workshop that serviced both private and government vehicles, including about 300 American and Soviet buses. It was well-supplied by U.S. AID, but Frank found that getting and using items from the storeroom was not easy.

David Fleishhacker Frank sought permission to get three trouble lights on extension cords from the storeroom to hang under a car's hood while servicing it. The natural light was no longer adequate now that the winter months were approaching. Frank was able to locate the trouble lights and take them from the storeroom, but there were no bulbs in them. It took two more days to get a new requisition from the company vice-president for the bulbs, but then, it turned out, the bulbs he was given did not fit the sockets in those lights. This time Frank simply lost all composure; he marched into the storeroom, over the protests of the man who guarded it, and found the correct bulbs. Triumphantly, he screwed them into the sockets and plugged the cords in. Nothing happened, except for some amused looks on the faces of the workers there. There were plugs in the shop, but the electricity had never been hooked up. Those plugs had always been dead. Nobody had bothered to mention it to Frank, because who knew when electricity might flow? That was in the hands of God.[5]

The Volunteers learned to work in this world of such different expectations from their experience. "It is difficult to believe that almost six months have elapsed since the Volunteers arrived in Kabul's forlorn airport," Steiner wrote in a memo to Shriver in February 1963. "In contrasting their first faltering efforts to adjust with their aplomb today, or the Afghans' initial reserve with their present reliance on the Volunteers, it seems incredible that six months could have produced such a change." He noted that the teachers had established "their identity and professional ability," the nurses had won respect as they dealt with the startling contrast between American and Afghan standards, and the mechanic with his Afghan colleagues had made the service department where he worked into a top money-maker.[6]

Volunteer Frank Brechin at the Zenda-ba-Non automotive workshop. (*Credit: January 1964 Peace Corps Volunteer*)

An evaluator from Peace Corps Washington summed up his findings in March 1963 saying: "The nine Volunteers in Kabul with Afghanistan-I are excellent, and all are busy performing needed tasks. They have enough Farsi to get along, and have created a favorable image even though, because of the delicate political environment in Kabul, they have not had the benefit of publicity or close personal relationships with the Afghans. Not a word, not even a suggestion, of criticism of the Peace Corps Afghan program did I hear in Kabul. Afghanistan-I presents a good case for a small, well administered project with high standards of selection and programming." He continued: "The present Peace Corps program has succeeded fundamentally on practical terms. They are all skilled and effective on the job. . . . That they are in addition creating favorable personal impressions is, as far as the Afghan government is concerned, only incidental."

The evaluation nevertheless emphasized that the situation was tenuous. "The Ambassador's comment, 'So far, so good,' is particularly revealing. The Ambassador is extremely enthusiastic about Afghan I. But his statement reveals the very delicate path we are treading. One slip and the Peace Corps may be through in Afghanistan. The suspiciousness of the Afghan government is exemplified by the close scrutiny to which the Volunteers are subjected. There is a policeman on the corner nearest each Volunteer's house, presumably not only for their protection, but to see and report on who enters and leaves. Servants of foreigners (and the Volunteers have servants) are questioned about visitors. Afghans are consequently reluctant to visit Americans. And the Ambassador believes that it is not unlikely that the Foreign Office keeps dossiers on the Volunteers. In short, this program is not like others where an incident may or may not come to the attention of the government, and even if it does nothing worse than the expulsion of a Volunteer is likely."[7]

CHAPTER 6 LIVING ON THE ECONOMY

The first months were also a time of working out how Volunteers would live in a way that allowed them to get to know and be known by Afghans. It was up to the Volunteers with the staff to demonstrate what this new kind of international relationship might be in Afghanistan. Besides providing mid-level skills, how might the Volunteers live to achieve the additional Peace Corps goals of building understanding across cultures, especially in a just-opening society with a functional literacy rate of not much more than five percent?

The intent of Peace Corps was for Volunteers to live like the people with whom they worked, in contrast to other Americans who often lived largely as they might have in the States by importing food, furnishings, and automobiles. Questions included whether to have servants; the choice of housing and furnishings, heating, and transport; and the level of the Volunteer living allowance. These first decisions were important in setting the tone for Peace Corps in Afghanistan.

As the handbook explained: "Only exceptionally does the Peace Corps permit you to have servants. In Afghanistan, it has been necessary to have them because of the time factor involved in shopping, the fact that all of you will be busy most of every day except Friday, and because most of your Afghan colleagues will have them."[1] Volunteers did not have refrigerators, which made shopping every day necessary. Nor did they have access to the Commissary on which the rest of the American community depended. The handbook said: ". . . [Y]ou are expected to work and live like your Afghan colleagues, provided it does not endanger your health and safety. As such, you do not have import privileges, nor are you expected to participate in activities which are not open to the Afghans." That included not only the Commissary but the thrift shop, the AID staff house, and the American swimming pool.[2]

The image of the Peace Corps for the American public in the 1960s was a Volunteer living alone, often in a village. That did not fit in Afghanistan with the first Volunteers living in Kabul where at that time most people lived in walled compounds with their extended families. Nor did scattering Volunteers around the city seem to make sense given that all in the initial group would be working in the same area of the city. The Afghans themselves questioned the Peace Corps view that Volunteers should live like their colleagues. Steiner recalled in writing for the *Peace Corps Volunteer* at the end of 1963: "Our first efforts to find low-cost housing met with almost universal opposition from the Afghans. As hosts, why should they be expected to help us find anything but the best?"[3] He needed help in locating places for the Volunteers to live, and he found Sami Noor. In response to an email in the fall of 2011 from Steiner, he recalled how he came to work for Peace Corps.[4]

Sami Noor *Based on your request, the Afghan Ministry of Mines and Industries—Labor Employment Department—introduced me to you. It was not an easy start. I had just graduated from the Faculty of Economics—Kabul University—and got an assignment as an assistant instructor at Kabul University. Besides working for the*

University, I was looking for a part time job for feeding my family. I preferred working for some foreign organization, which was quite rare at that time.

Though I had already found a job at the ICA [International Cooperation Administration, precursor to AID], *I could not get the clearance from the "Secret Police." The condition for the clearance was my obligation to report regularly to the Secret Police. I did not accept this obligation, and lost the job. In the case of Peace Corps, somehow, no clearance was required. You offered me some 2000 Afghanis (then about 50 dollars) per month. In the absence of an alternative, I accepted this low salary, which I do not regret to this day.*

Steiner had located an office in Shar-i-Nau [new city] for the Peace Corps with the help of the embassy real estate person and built a small staff that first fall.

Fran Irwin *And the Peace Corps staff that first year, you and Sami and Naim?*

Bob Steiner *And Roberta Auburn, who was the secretary. She was the wife of an AID official. She was there the entire time I was. She was an able and very key person.*

Sami Noor *Naim was working for Point Four, a U.S. program that provided food for work. Later on he joined the Peace Corps, and was quite satisfied working for you* [Steiner]. *At that time we had only one vehicle, and he was our driver. Since I could also drive, it helped us building a good team. Naik Mohammed was our janitor, Mrs. Roberta was the chief secretary. This means that the whole team consisted of five persons.*

The salary was real low, but the atmosphere and your treatment of the employees were worth more than any financial rewards. You had delegated lots of responsibilities, right from the beginning, and I had to cope with all the difficulties.

Gradually, I noticed that I had to work independently and get things done, without bothering you every moment. The style of your leadership was really marvelous!

Naim, the Peace Corps driver, with the Jeep in front of the Peace Corps office, a series of second-floor rooms near Zarghoona Square in Shar-i-Nau. (*Credit: Bob Steiner*)

Bob Steiner *I gave Sami the guidelines Peace Corps had for housing—that it was supposed to be similar to the counterparts'. He was superb. I said, "please go find some housing and let me go with you. The only thing I want is some kind of flush toilet." He would find some houses and*

I would go look at them and if they seemed to fit, we would bargain for the rent. That's how we found the housing.

Sami Noor *The criteria for finding the houses were: no luxury, low rent and preferably not support the rich by renting their fancy houses. Sometimes we even paid advance rents, so that landlords could get the houses ready for rent. This aspect helped quite often in finding comparatively suitable houses, and in the meantime helped some poor landlords receive some rent.*

I was responsible for providing the list of the houses in Kabul and later the provinces. At that time, it was not easy to find houses with some western sanitary style facilities. To furnish the houses you had decided to make use of the local products like charpaaees (rope beds), geleems (flat-woven rugs), and other easily available and relatively inexpensive furniture.

Rosalind Pace *I remember a really nice small house we looked at. I could even draw a plan of it, I think. I remember it had a nice sunny feel to it, but of course there was no bathroom and no kitchen, so we all went to a house in the old bazaar that had a lot of rooms more or less connected, and I think it had a courtyard. It would have a common kitchen. I remember discussions about how Afghans would view unrelated men and women living in the same house.*

After several months of living in the Kabul Hotel and eating at the nearby Khyber Restaurant, the Group I Volunteers divided up into two houses and an apartment relatively near to each other and their jobs. Then there was the issue of how they would heat their homes as winter came to Kabul, which at an elevation close to 6000 feet can get cold. The decision was to use kerosene for cooking but to burn sawdust to keep warm. Oil was imported and using it for heat would have been expensive.

Bob Steiner *I did a lot of research on heating devices to find something that was cheap and reliable. Naim, the driver, knew about using sawdust stoves and so we went around and enriched the bukhari (stove) makers.*

Sami Noor *The heating system in all our houses was based on bukharis—for warm water and heating of the rooms. Use of sawdust was common in ICA buildings. Very few Afghan families were making use of sawdust, which was the cleanest form of heating. Peace Corps could not afford kerosene (oil) heaters, and was looking for an economical fuel. On the other hand there was not so much demand for the sawdust in the country. I remember discussing how to heat the rooms. We thought burning wood would not be advisable—environmental arguments—and more expensive. Sawdust was a by-product, and relatively cheap. I think Peace Corps contributed towards the fact that later on more and more Afghans got used to sawdust as a good means of heating.*

David Fleishhacker *It* [the sawdust stove] *was a cylinder about a yard in diameter and four feet high* [many were smaller], *with a smoke vent at the top and an inlet vent at the bottom. A large canister, open at the top, and with a round hole about four inches in diameter in the bottom, was built to fit snugly inside. One then took a large wooden dowel, about four feet long, to fit in that bottom hole, inserted it, and packed the sawdust tightly around it. The canister was*

Stoves on display in a Kabul bazaar. *(Credit: Will A. Irwin)*

placed in the stove, the wooden dowel carefully removed, and a piece of newspaper inserted in the resulting tunnel in the sawdust, after which the top of the stove would be covered. Lighting that paper through the bottom vent would light the sawdust, which would then burn slowly from the inside of the cylinder outward. . . . Ordinarily it took about six to eight hours for all the sawdust to slowly burn, enough time for us to enjoy sitting in our living room in the evening and go to sleep well before our apartment cooled. By morning, of course, the rooms were freezing, but we could use a small electric heater for the brief period before we left for work.[5]

Volunteers needed to learn how to use the stoves. Group II Volunteer Doug Bell wrote extensive guidance, cautioning that no two were alike. He covered installation, lighting, burning time (6-12 hours, depending on size and draught), and trouble-shooting ("Most problems are due to insufficient draught," either from improper installation or because the pipes are clogged with soot.). The final words of caution were: "If you value your eyesight, keep your face away from the bottom of the stove at all times, and never try to encourage a balky stove with kerosene."[6]

In his report, the Peace Corps evaluator commented on Steiner and his staff's shopping and bargaining in the bazaars for items such as rope beds for the Volunteers. ". . . [T]his is certainly far preferable to reliance on AID. He is able to save the Peace Corps money, and to create a very favorable image of the Peace Corps by his faith in local materials, knowledge of ways of obtaining them, and by giving the impression of an American organization which is not spendthrift."[7]

There was also the question of how Volunteers would get around the city of then perhaps 350,000 people. Rosalind

Pace recalls that when Volunteers first arrived they tried the Afghan buses. Volunteers were briefly known as the Americans who rode the Afghan buses. No other technical assistance people did, although the Russians traveled in their own buses. Once they were able to travel outside Kabul, Volunteers frequently traveled by bus—as well as truck and taxi—between cities. They learned that it was an art to choose which bus among several waiting at the departure spot would fill up and leave first. Where to sit was also a question. Some imported buses had been refitted with wooden benches about four inches from the floor, comfortable if you were used to squatting, not if you were used to sitting. Sitting on the roof might be a better choice. The stops were likely to be frequent with no certainty about the time of arrival.[8] While bus rides around the country provided grist for Volunteer stories, within Kabul and other cities Volunteers became known as the Americans who rode bicycles.

Bob Steiner *Afghans rode bicycles. They were so much more versatile than was a bus. You get around and see more and do more than waiting for buses. I didn't think riding a bus in the city was all that terrific.*

Sherry Steiner *With motorcycles, Volunteers would have had to buy gas, which was expensive.*

Sami Noor *The Volunteers moved back and forth with bicycles. That paved the way for them to get more contact with the people. They were not arrogant, like some foreign experts, and believed in their assignments. Their approach was help the people in Afghanistan and gain experience and knowledge from the rest of the world, and make use of it for a better understanding among the nations back at home.*

That bicycles were by far the most common mode of transport in Kabul at the time other than walking is confirmed by a report in the *Kabul Times* giving Kabul Traffic Department figures of vehicles in the city at 40,000 bicycles, 1,251 motorcycles, 2,850 trucks, 850 buses, and 5,735 cars.[9] Len Oppenheim, a Group IV Volunteer who taught in Kandahar, still has the form he signed after receiving his Raleigh Bicycle with License No. 31070 on October 26, 1964.

The handbook was very clear by the time Group IV arrived: "Bicycles are definitely in, cars very definitely out. . . . *No Volunteer may drive a motor vehicle in Afghanistan without written permission from the Peace Corps Representative.* Due to the circumstances here and the laws of this country, this is a hard and fast rule to which there will be *no exceptions.*"[10]

Fran Irwin *I wrote in a letter that when we arrived we were told it was 4 Afs to get a bicycle tire fixed. I liked being able to ride on mostly flat roads through the city while looking at the mountains. My pictures show that the roads were sometimes almost empty—hard to believe now with what we hear about traffic jams. At other times, there could be lots of people walking and riding bicycles as well as Russian-made taxis, painted trucks, the buses, an occasional camel caravan, a good many donkeys. By then, there were not so many gadis—the two-wheeled horse-drawn carts—in Kabul, but still human power—men pulling wood platforms with two rubber-tired wheels.*

Will and I got to know each other riding our bikes. We never made a phone call to each other in Kabul. We both loved riding bicycles—despite the occasional dogs to deter. When the Kabul Times moved to a new building off the airport road my second year, I started getting a ride to work with other staff members in a government car. By that time Volunteers were living in many parts of Kabul. I had been living in Karte Char (fourth quarter) but later I moved to Shar-i-Nau to be nearer work.

Pat Higgins and Phil Weeks were among the first Peace Corps Afghanistan Volunteers to marry in Kabul. Bob Steiner was "father of the bride." Pat wrote in a piece in the PC newsletter: "When Afghan II came to Kabul, a mountain separated the single boys from the single girls. The bicycle ride through the mountain pass was certainly a stiff endurance test for those in pursuit of romance. . . . The happy couple settled in Shar-i-Nau and the groom put his bicycle away for the duration with a sigh of relief."[11]

Bob Pearson *Not all Volunteers were experienced cyclists. Not long after our arrival some of the nurses went for a bike ride in the bazaar, and one of them had only a cursory knowledge of bikes. So, in the crowded conditions of the bazaar she lost control of her bike and crashed into, and upset, a mobile fruit stand. Suddenly there was chaos, people on the ground, fruit rolling around. And then a large black Mercedes pulls up and stops. What is going on? An elegantly dressed young man descends from the car, and walks over to see what has happened to the foreigners. It is the crown prince of Afghanistan to the rescue! And here were these supposedly highly trained "CIA agents" unable to even guide a bike through a bazaar!*

A Cross-Cultural Studies Manual, prepared with the help of Louis and Nancy Hatch Dupree in the mid-sixties by Rosalind Pearson and Janet Bing, who had been Volunteers in Group I, recounts a bicycle story. "There were three Volunteer women teaching in Kandahar. All of them rode bicycles to school and were the only women in the city who rode bicycles. It was rare even to see a chadried woman on the streets, and never an Afghan woman on a bicycle. One of the Volunteers taught at the girls' school and became extremely good friends with most of the women teachers there. One day one of the young teachers came up to her and confided to her with a blush that she had persuaded her husband to buy her a bicycle and did she think the Volunteer could help her learn to ride it. So in the privacy behind the high compound walls of the school-yard, the young teacher received bicycle riding lessons and in a short time was able to ride her bicycle to school for the first time—the first Afghan woman in the city to appear on the streets on a bicycle."[12]

Bob Pearson *Steiner made it clear that Peace Corps was not there to change the Afghan culture but rather to respect their ways and let them make cultural changes on their own. This story about bicycle riding was the kind of thing Steiner was promoting. We do our thing, and if they wished to adapt it to their culture, then they could.*

Besides each being provided with a bicycle, Volunteers received a settling-in allowance to help furnish their houses from the bazaar. Volunteers also received a monthly living allowance to buy food, clothes, and other items in the bazaar. Landlords in Kabul at that point received their rent directly from the Peace Corps. In the fall of 1964 the living allowance was $90. Volunteers were not to receive extra money from family or friends or add to their income by taking extra jobs.[13]

Doug and Pat Bell put out a six-page list of what to bring and not bring based on suggestions by members of Group II for Group III, then in training. Noting that there was a "great diversity of opinion," they included: color film (easy to find but extremely expensive) and perhaps a "skylight filter to compensate for Kabul's 'high altitude blue;'" a full two-year supply of skin lotions and cream ("Kabul is extremely dry and dusty"); an "abundant" supply of women's underwear and stockings ("the rough furniture here makes torn stockings an almost daily occurrence, as does bike riding") . . . ; an all-season suit for men ("in selecting clothing, keep the DUST in mind—do not bring very dark blues and blacks"); a portable typewriter; and a good sleeping bag, "especially if you plan to travel.". . . [14]

Newly arriving Volunteers also got advice on furnishing houses from the bazaar. "The wool rugs are attractive but expensive," the memo advised. "Cotton rugs for the average room should cost less than $5.00 or about 20 Afs ($.33) per square meter." To order and buy curtains and furniture, it suggested: "Begin by drawing a good sketch of what you want made. This is then submitted to two or three carpenter shops."

Using the exchange rate of $1 to 60 Afghanis (Afs), the Volunteers also learned what prices they should expect to pay in the bazaar: a set of six aluminum sauce pans, 150 Afs; 2-quart teakettles, 45 Afs from India or Pakistan or 20 Afs for "Kabul-made;" 7 oz. Duralex glasses, 13 Afs ; 1 quart water pitcher, Bulgarian, 35 Afs; chrome-plated flatware, 1 ½ - 2 Afs each. The list included prices for food staples: 1 lb. olive oil, 60 Afs; peanut butter, 60 Afs; shortening (5 lbs. Spinzar), 90 Afs; margarine, 5 lbs., 110 Afs; 1 ½ lbs. imported salt, 24 Afs. [15]

Fran Irwin *I noted in a letter in 1965 that the living allowance had been reduced because you had found that it was more than we needed. I wrote that we had learned that our Farsi teacher was living with his entire family of nine people on about the same amount we were. That brought* *home to us how little money people had. Government and university jobs paid very little.*

Bob Steiner *You know, I never took the Peace Corps guidelines on that too seriously. I didn't see that anything was being gained by poverty. You lived like the Afghans did. Now, you had many benefits such as health care that they did not have. But, by and large, you got to know how they lived because you had to carefully budget your money; so I thought that was really more important than the exact amount.*

The Steiners recalled their own living situation.

Fran Irwin *You had had experience living in Iran in the early 1950s?*

Sherry Steiner *That's right. And Kabul was not the shock it would have been if it had been the first time. We had a house in Shar-i-Nau—at the edge. It was country-side beyond our street. The house was small, but adequate for us.*

Bob Steiner *The embassy supplied us with a car, so that we could get around. And they supplied the water. Other than that, I had to keep them from giving us all the things that they gave to AID people.*

Fran Irwin *How about food? I always think first of fresh nan, tea with cardamom and then pilau. How did the food compare with your experience in Iran?*

Sherry Steiner *Our cook shopped for food. It was fall when we got there and we had only the winter root* *vegetables. By the time we left in 1966, there was an agricultural program in Jalalabad (which was located at an altitude of about 2000 feet where vegetables could be grown in winter) and we were beginning to get things like broccoli, a real blessing since we did not use the commissary.*

Fran Irwin *It did seem like we had carrots in stew all winter. In the spring, we made jam using apricots from a tree in our compound, and we had rhubarb instead of lentils on our rice at work for lunch. And, of course, in season there were wonderful melons and pomegranates... Not using the commissary was a real difference from AID.*

Sherry Steiner *We used to get red oranges from Pakistan, and they were so good. Our sons ate peanut butter sandwiches. We could get peanut butter when families left and sold their extra canned goods. So the boys would have peanut butter sandwiches until they could not stand them anymore and then they would swap with their friends whose families had use of the commissary. So as far as food went it was not a surprise, it was familiar though not as varied as the Persian diet. We did have embassy water. Did Volunteers have it?*

Bob Steiner *Yes, they could use it. They could get it from the embassy if they took their own vessel. It was in the tanks in the back of the compound. It was a deep well.*

Fran Irwin *Health, overall, of the early Volunteers ...*

Bob Steiner *It wasn't a problem. Volunteers had training in this, they observed it, they boiled their water* *or they got safe water. Even the ones later out in the boondocks stayed pretty well most of the time.*

Fran Irwin: *We seemed to stay amazingly healthy, though I did find I had amoebic dysentery when I left as I think many others did.*

CHAPTER 7 A PROGRAM READY TO GROW

"The success of Afghanistan One can be measured with several yardsticks," Louis Dupree wrote. "Probably the most important would be Afghan reactions. In private, Afghans were before long expressing admiration for the accomplishments of the nine PCVs, as indeed also were most foreigners—often grudgingly. The Afghan government, however, made no official statements until the spring of 1963, when the Peace Corps Representative in Kabul asked if they would like additional Volunteers. The Ministry of Planning politely received his request, sent it to the various ministries for their requirements, and returned the list to the Representative. He glanced at the requests, stunned. He had hoped the Afghans would ask for at least another seven or eight. Instead, the various ministries put in bids totaling between seventy and eighty! While part of this new enthusiasm is perhaps ascribable to a change in the Afghan government in March, there is little doubt that the primary reason was that the Volunteers had gained the confidence of Afghanistan's leaders. The Representative realized that seventy or eighty would be too big a jump in personnel, but he pleaded with Washington for as many as he could get."[1]

Sami Noor *Since Peace Corps was a new idea for Afghanistan, we needed to convince the authorities and* *prove that such a program would suit the needs of the country. Specially the devotion of the Volunteers contributed to our success.*

Bob Steiner *The Afghans were truly astonished. I mean, Peace Corps was something they had trouble conceiving, why any American would come out there and put up with the problems they had, and do it so gracefully. It was just astonishing to them, so that when I went around to the offices and said do you know anybody, any schools that need teachers, nurses, and so forth, they were more than glad to help out and suggest something – usually more requests than we could fulfill.*

Will Irwin *Was most of the impetus of those requests from the Afghan government? It wasn't Washington saying, Bob, you need to take more people?*

Bob Steiner *No, just the opposite. The Afghans wanted them. Within six months we started getting more and more requests. The demand was most encouraging. It was Washington that began dragging its feet.*

Will Irwin *Did you have to persuade Washington that the Afghans want this, we can justify this, give us the people.*

Bob Steiner *We had to compete with world-wide requests for the same skills. And Afghans did sometimes ask for people who had technical skills beyond anything the Peace Corps offered, but they soon found out what was out of our ball park.*

Fran Irwin *It was limitations on the recruiting end.*

Bob Steiner *That's right. Particularly for teachers. And medical personnel were even more difficult to find and recruit. I recruited Dr. Jim Chapman, our Peace Corps physician. I went out to Idaho to see if he would make it in Afghanistan. They had a lovely home. He was head of the medical association in Idaho. He was comfortably settled there. And I thought, my God, is this man going to come to Afghanistan and be happy? But he did. Great guy.*

Fran Irwin *Do you have any memory of how you heard of someone wanting a Volunteer at the Kabul Times? How did that happen?*

Bob Steiner *I wish I could remember. Who was the editor?*

Fran Irwin *Sabahuddin Kushkaki.*

Bob Steiner *Kushkaki. Okay, he was the one. I met him somehow. He asked me about getting a journalist. They wanted a Volunteer, we asked for one, and I didn't think we'd get one, but we did. Washington was always surprised at the variety of skills that we were interested in. Nurses, secretaries, printers, accountants, mechanics, rural development. . . .*

Fran Irwin *And at least sometimes ministries did pay part of the cost—equal to what they would have paid an Afghan.*

The Dari and English brochure distributed by Peace Corps in 1964 notes that under a new arrangement, the Afghan government would pay a part of Volunteer living allowances.

Fran Irwin *Were there discussions with Washington about how much it cost to place a Peace Corps Volunteer in Afghanistan?*

Bob Steiner *You know, on thinking back on this . . . ever since the 50ᵗʰ [Peace Corps] anniversary . . . the whole question of money was never an issue. Never. I wonder why, but I didn't have to worry.*

Fran Irwin *How about budgeting?*

Bob Steiner *I didn't do a budget. I just said I want this many Volunteers. Our desk officer at that time was Pat Sullivan. She did much in terms of getting the Afghan program everything it requested. She was just absolutely outstanding, moving mountains to do this for us. She was very, very good, and she was there for the critical early period.*

Budgeting was handled in Washington. Pat Sullivan Meyers remembers that the desk officers put together budgets for country programs, starting with boilerplate numbers covering such basics as rental for the Peace Corps office, Volunteer allowances, and household furnishings.

One document in the National Archives with financial information is a project approval signed by Warren Wiggins, who ran the program development office, in December 1964. It authorizes 24 Volunteers for the education program in Afghanistan at an "estimated 24-month cost of $282,072." That year for its overall budget Peace Corps was estimating an annual cost of about $8200 per Volunteer.[2]

Steiner made a trip back to Washington in April 1963 to discuss how the program was developing. Minutes of a Peace

Corps Director's staff meeting record that he "began his report by pointing out that Afghanistan had been closed to most foreigners, regardless of their nationality, until recent years. Travel outside of the capital city of Kabul is controlled and Afghans are still hesitant about associating with foreigners. This has had a direct effect upon the ability of the Volunteers to carry out the second and third purposes of the Peace Corps Act. However, the Peace Corps has been extremely successful in accomplishing the Act's first purpose because:

a) There is a great need for the technical skills that the PCVs possess;
b) The Afghan government has a rigid, traditional way of doing things and they don't ask for PCVs unless they have jobs for them;
c) The Afghans look at the Peace Corps strictly as a technical assistance program and are quite forthright in saying that they do not understand the other two purposes."[3]

Gradually, however, some undefined attraction for the Volunteers seemed to take place in Afghanistan, a report prepared in Peace Corps Washington suggested. "Technical assistance, yes; the Volunteers appeared after all, to be skilled and efficient. But more than that. They spoke passable Farsi; and that alone set them apart from other foreigners. Then, they had an enthusiasm for their jobs; they weren't glory-seekers. Even more disarming, their public conduct belied the libertine hero of American movie fame." The report quotes Steiner: "Perhaps it was partly the lurking allure of novelty that prompted the Afghans to ask for additional Volunteers . . . ."[4]

The second group of Volunteers, also trained at Georgetown University, reached Kabul in June 1963, ten months after the first. It consisted of 26 Volunteers, mostly teachers but also five printers. A third group of 31 Volunteers came in January of 1964. It was split between teachers and those who would work in government ministries in roles such as secretaries and accountants. Most of these Volunteers were still placed in Kabul but as the months passed a few Volunteers from early groups began to test the possibilities in major provincial cities such as Jalalabad, Kandahar, and Mazar-i-Sharif.

More Volunteers meant a need for additional staff to support them. Robert S. (Bob) McClusky came to serve as deputy director for the Peace Corps Program in Afghanistan.

Fran Irwin *You had been working in Peace Corps in Washington? How had you landed that job?*

Bob McClusky *In the spring of 1961 I was in Washington on home leave after three years as CARE Representative in South Korea and India. The Executive Order establishing Peace Corps had just been signed in March. I was offered a spot in the Peace Corps Far East Program in June. I had worked in both humanitarian and self-help development programs with CARE in New Delhi and Seoul and also managed regional offices in Pusan and Madras* [now Chennai].

I had majored in government relations at Oberlin College and gotten a two-year Masters in Public Affairs at Princeton's Woodrow Wilson School of Public and International Affairs. My interest in international affairs was shaped by my Dad's work and his sudden death from a heart attack in 1950. He served on General Clay's staff during the rebuilding of Germany after World War II, and I attended 7th and 8th grades at the American school in Berlin. At 13, I remember

*the American Ambassador to Holland spending an hour de-
scribing to me the then still-emerging Marshall Plan.*

*At Peace Corps I got involved in initiating programs
in Burma and Thailand. Burma was reluctant and a program never got off the ground there, but Thailand had
no such reservations. One opportunity I had was to visit
early Volunteers on the job in Thailand and use that experience to foster collaboration between the field and those
recruiting and training Volunteers going to Thailand to
teach English. The report became a model for describing
proposed country programs. In the summer of 1963, I told
Warren Wiggins—he was running the program office—
that I wanted to get back overseas.*

Will Irwin *And how did you end up in Kabul?*

Bob McClusky *Shriver had decided that a Peace Corps
staffer, rather than someone from the local embassy, would
be asked to stand in at posts when a director went on leave.
Bob Steiner planned to take two weeks of vacation with his
family and that provided an opportunity for him to consider me as a deputy and me a chance to assess the opportunity. Just before I was to go back to the States after those
weeks in Kabul a Peace Corps cable came asking me to go
to Nepal. Willi Unsoeld, deputy director there, had climbed
Everest—up one side and down the other, a feat never before accomplished. He had lost nine frozen toes in the process and was in bed with hepatitis. I helped out until new
staff came later in the fall and then flew home with Unsoeld,
who recovered at Bethesda Naval Hospital while I prepared
to go to Afghanistan. I was in Washington when JFK was
assassinated. I got back to Kabul at the end of December,
about a month before Group III arrived.*

Five months later came another sign of the maturing program: the departure of the first Volunteers. A conference as they left in May of 1964 found that "this group saw their roles as PCV's almost entirely in terms of accomplishing their specific job assignments." Although all agreed that their work experiences had been frustrating, they were all also positive about their experience, saying that they would volunteer again to serve in Peace Corps in Afghanistan.[5]

Bob Steiner *The first group got a lot more staff support than the ones that came later.*

Sherry Steiner *Of course, we were learning, too.*

Will Irwin *I have the sense that the Volunteers were, in addition to your boys, an extended family.*

Sherry Steiner *Oh, they were! They really were. They were at our house lots of times. And any holiday, we always invited them. The whole group of us would get together. There were just nine of them and they all seemed to get along very well with each other. David Fleishhacker and Jan Mueller both played the guitar. We would spend evenings sitting around while they would sing and tell tales and put on skits. We enjoyed them thoroughly. But after that first group there were too many Volunteers to do that.*

Bob Steiner *And the Volunteers became busy supporting the new groups coming in.*

Fran Irwin *New groups coming also meant entertaining for you, Sherry.*

Sherry Steiner *I learned that you could entertain simply. We had so many coming and going. We didn't have the facilities to do anything fancy. So you just did it. You just didn't worry about it.*

Sherry Steiner and Jack White (Group II) drink tea at a picnic to welcome Group IV in late October 1964. (*Credit: Bob Steiner*)

CHAPTER 8   PARTICIPATING IN THE AFGHAN COMMUNITY

Sami Noor *Until the arrival of the Peace Corps Volunteers, the Afghans were thinking that the Americans and Europeans are human beings of higher status and not reachable. Peace Corps Volunteers proved it otherwise . . . trying to establish contact with all Afghans and help them in whatever way possible. In other words, they proved that it was not only the privileged who should benefit from the so-called "foreign-aid." The contacts established by the Volunteers were mostly with middle class Afghans, not the high society. The Volunteers never showed that they knew more—know all, and considered the Afghans as ignorant! They would drink tea and take time to talk with the Afghans, as friends.*

The handbook for Peace Corps Afghanistan emphasized to Volunteers arriving in 1964 that "success or failure is dependent on *your* ability to create a meaningful assignment, to establish informal working and social relationships with host country citizens and to become a participating, active, involved member of the Afghan community."[1] When the first Volunteers arrived in 1962, it had not been at all evident how they might achieve the Peace Corps goal of getting to know

Afghans and their culture beyond doing their jobs. Could they move beyond "guest" status?

Looking back over the first 15 months or so, Steiner wrote: "Foreigners are considered to be guests—and are expected to conduct themselves as guests. The Peace Corps Volunteer, whatever the literature said, was no exception. . . . The first group of nine Volunteers who arrived in September, 1962, although well prepared, found the courteous but distant reserve of the Afghans a far cry from the open-armed welcome which would have eased the way. Whether English teachers, nurses or the lone mechanic, the Volunteers went about their tasks patiently waiting to be accepted, yet careful not to abuse their assigned—but unwanted—role as guests. And the Afghans watched and studied and kept their distance. But gradually, there was a change."[2]

Bob Steiner *One thing that was great about the early Volunteers: Kennedy's "ask not what your country can do for you, ask what you can do for your country"—that was the keynote for them. And that is one of the reasons that I encouraged them early on to put on performances for the Afghans. Of course, Americans were also invited.*

A Hootenanny or folk concert was a common American approach to entertainment in the early 1960s. During their first year, the Volunteers decided it was one way to introduce themselves and connect to their students. For the early groups, Hootenannies continued to be a way to reinforce classroom English learning. They were effective in establishing rapport and exposing students to American culture.[3]

The first concert in early 1963 featured Group I guitarists Janet Mueller and David Fleishhacker perched on a ping-pong table before several hundred Afghan men. Janet described the experience: "An Afghan acquaintance of ours introduced our program in Farsi. . . . .

"I don't know what did it, the introduction or the novelty of our music, but the Afghans seemed thoroughly to enjoy the songs. They laughed at our less-than-perfect Farsi introductions, finding our explanations of the stories related in the songs very droll (perhaps they gained something in translation) . . . .

"After a few songs, we had requests from students familiar with a few songs in English. Although momentarily taken aback, we managed to fill requests for Twinkle, Twinkle, Little Star and Row, Row, Row Your Boat with our customary virtuosity.

"The real success of the evening though, came from our inducing the audience to participate in several songs. Goodnight, Irene was the big hit.

"The audience soon discovered that in tough songs like Three Blind Mice they could clap where they couldn't sing. At one point, a man jumped up and said, 'I want to sing,' and proceeded to make up and sing two songs with great enthusiasm and some talent.

"Our finale was met with much applause and hand-shaking. Our own students of English had gained a new conception of us, and many of the other students who would be going home to the provinces after the winter session would take with them some idea of the Peace Corps. We hope we have more opportunities like that."[4]

Volunteers also found that fellow teachers might become friends.

Bob Pearson *We were invited to several Afghan homes. The women teachers in our group made friends* *with the women teachers in their schools, and one or two of them regularly invited us to their homes for dinner or small parties. Perhaps because I was married it was okay for me to visit Afghan women teachers' houses. We also had lunch once a week with all the teachers working with the Columbia team, and got to be friends with one or two of the men. Perhaps because they had a bit more money, we were invited for dinner on several occasions, and this continued for me once I was desk officer in Peace Corps Washington and would come for a visit to Afghanistan and would be invited to my old friend's home.*

In some cases, socializing did not work out so well.

Bob Pearson *On a couple of shocking occasions we were invited to Afghan parties where Afghan men who had lived in the States brought their wives. There was close dancing at those parties, and I was shocked and scared when one of these wives would snuggle up to me while dancing! This didn't last too long. It may be that we told Steiner and he told us to stop going to such parties. . . . Steiner had made it very clear to us that we were not to date Afghans.* [By the end of Group I's two years in the country, women Volunteers were dating Afghan men. Although male Volunteers were told not to date Afghan women, the first marriages of former women Volunteers to Afghan men were only a few years in the future].

Bob Steiner *One of the problems we encountered with the nurses was with the Russian Embassy. They were inviting the nurses over to their homes and then trying to get them tipsy on vodka. That had to be stopped when some of the nurses had too much to drink.*

Fran Irwin *You saw what worked and learned from that rather than having blanket rules.*

Bob Steiner *That's right. Volunteers were expected to socialize with Afghans and get to know them as people as well as students or as colleagues where they worked; many of these relationships worked well.*

And gradually there was a change, perhaps particularly after the arrival of Group II in June 1963. Steiner wrote: "Some observers think that the coolness continued until after the arrival . . . of the printers, the physical-education teacher, and the additional English teachers of the second group of Volunteers to Afghanistan. . . . Sensing that the time had come to accelerate the pace set by the first group, the new Volunteers, after about three months of settling-in, have appealed to the Afghan's desire to learn more about cameras and art, social institutions, and informal, conversational English by accepting invitations to join groups meeting in the schools, the printing plant, or the Khyber Restaurant . . . ."[5]

It was performances that continued to break the ice. They proved to be an especially effective way of communicating. They ranged from a class play to a solo at a royal wedding, from jazz concerts at the university and the Khyber to more Hootenannies and a musical.

A student play worked well for Bob Pearson teaching in the spring of 1964 in Kandahar.

Bob Pearson *I took an Indian book in English on the life of Babur and turned it into a play in English. I gave my best English students from my four classes parts. The good* *guys had green hats and the bad guys red hats. There was a kind of stage made of mud bricks behind the school and the students really got into it, making costumes, suggesting changes to the script. We then put on a performance for the school, the parents and local dignitaries. It was such a success they decided to do it again.*

Many years later, a friend of mine, who was working for UNICEF in Quetta, wrote that he had two interpreters who had had a Mr. Bob as a teacher in Kandahar. Not only were they my students, but I had photographs of them as they had been in the play. I sent them the pictures.

Music brought the first meeting of Peace Corps Volunteers with His Majesty Zahir Shah. Pat Weeks was invited to sing with an Afghan group at the wedding of Prince Mohammed Nader in February 1964. (Another musician and Pat's husband Phil were the only other Americans invited.) Pat sang a solo in Farsi and a duet with an Afghan star. As Steiner later wrote, the King told her that "he was most pleased with this, his first personal contact with a member of the Peace Corps in Afghanistan about which he had heard so much. . . . [T]he work of the Peace Corps had been of the finest type and that, speaking on behalf of the Afghan people, he wanted her to know that their contribution and their willingness to work with and for the Afghans was known and appreciated by his people. . . . [T]he Queen interjected that she was delighted that Pat Weeks had sung an Afghan song in Farsi."[6]

Bob Steiner *Some Volunteers performed at a nearly professional level. Toby [Herbert Tobias in Group II] played the drums. He was a physical powerhouse. Huge muscles. The Afghans sat entranced as he pounded his percussion instruments in some of the shows.*

Toby, who was All-American in football and basketball and had played the drums professionally, was teaching physical education and physical therapy at Kabul University. He and another Group II PCV, Jack White, an English teacher at the university who played bass viol, teamed up with two Britishers in early 1964 to form a jazz quartet. In July, they gave a concert at the Kabul University auditorium. The 400 students "refused to let them go until they had played several encores. One of the highlights . . . was Toby's playing of the Conga."[7]

The Peace Corps performances built on other efforts to introduce various types of western music in Afghanistan. For instance, in September 1963 Duke Ellington had performed in Kabul as part of a cultural program organized by the Afghan government.[8]

Steiner summarized in a memo how the popularity of White's jazz group had spread like wildfire in the fall of 1964. The Khyber Restaurant asked the group to play dance music one evening on an experimental basis to a carefully selected clientele. The affair was an immediate success, and the Ministry of Finance, which operated the Khyber, secured official sanction for the continuation of this dance program on a regular basis every Thursday and Saturday night. In December, the Ministry of Press and Information held a big ball. White's band was turned to for the music. The event was a great success, financially and otherwise.

In January 1965, the Minister of Finance decided that Jack White should receive an award for his extracurricular music activities; he presented a medal, inscribed on the back with the word for "art," to the U.S. Ambassador, with Steiner present. Another ceremony was set for the U.S. when White arrived home; he had completed his service and was traveling.

"This event [the December 1964 ball] climaxed and dramatized White's tactful but persistent efforts to make jazz popular, but, more particularly, make it respectable in the eyes of Afghans. It should be noted that social occasions such as dancing and popular music for the public are strictly novel to Afghan society. Co-mingling of the sexes has been taboo until very recently. Jack White's success symbolized the emergence of the Afghans from the chrysalis defined by local convention. The accolade which Jack White earned may perhaps be explained by the Afghans' gratitude for his help in allowing them to break gracefully with tradition, or there may be other explanations."[9]

Thirty Volunteers took part in a Peace Corps Hootenanny in 1965 that included skits in Farsi—The Thrice-Promised Bride, folk songs in Pashto, and "Old MacDonald Had a Farm," sung in Farsi.[10] The performers tested the show first at an orphanage before 100 children. Next came two performances at Kabul University that attracted more than 2000 people. A final show was performed during Afghanistan's independence celebration in August at the request of the Ministry of Press.[11]

The next year PCVs from Groups IV, V, and VI collaborated in a June production of the 1960 off-Broadway Sullivan Street Playhouse musical "The Fantasticks" (book and lyrics by Tom Jones, music by Harvey Schmidt). Mary Lison played The Girl, Buddy Oldakowski The Boy, Craig Shulstad The Narrator (El Gallo). Other cast members were Mike Albin and Steve Gallen (the fathers), Linda Abrams (the old actor), Sheilah Kristiansen (the old Indian), and Gordon Hansen (the mute). Sharon Rollinson and Eileen Peterson accompanied on piano, Phyllis McDowell on drums. Barry Hammel, Carol Sanger, Ellen Kaulisch and Margarete Silberberg assisted with lights, props, and prompting. Bernice Stortzman directed: "[S]he cajoled and coaxed and quietly said, 'Yes, you can,' until they did."[12]

Bob Steiner *The performance of "The Fantasticks" was an outstanding success. The Afghans loved it. We tried in these activities to integrate the volunteers socially and professionally with the total community, including international professionals.*

Sports provided another way for Volunteers to make the Peace Corps visible to Afghans and to get to know their students. Volunteers in early groups formed a basketball team including John Borel, David Deeds, Peter Fitzpatrick, Donald Hill, Bob Pearson, Toby Tobias (who was the Kabul University team's regular coach), and Jack White. They beat the Kabul University team 62 to 48 as part of the independence celebration in 1963.[13]

Coaching became part of teaching for some Volunteers. Two examples: Bob Pearson, then in Kabul, took over as Naderia's soccer coach after its Afghan coach suffered a heart attack, and Dennis Egan coached the boys' basketball team after school at Lycee Sultan in Herat.[14] Perhaps best-known, Tom Gouttierre coached the Habibia basketball team as a Volunteer in Group V; that led to his being asked to coach the first Afghan national team. He also held workshops in Kandahar and Herat where he trained fellow Volunteers to coach the game. When he later returned to Afghanistan on a Fulbright fellowship, he was asked, on short notice, to coach a second national team. It defeated a team from China, 58-39, in 1970.[15]

Performances and sports were one thing, but what was the balance between trying to be "ordinary" and being recognized on the job and on the street? It varied by Volunteer, of course. Group II Volunteer John Borel wrote about his attempt at an inconspicuous approach as a six foot two, 200 pound

American. Sometimes one could be a bit too inconspicuous. Bicycling home after dinner one night, he and his roommate were struck by a car. The driver did not stop and two policemen watched.[15] (Read the story on pages 204-206 in Part II.)

By the end of 1963, Steiner could write that the "lines separating the hosts from the Volunteer guests are being obscured,"[17] but caution remained, especially in individual relationships.

Sherry Steiner *It was a rare occasion when we socialized with Afghans. I did teach English to a group of middle-aged Afghan women. Middle-class Afghan women did not volunteer. It was just not part of their culture. The fact that I would volunteer to teach them English was a little strange to them.*

Fran Irwin *I remember that the idea of volunteering was being promoted by some members of the Royal Family and a women's society or institute; we had articles about that on the new women's page at the Kabul Times. Where did you teach?*

Sherry Steiner *In the schools in the afternoon after the students had gone home. In the wintertime, and it was freezing. They never heated their schools and it was awfully cold. But they loved to have me come.*

Fran Irwin *These were teachers, or they were . . . ?*

Sherry Steiner *No, they were housewives who were interested in learning a little bit of English. They were a group of maybe six or eight. We met every week and* *would have an English lesson. It was perhaps as much of a social get-together as a lesson. And I had taught English, when we first arrived, at the international school to children of diplomats from all the different embassies.*

Fran Irwin *Did you find that you were invited to Afghan homes?*

Sherry Steiner *Not too much.*

Fran Irwin *Did you invite Afghans in your home?*

Bob Steiner *Yes, but Afghans were very cautious about appearing to socialize too frequently, or to invite us to their homes.*

Sherry Steiner *In some cases, they may not have really known how to entertain us. What should they serve us? They were uneasy about entertaining foreigners.*

Bob Steiner *That's true, but also the Afghan government had restrictions on their people and the extent to which they could socialize with foreigners.*

Fran Irwin *And did that change over the time that you were there? I see I report in one letter that I had been in three Afghan homes in 24 hours. No doubt I mentioned it because it was unusual—but perhaps it was easier for Volunteers.*

Bob Steiner *It was much better at the end than at the beginning of our time. At first, both sides had to test the waters, study the rules of behavior. The Afghan government*

*did not encourage the Afghans to mix too much with for-
eigners. They never did as long as we were there. They
relaxed it, but it was always tense, uneasy.*

Sherry Steiner *Very different from Iran where we
went out a lot.*

Bob Steiner *But also I think the Volunteers opened up
this relationship. Every case didn't flower. Nevertheless,
the fact that Afghans were able to meet Americans who
treated them as equals, I think was an eye-opener to many
Afghans—it made all the difference in the world. That's
why Dr. Ashraf Ghani* [an economist and anthropologist, a
former finance minister and chancellor of Kabul University]
*was able to tell Bill Moyers the names of his Peace Corps
teachers—Linda Abrams and Craig Shulstad—when he
participated in the 50ᵗʰ Peace Corps anniversary panel.*

n September, just ten weeks before the assassination, King Mohammed Zahir and Queen Homaira visited the United States and met with President Kennedy. The communique issued by the two leaders after the meeting said that the U.S. supported Afghanistan's territorial integrity and its policy of non-alignment.[1]

Fran Irwin *At the beginning, many Volunteers were responding to Kennedy's "Ask not" call.*

Bob Steiner *Yes, I am surprised how many remind us of that.*

Fran Irwin *Rosalind remembers exactly where she was when she heard about Kennedy's assassination.*

Rosalind Pace *We were giving final exams at Zargoonah* [a girls' high school] *and we were in the big exam room. I remember Jill Rindelaub* [another Group I Volunteer] *looking stricken and saying that something terrible had happened. I remember hearing some of the students crying in the courtyard below. Then she told me. After the exam, we raced to the American embassy on our* *bicycles. Afghans poured out of their shops wringing their hands and calling to us: "Kennedy, Kennedy."*

Fran Irwin *Do you remember how you heard the news?*

Bob Steiner *Vividly. Yes. We lived in a compound with walls; next door was another American we didn't know very well, but for some reason I'd put a ladder up to get on top of the wall. The neighbor was out and he said: "Hey, Bob, did you hear the news?" And I said: "What news?" And he said Kennedy had been killed. Whew! We had no details, but I came down and of course it became the subject of all conversations, Afghan and American.*

Chip Steiner *Sleet darkened an already cold and dreary morning. Our bus stopped in front of the American Embassy where, oddly, an adult boarded and staring back at this brood of high school and elementary age kids, informed us that John Kennedy had been shot. School is cancelled. . . .*

Afghans on the street were in deep and obvious mourning. Their flags flew at half-mast. Many approached us saying "Amrikoyee" and they would gently hug us. In my teenage obsession with nothing but myself, the emotions of others usually got short shrift, and I was stunned by the kindness and caring and sophistication of these Afghan people. How could it be that they (who, after all, we Americans were trying to lift from abject poverty and ignorance) seemed to understand better than I the import of Kennedy's assassination, and who were giving succor and consolation and sympathy

*and support to us!! To almighty Americans!! It was a
lesson of the greatness of human understanding—I think
Afghans and Afghanistan identified with Kennedy's ideals for a peaceful and united world in a way that I had
not even begun to grasp at 15.*

*Americans—embassy personnel, Peace Corps staff
and volunteers, AID employees, members of the Wyoming
and Columbia University teams, UN personnel—all of
them it seemed—wept openly or pounded desks with furi-
ous, helpless anger. . . . Things were not so perfect after
all. The United States way of things had flaws, murder-
ous flaws.*

Louis Dupree was scheduled to participate in the Group III
training program in Vermont on the day after the assassination. " . . . I telephoned and asked what to do. Officials at Putney
said, 'Come on up. Shriver has said for all training to continue.
The President would have wanted it that way.' So I flew up.

"The trainees held a brief, simple service on the day the nation
buried Kennedy. The Afghan language instructors bought a wreath
and placed it around a portrait of the late president, and at the end
of the service asked if they could say something. One of them read
a moving poetic tribute in Persian. Then, the training continued."[2]

Pat Sullivan Meyers, desk officer for Afghanistan, was in
Philadelphia recruiting for Peace Corps that day. The 18th person
hired by Peace Corps, she, like many others, remembers it as the
best job of her life. She cites Patrick Moynihan after JFK's assassination: you "know the world is going to break your heart eventually. I guess we thought that we had a little more time . . . heavens,
we'll laugh again, it's just that we will never be young again."[3]

Volunteers who served in the mid-sixties found that
Afghans across the country knew about and remembered

Kennedy. His message to "citizens of the world" seemed to have reached them.

Fran Irwin *I wrote in a letter home that our cook, Corban, from the Hazarajat, asked whether a photograph was of Kennedy. I was surprised—this was not until late 1964—that he knew about Kennedy.*

Betsy Thomas Amin-Arsala *In July of 1966, during a summer heat break from teaching in Herat in western Afghanistan, several of my cohorts and I took a trip to Maimana in the north. Though Herat and Maimana were only about 250 miles apart, it took us four days and four nights in each direction, traveling on whatever buses and/or trucks would pick us up. The route was exciting and breathtaking as well as dusty and exhausting. Finally reaching a lovely village called Murghab on the Murghab River, we gratefully paused at a teahouse while awaiting the next leg of our journey. Teahouses were the only public places to eat or drink. Even though they were reserved for men, Volunteers—male and female—had to stop there for food. This particular teahouse was unusual— beautifully painted with real paint instead of the commonly-used tinted whitewash. And there were even lovely flowers painted on the walls.*

On one side I noticed a photo of President Kennedy, clipped from a magazine. Many times before I had seen photos on walls in people's houses and discovered that the owners often did not know what the picture was; they just liked the look of it. So I asked the teahouse owner "Who is that in that photo there?"

The teahouse man looked at me somewhat incredulously and asked "Aren't you an American?" I nodded, and he asked: "Well, don't you know who that is?"

I said: "I know who it is but I was wondering if you do."

The man drew himself up and rather proudly said, "Why, that is President Kennedy. He was the President for the whole world!"

This was a time when the only connection with the outside world in a place like Murghab was the radio. And in 1966 most Americans had either never heard of Afghanistan or thought it was in Africa.

Fran Irwin *The early Peace Corps Volunteers met with the King?*

Bob Steiner *Yes, he invited all of them up to Paghman, in the foothills above the city. . . . We have some pictures of that. I remember the CIA chief was a little burned up. . . . "Who do they think they are?"*

On August 19, 1964, King Mohammed Zahir and Queen Homaira invited all 60 Peace Corps Volunteers then serving in Afghanistan to a reception. It was held in the King's (Tepa) Gardens in Paghman. *An Historical Guide to Kabul* describes the gardens as they were in the 1960s. "Stately trees shadow well-kept terraced lawns and flower beds beside large fountains; arcades grace the lower terrace from which one may look down upon the Kargha Lake and Kabul spread out at the foot of the Sulaiman Mountains which recede into the distance, range upon range. On the opposite side from the car park, steps lead down to a large swimming pool on the terrace in front of another palace. The gardens continue from here in a more natural state, dotted here and there with artificial lakes and ponds."[1] The district was designed after King Amanullah's visit to Europe in 1927-28, and includes an arch marking Afghanistan's independence.[2]

Since Bob Steiner and his family were on pre-scheduled home leave in the U.S., it fell to Bob McClusky to represent the Peace Corps staff. The U.S. Ambassador to Afghanistan, John Steeves, was also present.

Bob McClusky *The reception was held on one of the upper terraces and shaded by a large tent replete with Afghan carpets covering the ground beneath it. Tea was served by palace staff. Rather than a formal reception line, the King and Queen opted to move from Volunteer to Volunteer. As they did so, I introduced the Volunteers to the King and Queen by name, telling where each one worked. Frequently there would be an exchange between the King and the Volunteer or Volunteer couple.*

Later, there were conversations, in English and Dari, in small groups, the men with the King, dressed in a suit and smoking a pipe, the women and some of the married Volunteer couples with the Queen, dressed in a white suit with black polka dots. As the nearly three-hour event drew to a close, a photo was taken of all assembled, the King and Queen at the center, the Volunteers to the left and right, all dressed appropriately for the occasion.

The King expressed appreciation for the Volunteers' service and their effectiveness in promoting better relations among nations. Louis Dupree also subsequently reported that in his remarks to the Volunteers, His Majesty said, "I do not wish to make light of the American Ambassador, but I do wish to say that you Peace Corps Volunteers are the true American ambassadors in Afghanistan." Dupree viewed it as "a memorable event (which) symbolized the success of the Peace Corps in Afghanistan . . . since no other development group had received such recognition from the King."[3]

King Mohmmed Zahir and Queen Homaira with Peace Corps Volunteers at the Paghman Gardens, August 19, 1964. *(Photographs provided by Bob McClusky; photographer unknown but may have been taken by U.S. Information Service.)*

Bob McClusky *It was unusual. The King was not known for this sort of public gesture. But it was not just the King making the gesture; he was accompanied by his wife and members of his family. The interaction between Volunteers and members of the royal family was relaxed and congenial. The Volunteers answered questions and talked about the work they did and their life in Afghanistan.*

The Peace Corps had been in Afghanistan for just short of two years. The original group had convinced the doubters that Americans could live and work within the Afghan society, under Afghan supervision. Requests for more Volunteers had followed upon the work of the first group, as did requests from the provinces. Individual Volunteers had made the difference. The reception was essentially in their honor as well as to recognize Steiner and the character and tone of his low-key, in-the-background leadership.

King Mohammed Zahir and Queen Homaira are introduced to Volunteers Herbert (Toby) and Barbara Tobias by Deputy Peace Corps Director Robert McClusky, center.

Queen Homaira talks with Volunteer Alice Kapell as her husband David listens.

CHAPTER 11   GOING TO THE PROVINCES

By the fall of 1964, Afghanistan was ready both to increase the numbers and to expand the locations of Peace Corps Volunteers significantly. The country was continuing to modernize. The new terminal at the Kabul airport was in use. The Afghan Air Authority's school in Kabul was looking for a Volunteer to teach students who were learning English so that they could talk to pilots as air traffic controllers from provincial airports. The Soviet-built Salang Tunnel slicing through the Hindu Kush at 11,000 feet to connect Kabul to the northern cities was about to be inaugurated. The tunnel cut the distance through the mountains between Jabul Seraj and Doshi from 192 to 67 miles. The trip from Kabul to cities like Pul-i-Khumri, Kunduz, and Mazar-i-Sharif could now be measured in hours instead of days.[1] At the same time, the number of students in schools at all levels was growing rapidly. A new campus for Kabul University funded by the U.S. had opened. Political change seemed to match the physical changes. A Loya Jirga, a grand assembly, met in September to approve the new Constitution. Representatives came from various ethnic and tribal groups and included four women.

The control tower and a directional sign at the Kabul Airport in 1965. *(Credit: Will A. Irwin)*

Peace Corps was improving its ability to meet the needs identified by Afghans as training and placement benefitted from the experience of earlier Volunteers. Group IV would be the largest group yet with 56 Volunteers, and for the first time nearly half would be immediately assigned to serve outside of Kabul. Steiner noted the turning point for the Peace Corps in Afghanistan in a newsletter, written and edited by Volunteers already serving in Afghanistan and issued at the end of October as the new group arrived. He wrote:

> It is appropriate that the arrival of Afghan IV would be heralded by this, the first issue of a PC/Afghanistan newsletter. For it is those who preceded Afghan IV, and who initiated and prepared this newsletter, who made Afghan IV possible. And that is fact!
>
> The Afghans have always liked the idea of the Peace Corps; but like realists everywhere, they had to see its application to measure the benefits against any attendant headaches. They started slowly, cautiously. Afghan I, II, and III were on trial; they have fulfilled the hopes, dispelled the fears.
>
> In this sense, you, all of you in Afghan IV, are the tangible evidence that the efforts of your predecessors have not been in vain. You have doubled our size (the number is not important but the fact is), the provinces have been opened to you! We welcome this newsletter, and through it we welcome you! Good luck![2]

Volunteers in Group IV went to more than a half dozen provincial cities and towns. The largest numbers went to Kandahar (10) and to Lashkargah (8). Others went to Mazar-i-Sharif (4), Pul-i-Khumri (2), Tegari (2), Farah (2), and Jalalabad (3).[3]

The first opportunities for Volunteers to work outside of Kabul had opened up at the end of 1963. Prime Minister Mohammed Yousuf's government, formed in March of that year, saw in the Peace Corps a potential force for social change.[4] The initial assignments to the provinces were tentative. Seventeen Volunteers from the first two groups spent between two and five months on temporary English teaching assignments in provincial schools during the first six months of 1964 and four of them remained until December.[5]

Bob Pearson *Some members of Group I went to the provinces after our first year in Kabul. After we returned from our winter vacation, four of us (Bob and Rosalind Pearson and Jan Mueller and Jill Rindelaub) went to Kandahar to teach until June of that year when we had our termination conference.*

David Fleishhacker, also in Group I, remembered going to teach in Mazar-i-Sharif at the end of 1963. A major purpose of his months there was to prepare the ground for later English teachers and to demonstrate that the presence of Volunteers in northern Afghanistan would not threaten Afghan-Soviet friendship. He also got a first-hand look and experience of the "core of the country" as "a mass of mountain peaks cut by steep, rocky gorges." The trip north from Kabul could, and did for Fleishhacker, take days, or could mean waiting weeks for a plane, depending on the weather, since the road was not yet paved nor the Salang Tunnel completed.[6]

As Peace Corps Volunteers moved into the provinces, whether to Maimana in the northern plains or to Farah in the southwestern desert, Volunteers and staff learned first-hand about the landscape and the nature of travel.

Bob McClusky *For one trip to check out a Volunteer site, we took the Travelall, an enhanced station wagon with four-wheel drive. I think there were four of us: Walter Morgan, the doctor, and Sami and Naim. We took turns driving with Naim indicating the direction. We drove across open plains from Kunduz to a small bazaar midway between Kunduz and Kholm, then on to Kholm and Mazar. We were making our own track mile after mile. It was like being at sea and charting your own course.*

Fran Irwin *Who made the decision that Peace Corps Volunteers could work outside of Kabul?*

On the way to Band-i-Amir Lakes in central Afghanistan. (*Credit: Bob Steiner*)

Bob Steiner *The Afghan government made the decision—for example, for the teachers, the Ministry of Education. Dr. Saif Samady, then the director of technical and vocational education and teacher training, was the critical first Afghan with whom we mostly worked. He was fairly familiar with the schools and would suggest I go visit whatever schools it was he was thinking about. And I'd go visit them and talk to the principal. Toward the end of my time there, they began to hear about the Peace Corps and it was no big problem. At the beginning . . . getting the first Volunteers placed . . . it took some explaining and some very dubious "yes, well, you damn Americans" sort of thing. But inevitably they were very happy with it . . . with most of them. We had some problems, of course.*

Fran Irwin *So initially it was Mazar-i-Sharif and Kandahar. I think of Kandahar being more conservative.*

Bob Steiner *Yes, it was, and it was more difficult for the Volunteers.*

Fran Irwin *But Kandahar schools weren't behind in requesting them?*

Bob Steiner *They were among the first in requesting them. And then the Helmand valley. And finally, almost every city, any place, in the country. At the end of the second year I think all restrictions were lifted. At that point Afghanistan was big. Once they lifted the restrictions it wasn't a question of I'm dealing only with Kabul. By working with some of the larger cities, one dealt with many places. Eventually, I didn't need to search for business.*

Fran Irwin *There were some problems in the provinces?*

Bob Steiner *There was the problem of getting to see the Volunteers on the job. In Kabul, I didn't have to worry. Volunteers did very well, no problems. But out in the provinces it was more difficult, and we tried to get out once every two or three months to see them. That took a lot of traveling and planning and, inevitably, when we went, there had been problems of one kind or another. So those had to be settled. But generally, fortunately, I made assignments, the really tough ones, to the right people.*

Fran Irwin *That was the key.*

Bob Steiner *Yes, it really was, because some of those spots were difficult, like the one way down—Farah down in the southwest corner—the McGaffeys just performed beautifully. He later joined the Foreign Service, and she did, too.*

Fran Irwin *Volunteers were facing different kinds of challenges than ones in the city?*

Bob Steiner *Right. Different kinds, some more intense, some less intense, than in Kabul. They were usually the lone American figures in a town. Their every move was watched with great care. And the Volunteers sometimes didn't know they were being so intently watched. It was only when I got there that we learned that this guy or that gal was behaving in ways unacceptable to the Afghans.*

Fran Irwin *I certainly wrote in letters frequently about how it was to be a Volunteer in the city, in Kabul,* versus the provinces. Being in the city was different from the traditional Peace Corps image. It wasn't that we weren't spending time with Afghans—we were—but that there was also such an active international community to distract us, and it could be hard to spend time with Afghans after work. Dinners might be late and transportation uncertain if not in bicycle range. It was harder to spend time with women in the evenings. There were exceptions, and sometimes we were able to get to know women through their husbands. Our Farsi teacher got married and we arranged for him to continue to teach my housemate—who was way ahead of me—and I studied with his wife—and so they'd both come.

Bob Steiner Yes, there was a big difference between the problems of those of you in Kabul and those out in the provinces. It was a marked difference. And much tougher in the provinces.

Will Irwin How was it tougher?

Bob Steiner Well, things like Fran's mentioned. Getting to meet socially with the Afghans. The Afghans were very cautious about being seen too much with foreigners. So it was often a much lonelier job in the provinces, of course, than in Kabul. And the Volunteers who were there, I think, had to make a much greater adjustment than you guys in Kabul. It was usually important to send a couple to the provinces because they could support each other. Single ones often invited trouble. Some Volunteers refused to abide by Afghan rules of conduct and thought they could get away with it. Well, of course, the Afghans knew immediately what they were doing and *when. Afghan complaints to their supervisors would mean a call to somebody in Kabul and then I would get a call. A couple of Volunteers who refused to respect complaints had to be terminated.*

Will Irwin *What was the issue?*

Bob Steiner *Well, they were climbing over the wall between their houses and co-habiting of a night while believing the Afghans didn't know what was happening. The Afghans were saying these guys should not be doing this. These Volunteers chose to disrespect Afghan customs.*

As Volunteers gained experience, they were rapidly becoming responsible for tasks that the staff had previously performed. The handbook now stated that Peace Corps housing in the provinces would be up to the Volunteers, noting that usually Afghan colleagues would assist in finding modest housing. "Depending on location, housing should not cost more than 800-1000 Afs per month/per Volunteer. You should insist upon screening of all doors and opening windows." In Kabul, the Peace Corps was paying an average of 1500 Afs a month per Volunteer. The fall 1965 newsletter in welcoming Group VI noted that the Peace Corps office wanted to get out of the housing business and give Volunteers in Kabul as well as in the provinces more responsibility for locating and negotiating housing and also for supervising routine maintenance, tasks that had taken much staff time.[7]

A Group VI Volunteer who initially taught in Kabul and then moved to Herat recalls finding housing largely on her own.

Betsy Thomas Amin-Arsala *Upon arriving in Herat I stayed for several weeks with two PC nurses who were already living there. Somehow, totally on my own I found out about available houses, went to see them on my bike, interviewed the landlords and finally settled on a brand new house. Well, it was 18 months old but had never been lived in. In fact, the well had to be dug—by hand—after I moved in. The window glass was also not put in until after I had signed the lease. Two months later when bug eggs started hatching I discovered that many had been laid INSIDE the window pane-less house!*

Volunteer letters, presentations, and oral histories record how it was to be among early Volunteers to serve outside of Kabul. These three examples provide a glimpse of life in Ghazni, Kandahar, and Farah.

Dennis and Susan Aronson in Ghazni

Dennis and Susan Aronson had come with Group III in January 1964 and taught the first year in Kabul. When they learned there was an opportunity to teach in the provinces the next year, they jumped at the chance and were assigned to Ghazni, a provincial capital southwest of Kabul. They put their bicycles on a local bus and moved to Ghazni, apparently the first foreigners to live there.

In a presentation Dennis made in 2009, he described how it was to settle in. Their water was delivered in a goatskin bag. The stove burned wood instead of sawdust and had a tank on top for heating water. He had found a toilet seat in the Kabul bazaar and made the commode out of a kerosene can. A student taught them how to deal with their leaking roof. Tack a bed sheet to the ceiling, cut a slit in the middle, tie a rope in the hole, tie a rock to the rope to make the sheet taut. The water saturates the sheet and runs to the rope and down into the bucket. It worked for the rest of the winter. They also learned that a little salt mixed with mud kept weeds from growing and creating cracks in the roof.

Dennis Aronson with his class and principal at Lycee Sanai in Ghazni. (*Credit: Bob Steiner*)

Their 7th to 12th grade students were highly motivated. Many came from nearby villages when they could be spared from work in fields or shops. Boys and girls went to separate schools. The girls wore standard black uniforms with white scarves. The women teachers wore modern dress and the religion teacher, the only man in the school, traditional dress. Dennis was once invited to give a special lesson on aerodynamics he had prepared for a boys school science class at the girls' school, an unprecedented event. Some classes had as many as 60 students. Fifteen might be absent, and a different group every day. Students remained in their classrooms while the teachers moved from room to room each period carrying their teaching aids with them. There was no electricity so they used pictures, hand puppets, and flannel boards. Nor was there heat, so exams might be given outside in the sunshine.[9]

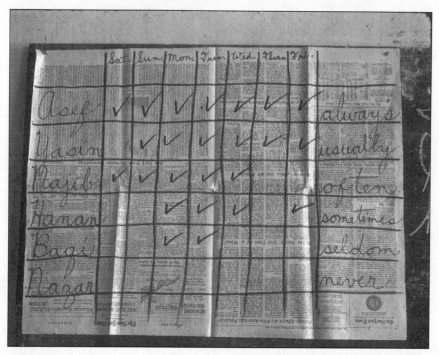

Dennis Aronson used this as a visual aid for teaching the terms for frequency in English. It is drawn on a *New York Times* dated April 14, 1965. (*Credit: Bob Steiner*)

Leonard Oppenheim in Kandahar

Len Oppenheim wrote in letters home in early November 1964 within weeks of his arrival about his early impressions of Kandahar—an oasis in the desert with quite a few fir trees, no buildings with over three floors, a huge and totally unpaved bazaar, one movie theater, few cars but hundreds of gadis (carts) with horses highly decorated in red pompoms.

Apartment 2, which Len and another Volunteer shared, was in the Marastoon complex built by a foreign firm and later handed over to the city to be used as a poorhouse. The rents, fairly high by Afghan standards, were used to support the poor. Employees were also supposed to be poor people. It was located next to the Darwaza Id-ga, an arch providing the gateway into the bazaar. "In front of the apartments is the main paved highway, but between the highway and the building runs a wide parkway with paths and flowers and then a dirt road, which could possibly eventually become a beautiful four lane divided highway, although now its main use is for the hundreds of camels and sheep and donkeys that are driven past by their owners daily. . . ."

"Outside the door to Marastoon complex 2 apartment stands a policeman. Sometimes he sits on the next doorstep and sometimes at night he builds a fire on the small stoop leading into the tailor shop on the right. But there is always a policeman there. We have a 24 hour guard which must change about four times daily. I don't know what they are guarding us from or if they are guarding us or the apartment or what, but it certainly is a kind of status symbol of some sort, don't you think? . . . They must be totally bored and also extremely curious as to the goings-on at No. 2."

As he got to know Kandahar, Len was eager to show his students, tenth and eleventh graders learning English so that they could become surveyors, what the United States looked like. "[P]lease try to find a wonderful picture book of America including scenery, industry, peoples and everything possible. No one here has any concept whatsoever of America and what it looks like. Only perhaps two of my students have ever been outside of Afghanistan and since they don't see American movies or magazines or pictures of anything like it they have absolutely no idea of what else exists in this world. None have ever seen a railroad train, and only one has been on a plane. They have only seen Kabul and that's the only city they know. To them, Kabul is the best in the world and what else is possible? Please try to find such a book (with some color pictures). It will mean so much to me if I can show them."[10]

On one occasion Len did not need to depend on a book to show his students about his country. A plane carrying Averell Harriman as a special U.S. ambassador landed at the Kandahar airport. Len and another Peace Corps English teacher decided it was an opportunity for their students. They negotiated permissions and transport for 120 10th graders to go to the airport. The students got what was for most of them their first look inside a modern western building and inside a jet plane. Then, as the plane took off, the students heard the loud roar of jet engines for the first time. None of them had heard anything louder than a truck horn. "It sounds corny, but the friendliness of just plain Americans, and their skill . . . was really an impressive thing. And then we all had a surprise. The Afghan colonel told us that as a special favor to the PC and our class, the pilots of the jet had radioed that they were going to circle the airfield and come down very low and go real fast . . . as a special salute to us. This they did with the whole class watching. . . . In three weeks they will be going home to their villages all over the country, and I'm sure this is one of the first stories they will tell about their school. . . ."[11]

David and Elizabeth McGaffey in Farah

David and Betty McGaffey wrote about their life in the southwestern province of Farah in letters home between late

1964 and 1966. "Farah is a mud-brick town on the edge of the desert, composed of equal parts of high walls and gardens. Behind it are fantastically sharp and lifeless slate mountains, and as travelers emerge from this sharp desolation, they are met by a two-mile long, absolutely straight avenue of trees. . . . All growing is by irrigation, so not dependent on rainfall, and with a one-month winter, which only usually gets down to freezing at night, and averages 60 during the day, the city remains green all year round. . . . Just outside the city lies the old city of Farah (about three thousand years old) in which little remains but the tremendous walls, five miles in circumference and sixty to eighty feet tall, and mounds which were homes. . . ."

In a later letter, they describe their house. "It's adobe brick and mud plaster, whitewashed inside. . . . A fence in our alley was cracked so they just knocked it down, added straw and water to the wreckage and rebuilt it. There are some beautiful bits of work with this basically rough material, an arched stairway up to our sun-roof, which is in beautiful smooth curves, and some of the doorway arches are great. The strange thing is that some of the walls around us, built no more than 5 yrs ago, look precisely like the walls standing in the old walled city outside of town, built some three thousand years ago. . . . Our living room floor is of earth concrete, while our kitchen and bedroom floors are dirt. Living room and bedroom are covered with rugs, and the kitchen floor is kept clean and hard by a daily soaking with water. It's great for spills. . . . We have electricity from 5:30 to 10:30 at night, very good 150 watt, and a pressure lantern for the rest of the time . . . ."

"The town seems to have accepted us well. Everybody knows us. . . . We have been to our neighbor's house for lunch (she wouldn't eat with us, but talked from a curtained doorway while we ate, but it was great fun), and to tea at the governor's, and are invited there for dinner. Our fellow teachers are great—all friendly, many eager to learn English, and all willing students. These kids are so eager to learn, and so interested that every class is a joy. Once we get books for them, it will be perfect. And they understand our Farsi."[12]

A year later, they wrote: "Our first rosy glow of assurance was replaced by something approaching sheer panic when we realized that they didn't really understand the book, and that most of the tidy little techniques of teaching we learned in the States just didn't apply here. Through painful trial and error, we have learned how to reach them now, and both they and we have benefitted from the experience. We've also learned to stop trying to 'figure people out.' We now know enough to know that Afghans are just as complicated as everyone else, and no more subject to 'interpretation'. We even dislike some of them. The first year, we thought we just didn't understand them, but now we just say we like or dislike them."[13]

A few months before completing their second year, Betty wrote: "Well, another experiment that didn't work. . . . I asked two of my students, the landlord's granddaughters, to come over to see my house, but he didn't give his permission. . . . So far, no woman from Farah . . . has ever seen this house. And only the doctor's wife and the woman who lived next door have even been here at all. Isn't that hard to imagine?"[14]

David's memories recorded 30 years later as part of an oral history for diplomats further describe their experience.

McGaffey: We were the first foreigners who had ever come to Farah to live. We were teachers in the sense of rabbi. The Peace Corps had one definition of what we were supposed to do and we did that plus a lot of other things: set up a science lab, opened the first high school for girls, dug wells and taught carpentry. Mostly we were being Americans in a place that didn't quite believe in those mythological beings.

Q: You said you helped set up a girls high school. I would have thought this would have run counter to much of what was going on.

McGaffey: No, as a matter of fact, it was very much what was going on. This was 1964. Afghanistan was very much a part of the exploration of limits and deciding what was new. They were trying to establish a central government for the first time but never quite succeeded. They did things like provided money for schools in all of the towns, built roads out, sent Peace Corps. So I was part of a modernist conspiracy that was myself, the principal of the high school, the governor, the chief of police, and the young doctor who was the first doctor ever in town, all trying to refocus the minds of the people in Farah.

Q: I would expect in that society it would have been very helpful to have been married, wasn't it?

McGaffey: The only previous person from the Peace Corps was a young man who had been sent down by himself and was installed in a hotel room. He came very close to having a nervous breakdown because the people were so hospitable, and so concerned for him, that they would sit in his hotel room for 18 hours a day just to keep him company and he never had any privacy. He reported that it was an unlivable town. So, yes, having a wife meant that we could have privacy and so it was very important. Elizabeth was also a teacher, which meant that she was ambisextrous. She was welcomed in both the male areas and the female areas. I was only welcomed in the male areas, except for a very few exceptions.[15]

Knowing how to speak Farsi easily from his years growing up in Persia was a significant factor in enabling Bob Steiner to build the Peace Corps program in Afghanistan.

Fran Irwin *You did know Farsi. Presumably, that helped a lot when you were explaining Peace Corps and talking to people about possible jobs.*

Bob Steiner *Yes, oh yes. Night and day. It made a big difference. There is no question about it. Of course, if they knew English they were much more anxious to practice their English than to improve my Persian.*

Sami Noor *Although he was in Afghanistan for the first time, Bob Steiner already had knowledge of the culture and tradition in Afghanistan. His command of the Farsi language was quite helpful in creating trust among the Afghans.*

Bob McClusky also emphasizes the advantage of knowing the culture and language—an ace in the hole for Bob Steiner.

Bob McClusky *Having grown up speaking the language was of inestimable value in starting the program* *and in providing guidance and timely insight as it grew. Most important was the word of mouth among Afghans regarding the sensitivities and instincts of the person sent to Kabul to embody JFK's new initiative.*

Yes, as Steiner told me when I came, the folks in the ministries spoke English and once I was there I could take lessons. I found English was in wide use, but it was not the native tongue. It would have been to my advantage had I known Farsi. I dialogued in English, worked at learning Farsi, and when necessary collaborated with folks like Sami Noor, who served as invaluable colleagues in relating to the complex world in which I found myself. But there is no doubt, Afghans were aware—as we were—that Steiner spoke the language and knew the culture. Yes, he had been in Iran, a different country, but that was not emphasized. As he says, knowing the language made a big difference when talking about jobs and assignments and even more so working out complications and confusions. Would that every director in each of the countries in which Peace Corps initiated programs very quickly had had a familiarity with the culture and some experience with a local language.

For Volunteers, the importance of learning the language was emphasized during recruitment and training and while in the country. The handbook spelled out the importance. "Language study is one of your most important responsibilities. Language fluency can make a significant contribution not only to your work, but also to the richness of your relations with the people of this country and to your own education and value."[1]

Sami Noor . . . *the Volunteers were trying to work as counterparts, not looking at the Afghans from the "top" to the* *bottom. They tried to convey the notion that they were there to cover the needs, and they treated Afghans respectfully. Learning the Afghan languages was compulsory, and had quite a significant effect on the daily work of the Volunteers.*

The training program for the first group that was started with only a few months' notice found an instructor who knew Persian well but not the version spoken in Afghanistan, as Bob Pearson recalls.

Bob Pearson *Our language instructor was a man named Dr. Jim Pence, who undoubtedly knew enough Persian to teach us, but he spoke very slowly and did not have a real Afghan accent. This turned out to be a problem because it was hard for us to get used to Dari [the Afghan version of Farsi] spoken at normal speed. . . . Our TEFL [Teaching English as a Foreign Language] instructor for our training knew nothing about Afghanistan and gave us a theoretical linguistics course based on his long experience in the Philippines. While it had some intellectual merit, it did not give us any real sense of the Afghan classrooms that awaited us. . . .*

A few Afghans thought the first group had been taught the wrong kind of Persian, that is, they had been taught the spoken language rather than literary Persian. However, it was Farsi as it was spoken in Afghanistan that would allow Volunteers to do their jobs and get to know Afghans.

Bob Pearson *I believe it was early spring 1963 that we were invited to a 'high level' meeting with some of the Afghan government ministers, a kind of tea party where we were to 'mix.' I remember talking to one of the ministers* *and he admonished me for speaking 'kitchen Persian.' He felt that it was a dis-service to not teach us the classical Persian that he found so beautiful. He felt it a waste to teach us such a demeaning dialect!*

Ehsan Entezar, who directed language training for Groups III, V, and VIII, produced a first manual for Peace Corps for teaching Dari.[2] Group IV used the new manual in its language training program that was led by Esmael Burhan. By then, trainees were getting a total of 325 hours of language, often 6 hours a day. Initially, all Volunteers studied Dari, but by 1967 training also began to include Pashto for those going Pashto-speaking areas.

Having begun to learn the language and experience the culture, Volunteers became an important source for future staff field officers. Jon Wicklund from Group II was one example.

Jon Wicklund *I wonder what those of us in the first and second groups missed by not having Ehsan Entezar and his terrific group of teachers as our instructors. One of my memories of Ehsan and how dedicated he was to his profession happened later—at Ft. Lupton, Colorado, in the summer of 1968. Trainees in that group wanted to go to see Eugene McCarthy give a campaign speech during the time they would ordinarily be studying Persian. I can remember Ehsan being adamantly against a change of schedule; I wished Bob Steiner were there to come up with a compromise.*

When I was teaching as a Volunteer in Pul-i-Khumri, I liked the principal at my school a great deal because he was always complimentary of my language skills. Earlier that winter, I had gone to Iran on vacation and was talking to an Iranian on a bus trip to Isfahan. At one point, he told me he couldn't take my "kitchen" Persian anymore, and we had to speak German.

A low point came when I was later working for Peace Corps. I was dealing with a school official in Maimana and it was apparent to both of us that my Persian was not up to handling the problem. My high point with the language was when I working for Walter Blass, giving a speech at the Jeshun stadium. I can't remember why I was giving it. I just remember one of Ehsan's instructors helping me with it. He probably wrote the whole thing.

Some Volunteers working in Kabul found that they used English in their jobs and felt less incentive to learn more than necessary to get along in the bazaar. However, Peace Corps encouraged further study by paying for instruction once Volunteers were in Afghanistan and also by testing their progress. The policy recognized different needs for vocabulary and dialect depending on the job and living situation. The emphasis was on effort: "What we are interested in is that the level of individual *effort* be uniformly high."[3] The focus of language in training was on speaking the language. However, once in Afghanistan some Volunteers also studied how to read and write.

Group VIII Volunteer Saul Helfenbein recalls: "Farsi was a fairly easy language. It was a branch of the Indo-European languages and had many recognizable cognates that made for a friendly and confidence-building initial encounter with it. Grammar and syntax were also fairly simple and standard without too many irregularities. For the most part, as we were expected to get to a certain level of spoken proficiency, learning mainly involved picking up new vocabulary. Written Dari was in Arabic script, but with a little practice and memorization I mastered the alphabet and could read. Writing as in all languages was more difficult as this took a different set of skills. By the time I left Afghanistan I was fluent and literate, but probably not as much as I could have been because we mainly spoke English at the *Kabul Times*. I didn't have to put that much effort into learning the language as I might have had I been in a local language working environment." Saul taught English during his first year in Kabul and notes that he learned to teach English as a foreign language by imitating his Farsi language instructors.[4]

The McGaffeys are an example of Volunteers serving in isolated provincial posts who became particularly skilled in Farsi. David wrote in a letter home about changes after being in Afghanistan a year: "For one, we have really learned Farsi. We received a 'professional proficiency' rating on the Foreign Service exam this summer, but we notice it mostly in our ability to share the ordinary conversation of the teachers and our other friends. After an evening of arguing about politics, religion, women, the weather, world affairs, hunting, school intrigues, I realize how much I missed that last year. All of you who know me, know that I'd rather argue than eat. Betty had a much harder time than I did, because she also had to overcome their reluctance to speak to a woman, but now they talk freely with her as well."[5] The McGaffeys also reached the "working proficiency" level in reading.

Describing his impressions of the embassy staff in his oral history interview, David recalled that when he was in Peace Corps "[n]obody there, with the exception of a man who I learned was the [CIA] station chief, spoke the language to anything like my capacity and my capacity was certainly limited. None of them left the capital. All of them felt that talking to the small inner circle of what we called the prop jet set gave them an insight to what was happening in Afghanistan, and they were wrong. . . ."[6]

The newsletters report on several Volunteers winning fellowships to further education in Persian, linguistics, or area studies. There were also Volunteers who made learning Farsi a major focus of their time in Afghanistan and then used it in their careers. For example, the newsletter in December 1966 reports that three Group V Volunteers in Kabul had passed the foreign student Farsi examination at Kabul University. That entailed a five-hour test before the Faculty of Literature including dictation, Persian poetry, composition, conversation, reading comprehension and translation. They had studied in the Dari Department and also with the Afghan Historical Society.[7] Deborah Klimberg-Salter became an historian of South and Central Asian art, including the art of Afghanistan; Charline Reeves served with U.S. AID for 40 years; and Dunning Wilson became a bibliographer of Near Eastern manuscripts at the Young Research Library at the University of California Los Angeles.

For Steiner, knowing the language also meant he could understand what was going on as he traveled the country.

Fran Irwin *Do you remember any specific examples of when knowing the language made a particular difference?*

Bob Steiner *This isn't exactly an indication, but I used to drive up to this most remote site in the northwest of Afghanistan. Maimana. There were two Volunteers there. Driving from Mazar-i-Sharif taking the regular road you went north and then south. It was the worst road in Afghanistan—a corrugated road. When one went in the Peace Corps pick-up it was a painful experience. Once Naim, the Peace Corps driver, took me straight across the unmarked plains of Central Asia, unscored by any road.*

*He said, "I know the way." It was absolutely smooth; the
grass would rustle across the bottom of the truck. It was
wonderful. It was a long drive. I think it was an eight-
hour drive across these steppes, and one had to find the
one place where a big moat could be crossed. It took a little
luck to hit it. In the evening, when darkness marked all but
the sky, the smoke from towers in the town of Maimana
became the target. No road, just the column of smoke to
guide the driver—an infallible one.*

*I determined that I was going to do that by myself the
next time. But I got cold feet just before leaving the road. I
usually stopped at teahouses along the road and if anyone
wanted a lift, I would put them in the back of the truck to
serve as a stabilizer. On my first solo trip I asked a couple
of them if they knew the road to Maimana. This one guy
said he did. Well, I was a little suspicious, but I said you
come with me, show me. So we went on, and as we stopped
at several teahouses, I suddenly found a lot of people getting in and I got more suspicious. The next time I dropped
some of them off at a teahouse, I said "How much did this
guy charge you?" "Oh, not very much." The rogue was
charging every one of these people as we went along, and
he didn't know his way across the steppes of Central Asia
any better than I did. In such circumstances my language
facility proved essential. I arrived in Maimana as the
lights were being lit.*

Not surprisingly, new challenges emerged as Peace Corps became more established in Afghanistan. In what jobs were Volunteers likely to be most effective? What did working within the culture really mean? What did being non-political mean as situations changed in Afghanistan and in the United States?

By May of 1965, Peace Corps Afghanistan had nearly 140 Volunteers teaching, nursing, and working in other fields such as accounting. The goal was 200 with the additional Volunteers all going to the provinces. At that point there were 89 Volunteers in Kabul and 48 in fourteen provincial locations.[1] As Volunteers began to serve in more parts of the country, they encountered a wider range of Afghans. At the same time, Volunteers were also getting to know a broader cross-section of Americans through the Peace Corps than many had encountered at home.

Education continued to be a primary focus of the Peace Corps as the Afghan government sought to meet the demand for schooling. The 1964 Constitution provided the right to free education for every Afghan citizen. The education law adopted under it stated the "aim of the government to reach a stage in which suitable educational facilities will be available for all individuals according to their capacity in institutions of primary education, literacy centres and institutions of vocational, secondary and higher education as well as centres for research and cultural activities."[2]

More than half of the Volunteers arriving in 1965 and 1966 came to teach—most English but also science, math, and physical education. They were filling a need during what Afghan Education Minister Mohammed Anas called "a very critical period." It is "a time when the Afghanistan educational system has tremendous growing pains—the majority of the people are understanding more and more what they lack, and the school population rises continuously."[3] During the 1960s and 1970s, the Afghan government was spending ten percent of its national budget on education with a particular focus on meeting the need for schools in the provinces. The number of students at all levels between 1950 and 1978 increased ten-fold (from 96,000 to 1,037,800)—with the number of women students growing by 33-fold (from 5,000 to 167,120). As the graph on the next page shows, the numbers were taking off just as the Peace Corps arrived. The numbers in secondary schools doubled between 1960 and 1965 and then more than tripled between 1965 and 1970. Higher education enrollment rose from 1700 (including 157 women) in 1960 to 12,260 in 1975 (including 1680 women).[4]

Volunteers debated both the methods and merits of teaching English in Afghanistan. Before they departed at the end of 1964, Group II Volunteers discussed their experience. Like the first Volunteers, the teachers had struggled with rote learning, discipline, cheating, absenteeism, disorganization, petty bureaucracy, low and inconsistent standards, and a curriculum that required students to study as many as 18 subjects at one time. "Even though Volunteers could do a good job teaching English, a number of Volunteers expressed serious doubts

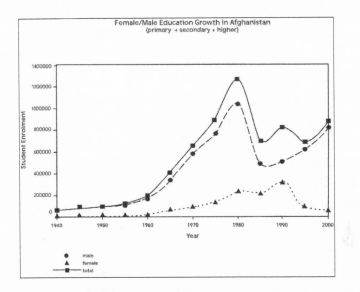

This graph from Saif R. Samady's report on Education and Afghan Society in the twentieth century shows the increasing student enrollment as Peace Corps Volunteers arrived in the early 1960s.

about whether English was worth teaching in Afghanistan where 85 percent of the people lived in rural areas. 'Wouldn't a Peace Corps agricultural project be more beneficial to the country?' Agriculture, they argued, is more essential than English because only five percent of the people would ever use English, while everyone would benefit by improved agriculture."[5] One counter argument was that teaching English, even to those who were not likely to have an opportunity to use it, provided a way into Afghan society, especially as Volunteers increased their outside activities—whether a Girls' Club in Herat or a pottery project in Mazar-i-Sharif—as ways to get to know students.

The health program also grew during these years. About 50 Volunteers came in 1965 and 1966 to work in the health area, mostly nurses but also several doctors and lab technicians. The first nurses, who came in Group I and then Group IV, had worked mainly in Kabul hospitals, but by 1965 attention in the health program was also shifting to the provinces. Peace Corps doctor Walter Morgan was particularly interested in rural medicine. He had come in 1963 and worked at a maternity hospital in Kabul while also serving as the doctor for Volunteers. He knew that Afghan medical students needed training to work in rural areas where the really tough issues were. To start addressing this need, he organized a Doctors Volunteer Program to work with the new medical school in Jalalabad that the Afghan government was establishing and spent the latter part of his three-plus years in Afghanistan working there.[6]

Afghans were also interested in training nurses in hospitals in other parts of the country including Mazar-i-Sharif, Herat, and Kandahar. They wanted both to improve nursing skills and to make nursing a more respected job. With the help of Peace Corps nurses already in the country, Bob McClusky helped lay the ground work for these jobs by scouting the settings in which nurses might be placed in the provinces. What were the needs? Were there any serious downsides to placement? How might they be handled? McClusky recalls one experience in Herat: "I believe Sami was with us. We were met by the ubiquitous property protector who assured us he would take us directly to the hospital director. Off we went down one corridor and then another until we arrived at what turned out to be the operating room. The head man was in the midst of performing an appendectomy: 'Sorry to interrupt. Why don't we talk later?'"

The World Health Organization in Afghanistan raised the idea of the Peace Corps helping with a vaccination campaign in the country in the spring of 1966. Cheryl Stetler, a nurse in Jalalabad with Group VII, remembers that during the summer of 1966 the hospital where several nurses were working closed except for a skeletal staff because of the heat. During that time, the Peace Corps nurses did a pilot project for the vaccinator program in rural villages, two outside of Kandahar and two outside of Mazar-i-Sharif.

The variety of skills requested by the Afghan government meant a significant minority of Volunteers were working in a wide range of areas beyond education and health. The Volunteer newsletters during 1965 and 1966 provide an indication:

- At the Group VI mid-term conference, Volunteers agreed that the accountants had been the most successful of the technical programs undertaken by that Group's members, both because of the leadership of the Afghan Finance Ministry and because of the nature and measurability of the program—introducing a new accounting system into ministries and provincial government centers.[7] The path toward having an impact was not a direct one, however. Accountants in Group III had moved among several ministries exploring ways to change administrative procedures of the "signature" culture. Dupree had expressed concern that the needed follow-through for the program had not come because there were no plans to include accountants in Groups IV and V.[8]
- A high school building in Laghman was nearing completion having started with the help of Group IV Volunteer Joe Basile and moved forward under Group V Volunteers Jim Keane and John Barbee. John also worked with the Forestry Department of the Ministry of Agriculture in Nuristan and then in Laghman acting as liaison among U.S. AID, the Afghan government, and local communities in building footbridges across the Alingar River.[9]

- Stu Schmidt and Farrell Walback, at the Teachers' Training College in Kabul, worked with their students to build a rock and sod dam that provided water for school gardeners as well as swimming for the neighborhood recreation center. They also built a kiln for firing pottery, which was to be replicated at teacher training institutes in provincial cities.[10]

- Working at Kabul Museum, Deborah Salter in Group V wrote about her work in archeology. She described how a visitor to the Museum could take a tour of the historic and artistic development in Afghanistan over the past 5000 years.[11]

- In June 1966, six hydrologists arrived to work with the Ministry of Agriculture in helping build 80 river gauging stations around the country.[12]

Group V Volunteers arrive at Kabul Airport in May 1965. Bob Steiner and Roberta Auburn (Peace Corps office administrator) are on the left. (*Credit: Sherry Steiner*)

Some of the challenges in 1965 and 1966 were directly related to dealing with the increasing numbers of Volunteers and wider geographic spread. The arrival of Group IV with 56 Volunteers had doubled the size of the program in October 1964. And the groups kept coming—48 in May 1965 (Group V), 41 in September 1965 (Group VI), 28 in June and December 1965 (Groups VIIA and VIIB), and 58 in May 1966 (Groups VIIIA and VIIIB)—but at a scale the country could absorb at the time.[13]

Jon Wicklund *After Group IV arrived, I recall a change from being in a small community where everyone knew each other to one in which it would be impossible to interact with everyone. Part of that must have been because so many in Group IV spent some or all of their time in the provinces.*

Bob Steiner *A big problem internally for me was remembering names. After a while, when there were about 200, it was kind of hard to remember every name. But I did pretty well.*

In a letter at that time, Steiner wrote that moods had "changed since those halcyon days when we could leisurely enjoy the PCV's impact and success." Now he had to "watch from a greater distance, observe and assess more academically, discipline more often than counsel, arbitrate more office disputes. But, on the other side, there is more programming to do (which I love), more talent and numbers to pour into good projects and thus greater leverage at our disposal to arrest souring projects." He noted that the project at the Nangahar Medical School would test Peace Corps skills to the utmost but if successful would be enduring and significant. [14]

Inside a mud-walled compound in Logar, south of Kabul. (*Credit: Will A. Irwin*)

The health of the Volunteers themselves had become a concern, especially as more Volunteers worked in the provinces. Volunteers joked about their health, the handbook noted, as it acknowledged that keeping healthy was not easy. "Without doubt, we are in a hazardous area in terms of endemic disease, spread by extremely poor sanitation and unclean foods. And Volunteers do spend considerable time—too much time—being sick." The handbook included guidance on immunization boosters; buying and storing foods; preparing and cooking fruits, meats and vegetables, and dairy products; obtaining, boiling, and storing water; and organizing kitchens. A September 1965 update added guidance on treatment of wounds and animal bites, on precautions against insects and scorpions, and on the health of servants.

A report of a late 1966 meeting of Volunteers, doctors, and the regional medical officer said that Afghanistan had the highest rate of illness and the highest rate of health expenditure per Volunteer per year ($700) of any Peace Corps country. Amoebiasis was the biggest single problem; an estimated 70-80% of Volunteers contracted it.[15]

In addition to discussion about what kinds of jobs Volunteers should be doing, there began to be some questions about how Volunteers were performing. One forum where these questions came up was a staff-PCV Liaison Committee formed to increase communication as the number of Volunteers grew. Minutes of a July 1965 meeting record a lack of enthusiasm among some Volunteers. Committee members first considered agenda items on responding to a request to help with a recreation project for university students and on making plans for a folk concert. Under the third item, Steiner noted, and members concurred, that "there seems to be a growing sickness among the PCV's. An attitude of cynicism and lack of enthusiasm for or interest in living up to the high Peace Corps standards which have been developed by our predecessors in Kabul has taken hold of many Volunteers."[16]

The change in the scale of the program combined with the shifting political and social climates in both the United States and Afghanistan brought increasing debate about how to work within the Afghan culture, and also the first brush with politics.

New Volunteers were learning how difficult it could be to work within the Afghan culture. A cholera epidemic that summer brought to the fore the consequences of not doing so.

Bob Steiner *In the cholera epidemic, I remember we had a medical team in Jalalabad. I was having trouble with them in terms of their attitude towards the Afghans.*

Doctors can be terribly arrogant. I was trying to get them to look at this and look at the situation from the Afghans' point of view before they tried to impose what they expected from the States. This one Volunteer doctor just refused; he kept ordering the Afghans to do what he, as an American, in America, thought was proper.

In the hospital in Jalalabad they had just a little amount of the saline solution – the only thing that will save one from cholera. This guy came in who was desperately ill and the American Peace Corps Volunteer doctor said now you give him what's left of that solution. They said, sir, he's going to die anyway, don't give it to him. But he insisted. And the guy died. The last of the solution was gone. And the next day a good friend of this doctor came in with cholera. There was nothing to give him, and he died. And the American doctor changed completely; from then on he'd learned his lesson. So he began to say if these are the conditions the Afghan doctor has to work under, so am I. He turned out very well. But it was a painful lesson.

In July 1965, Steiner sought to engage Volunteers in conversation about cultural change in a piece titled "Usage more than Reason." He wrote:

"During the 18th and 19th centuries, the British East India Company had a series of good and bad administrators, one of the best of whom was John Malcolm. Describing his philosophy towards the Indians, he wrote about 1810 as follows: 'to alter nothing that can be tolerated, to distrust as little as possible, to attend to usage more than reason, to study feelings and prejudices, and to make no changes but such as I am compelled to do. . . .'

"It may seem paradoxical that despite such a philosophy, Malcolm's fame was made because of the significant and enduring reforms introduced during his tenure. Over the years, his tolerance of local customs and mores (which, incidentally, were sharply at variance with his own personal code of conduct) gave him the necessary insights into and understandings of Indian culture to make his reforms durable because they were compatible with that culture.

"Some have suggested that there is much in common between Malcolm's stated philosophy and that of the Peace Corps. What say you? R.L.S".[17]

In the next newsletter, Margareta Silberberg, an experienced nurse, pointed to the difficulty of putting into action Malcolm's approach in the health arena. "Disciplined working habits do not exist. Reforms meet with prejudices, even hostility. Feelings are much hurt by reforms. Local customs are so much at variance with that which we are trying to achieve that their tolerance is going to jeopardize our goals. . . . Peace Corps may have the idealistic philosophy of a John Malcolm, but to have it applied to the down-to-earth working level of a Volunteer would, in my estimation, result in naught."[18]

At the fall liaison meeting, Steiner once more talked about the importance of creating the cultural climate that is a prerequisite to technical work and the role of generalists in establishing it. He stressed the Peace Corps was not just a technical assistance group.[19]

The following spring, after conducting an end-of-service conference for Group IV, Leslie Hanscom wrote: ". . . I believe the profoundest people-to-people encounter to be witnessed in Afghanistan is what goes on between the sick in Afghan hospitals and the Peace Corps nurses. To see them at work is to be struck by the power that can be exerted by a little common decency. Moreover, it is not just the visiting outsider who is struck but the Afghan hospital workers who are there to stay."

He concluded his piece on "The Magic of Caring" by noting that "Making the nurse respected is a major Peace Corps purpose in Afghanistan. Until lately, care of the sick was considered a debasing occupation. . . . The strong assault that Peace Corps nurses have made upon this prejudice is owing in large measure to their high qualities as human beings."[20]

Dupree wrote about Volunteers' frustrations in dealing with cultural issues such as rote learning in the schools and the lack of sanitary conditions in the hospitals. He described the value of Volunteers: "In the past, American assistance programs usually consisted of money (grants and loans) and technical assistance—without any guarantees of continuity. Under such conditions, the result can be a dam, a road, or a university left empty and functionless on the landscape of a developing country—a magnificent ruin. Tractors and buses with no provision for spare parts or maintenance often sit idle and useless for months. The Peace Corps Volunteers, especially in Afghanistan, try to fill these longitudinal needs, to continue the processes begun. They try to do this gently, within the cultural pattern, and not with a heavy, alien self-righteous hand. This patient day-to-day, face-to-face contact with their Afghan supervisors, assistants, and acquaintances will help to introduce and *perpetuate* the ideas which stimulate permanent technological change. It will also, incidentally, have some effect in the general direction of creating a literate, responsible, outward-looking middle class which some day might form the bulwark of a representative government."[21]

As discussions about how to work effectively to create a cultural atmosphere in which technical change could take place continued, political issues were also heating up in both the United States and Afghanistan. Volunteers were coming from a United States where opposition to the Vietnam War was growing rapidly and a social revolution was brewing, especially at colleges and universities. The Civil Rights Act was passed by Congress in 1964, the Voting Rights Act in 1965. The black power movement was emerging. Applications to Peace Corps began to reflect these changes. They had reached a peak in 1964 at more than 45,000; the decline was slow at first but in 1967 was down to about 35,000 and hit 19,000 in 1970.[22]

Early in 1966, Steiner forwarded to Volunteers a copy of a memo from the Peace Corps Director in India about letters from Volunteers in India that had been printed in the *New York Times* about the war in Vietnam and in *Newsweek* about the conflict between Pakistan and India. Steiner noted that a similar situation had never arisen in Afghanistan but suggested that "Mr. Ashabranner's comments stand as effective reminders of how much our success and ability to gain rapport with host country nationals depends on the Peace Corps remaining a completely non-political organization."[23] It was not until 1969-1970 that the issue of making the views of Volunteers in Afghanistan about the Vietnam War known came to a head around a visit to Kabul by Vice President Agnew.[24]

Volunteers were serving in an Afghanistan where the late summer of 1965 brought the first national elections for Parliament under the new Constitution. Marxist, Islamist, and nationalist groups were forming. In Kabul, classes paused while students went home during the election. When Parliament convened in mid-October, student demonstrations erupted as members of Parliament debated whether to approve proposed appointments of cabinet members. The response to the demonstrations on October 25th left three people dead.[25] The King named Mohammad Hashim Maiwandwal, then the press minister, to become prime minister. The next spring, in May 1966, Khalq, a newspaper that used Marxist-Leninist language, quoted a Kandahar deputy in Parliament as saying Peace Corps was adversely influencing the youth of the country.

Fran Irwin *The King had signed a new press law. As the private papers began publishing in the spring of 1966, some of my Afghan colleagues formed a service to provide English translations so I heard a good bit about what the emerging political groups were writing.*

Bob Steiner *When trouble broke out then, one of the Volunteers got involved with one of the competing Afghan political groups. That was the first real tension we felt in the political climate, I think. The minister of interior—Dr. Kayeum was the minister then and very friendly to the U.S.—called and said you'd better pull him in. That was the night the Volunteer showed up at our home at 2 a.m., very tight and nervous, saying he'd been chased out there. That was the only time any of the Volunteers had been involved in the politics.*

Fran Irwin *Lines could be hard to draw at that point. One of our goals was to get to know those with whom we worked. That some Volunteers knew teachers and students who decided to participate in the demonstrations was not surprising. If I had any question, my Afghan colleagues had a good sense of what was appropriate and safe for me to do. If I had any doubt, they made it clear that as a foreigner I would not be welcome around the Parliament as members debated whether the Khalq newspaper should be banned.*

The meaning of Peace Corps goals and operating practices was being worked out on the ground in Afghanistan. The goals were broad enough to support differing combinations of technical assistance and cultural cooperation. The debate among Volunteers about the relationship between doing the job and cultural learning would go on, whether working through how to handle getting supplies from storekeepers or what to American teachers was cheating in taking tests but to Afghan students was expected cooperation. Volunteers also continued to grapple with what being non-political meant and how Peace Corps could work with U.S. AID effectively, yet remain independent.

CHAPTER 14 FORCES AT WORK IN AFGHANISTAN IN THE EARLY 1960s

In some countries, Peace Corps might be able to ignore the Cold War, but it was very real in Afghanistan. Afghan leaders tried to balance the Cold War competitors in all kinds of forums.

Bob Pearson *Our Peace Corps basketball team was to play the Afghan university team in a big stadium for the King's birthday in August of 1963. We waited and waited (at least two hours) while the Afghan officials debated who should lead the parade to open the festivities (us or the Russian soccer team). Finally, after this long time we were told we would be second because the Russians had come all the way from Russia specially for this event while we were already in Kabul. That was fine with us, but Toby draped our flag over the Russian flag at some juncture.*

Fran Irwin *When I try to describe what Afghanistan was like then to people now . . . how do you explain what it was like at that moment?*

Bob Steiner *I think they were much more open at that time, both to America and to Russia, than they had been. They were always very cautious to make sure that* *the Russians were also doing something at the same time we were doing some project. But the Russians offered nothing like the Peace Corps, nothing. They could offer technical skills, they could build tunnels, they could build roads. But their people were persona non grata. Again, this was partly the attitude of the government, but then it was also the climate of international affairs at that time. The Peace Corps was there, I was there, at a time when Afghanistan was really reaching out to the outside world, in ways that they had not done before. Their experience had been mostly with the British, which was always troubled.*

Fran Irwin *One of my housemates painted a sign for Aeroflot as part of her work at the advertising agency. That created a bit of a stir, some comment from a visiting U.S. Senator. My letters also reflect that there were numerous times when I was wondering whether I was going to be able to continue working at the Times. That it would become too political for them to have an American there.*

Bob Steiner *I, too, was always worried about that, but it never became an issue. I think the Embassy at one point said something to me and I said it's up to the Afghans.*

Fran Irwin *Did you ever have any dealings with the Russians?*

Bob Steiner *One snowy night, my son Chip and a friend were out riding on the friend's motorcycle and came upon Russia's large plastic-paneled display window overlooking the Kabul River. They decided to pelt the plastic with snowballs. It broke and they fled. At 3 o'clock the* next morning I got a call from the embassy saying "Do you want to come down and get your son out of prison?" I could just see the headlines . . . "Peace Corps progeny attacks Russian embassy." I went down to the prison. They wouldn't let me in but I could see Chip sitting inside. My cocky son was smoking a cigarette. "Hi, Dad!" he cheerfully shouted. There was no evidence of guilt. Bill Brewer, deputy chief of mission, patched it over with the Russian chargé. Nothing happened, there was nothing in the newspaper that I know of, and Chip got out in the morning.

Will Irwin Did you have any trouble keeping the Embassy at a distance from Volunteers? For example, we'll invite a few Volunteers in and pump them a little bit for what they might be learning or observing.

Sherry Steiner One of them got involved with the CIA people.

Bob Steiner Oh, they were pumping him. They were calling him. That wasn't the Volunteer's fault.

Sherry Steiner You had to tell them to quit.

Bob Steiner I told the ambassador to get those Embassy guys out of there, and he did. That wasn't the Volunteer's fault.

Will Irwin What was your sense of Islam and of the ethnic divisions among tribes and regions at that point? What undercurrents of these kinds of forces were at work that you needed to be aware of then in setting up the program, in placing people, in talking to different people?

Bob Steiner *The conflict then was twofold. One was the conflict between Afghanistan and Pakistan, and the second—really part of the first— was the constant struggle with the Pashtuns and the Hazara-Tajik tug-of-war. Those struggles were always apparent in the Afghan thinking and planning. But, you see, that didn't affect the foreigner, it didn't affect us. For the Afghan, the Peace Corps Volunteer was not an issue. Volunteers were not a religious threat and so religion was a non-issue. This became apparent in the stories of Len Oppenheim. Lenny, a Jewish fellow in Kandahar, was accepted more totally by his students and their families than perhaps any other Volunteer. He was taken by them to Muslim celebrations, the wrestling games and dogfights. I don't think any other Volunteer or any other foreigner was so completely accepted by his Afghan friends. It was incredible. It was the genius of the Peace Corps concept—and Lenny—that religion never crept in. Certainly in Afghanistan the question was never an issue in programming. The Afghans wanted a teacher, a writer, or some other skill not present in Afghanistan. They were not worried about religion.*

Other Volunteers confirm this. David Fleishhacker writes that students never showed any interest in his religious beliefs. Most Afghans never expected to meet a Jew.[1] He did find a small Jewish community in Kabul.

Fran Irwin *So, Pashtunistanism, of course, that's part of being there at the right time – that was tamped down a little bit with the King's cousin Daoud out of power, but he was always in the background.*

Bob Steiner *Yes, he was just waiting to come back in.*

Fran Irwin *You could feel that?*

Bob Steiner *Yes, you could feel it. Afghans feared him. He was a known tyrant. There's a story—apocryphal, of course—that portrays him well. When the telephone line from Kabul to Mazar-i-Sharif was first installed, Daoud called the governor in Mazar to celebrate the occasion. The janitor in Mazar answered the telephone. It is the Afghan custom to establish rank by who first identifies himself by asking "Qi asti"? —"Who are you?" The answer is "Qi asti"—"Who are you?" It is a question of prestige as to who first must identify himself.*

So Daoud called and said I'd like to speak to the governor and the janitor said—and who are you, "Qi asti?" to Daoud. He replied "I'm Daoud." "Daoud who?" asked the janitor. He said "The Daoud," and then asked "Who are you?" The janitor realized he had insulted the Prime Minister and it was best to get lost—so he hung up and Daoud had to try again. It's an example of how they feared Daoud. The Afghans didn't talk much about politics to us. They consistently avoided it. But it could be felt.

Will Irwin *Could you feel tension between the kinds of advances and progress—women out of chadri, women in the schools—could you feel a tension between what the King was trying to do, that started in Kabul, and what mullahs and religious people or others in the provinces were uncomfortable with, perhaps even resisting? Was any of that dynamic apparent, and did it affect . . .?*

Bob Steiner *Not very. But it was there, it was there. But the Peace Corps mostly ignored it, as the Afghans did.*

Sherry Steiner *In Kabul, you didn't have any feeling of this at all with the women I met with who spoke English. Women without chadri were apparently quite free to do whatever they wanted.*

Fran Irwin *I remember being surprised at first to see women in chadri carrying briefcases. Volunteers in Group IV who worked as secretaries felt they had seen a difference over two years. More Afghan women were working in offices.*

Sherry Steiner *One difference between Iran and Afghanistan was that in Iran women could work as servants. In Afghanistan, women might be nursemaids but not servants.*

Bob Steiner *You were also asking about politics. The Afghans never talked to me much about politics. They were very discreet. And I never tried to raise it. Even with Naim . . . every once in a while I would try to probe. But I got no reaction. No way was he going to get involved.*

Sherry Steiner *Maybe it wasn't part of his life at all, it was something he couldn't influence.*

Bob Steiner *But I think the Pashtuns were much more reserved than the Tajiks. And, certainly, than the Hazaras. A few Hazaras were in government then, but not in important positions. Some of the Tajiks were there too. I could always tell from Naim, the driver. He was a Pashtun, and you could tell his sense of superiority every time we were dealing with a Tajik or a Hazara.*

Another change as Peace Corps moved beyond the start-up phase was the introduction of quantitative criteria for measuring success.

Will Irwin *A virtue of being a young program was that there was not a routine of planning, programming, budgeting, evaluation, justification . . . ?*

Bob Steiner *The US government soon wanted to apply PPBS to the <u>quality</u> of Volunteer performances.*

Will Irwin *The Program Planning and Budgeting System coming out of McNamara at the Department of Defense?*

Bob Steiner *Yes. They wanted to figure out the effectiveness of the Volunteer. They introduced that system. And Paul Sachs came out and found me a very stubborn opponent. I defied him to figure out how they could measure their effectiveness by assigning numbers to intangible qualities.*

Fran Irwin *What kinds of things were they trying to measure—numbers of contacts Volunteers might have had?*

Bob Steiner *Something like that. Everything that was a number they liked. This was McNamara's approach. I resisted. First of all, I didn't understand it. It was a lot of bureaucracy about what records you had to fill out and keep. We just dragged our feet until Paul Sachs came out to find out what was really going on. I think this system was tried the last two years that I was there.*

One example: The 4th Annual Peace Corps report issued in 1965 in describing the Afghanistan program says: "Peace Corps teachers reach nearly 40 percent of all Afghan students at the secondary and university levels."[1]

Will Irwin *Was there an association between that kind of management thinking and the increasing attention to economic development theory?*

Bob Steiner *Yes, but we were not measured by economic theory.*

Will Irwin *So, your answer would be if a principal asked me for a teacher, in Faryab, I gave him a teacher in Faryab. I didn't have to spell out how that would benefit the country.*

Bob Steiner *That's right. Nor did I have to justify it by the number of people he would influence or the students he would have.*

Fran Irwin *That is hard to believe now, of course. It was an assumption partly based on your growing up in Iran where your father was teaching. . . that you help improve education and health, different areas, and that is the way development happens.*

Bob Steiner *Yes, you know, it wasn't a question of a formula. This person is teaching in the school. He or she is going to have some kind of an influence. Anybody knows that.*

Fran Irwin *The influence by working closely, respecting people, on an equal basis.*

Bob Steiner *Working within their system. Making it work better.*

Fran Irwin *The thing about Peace Corps, in contrast to most foreign assistance programs, was that we were actually working with and for the Afghans and how revolutionary . . .*

Bob Steiner *. . . that concept was . . .*

Fran Irwin *. . . to many people, and what a difference it makes.*

Bob Steiner *That's right.*

Fran Irwin *For me, with fellow staffers, some of them . . . we were able to joke about what working on an equal basis might really mean. Every day we were figuring it out. We were colleagues. Some people who came under* *other programs and expected rapid change following their advice were frustrated. The difference in approach is hard to explain.*

Bob Steiner *It is . . . you don't have anything to put your hands on. There was an agricultural specialist with AID who worked with farmers on equipment. He put in a proposal to AID suggesting that instead of getting tractors and bulldozers why don't you supply money for metal tips for the plows. The project was turned down. You can't measure that. How can we sell this to Congress—telling them that we are putting tips on plows? They want to see American tractors over there that Afghans can use for one month and then they break down. There's nobody to fix them. They don't have the gas to run them and so forth, but his project was turned down. He loved the Peace Corps. He just thought you guys were revolutionary with no gadgetry.*

Fran Irwin *Some PC programs around the world now are working directly with AID?*

Bob Steiner *I think so. We started doing that. AID was delighted. It made their task much easier because the Volunteer knew what he was dealing with, so with the effective AID people the Volunteer was a great asset.*

Fran Irwin *. . . because we knew what was happening at the ground level. A member of the Columbia Team, Wilma Oksendahl, was helpful to us in starting the student page for the Kabul Times. From my point of view, that project was an example of an effective relationship between AID and Volunteers. She had a good sense of how it could serve as a resource in helping students learn English.*

Will Irwin *Did you have misgivings with getting involved with AID programs?*

Bob Steiner *Yes, I didn't want them to get too involved with us.*

Fran Irwin *After all, many people originally thought Peace Corps should just be part of AID.*

Bob Steiner *I saw nothing wrong with Volunteers meeting with people in AID or at the Embassy—except, of course, for the CIA. My gosh, they're our country's people.*

Fran Irwin *Presumably, the influence was two-way. We were influencing them, too.*

Bob Steiner *Absolutely. I think many AID professionals admired the Volunteer approach to technical assistance. They felt it was very effective. Some of them were even envious of what you were able to do. I thought the interchange was fruitful to both sides.*

Steiner continued to grapple with the goals of Peace Corps and how to measure the effectiveness of its programs after he became Peace Corps regional director for North Africa, Near East and South Asia in mid-1966. He wrote a memo in February 1969 to country directors in the region in which he dealt with issues ranging from ending paternalism to moving toward binational staffing. Primarily, however, it explained his view of Peace Corps goals.

. . . When the PPBS system was reluctantly applied to Peace Corps programming, it was adopted but not adapted. We didn't know how. Traditionally, it had been used in a hardware or at least economic context. It was said that unless we set our sights on the "economic jugular," we were not relevant. Though this was modified, our target became some well-defined segment of the economy. All 104's [*Form 104s were basic documents prepared to describe, justify, and budget a country's request for a new PC program.*] now point to that target and suggest ways of measuring project success. Today we are justifiably being asked and pushed to come up with the measurement figures. We are about to be hung by our own petard unless economic development is indeed the Peace Corps' goal. (And even if it were, there is something completely spurious about the assumption that because a project is a success, it was because of Peace Corps' involvement—or vice versa).

But I would submit that economic development is not our goal. At the risk of sounding corny, I contend that our goal has been, and today even more clearly is the amassing of information about how to wage peace, about inter-cultural and interpersonal relations, about the process of economic development, about how diversity between peoples can be used to enrich, not homogenize or destroy. Ours is the business of enabling those who share these objectives to learn the process firsthand through a personal involvement in and contribution to the developmental activities of the host governments.

It has been said that it requires men of courage to act in the face of ambiguity. That's us. So far, however, our best efforts have gone into pretending the ambiguity is not there, that we are not dealing with two goals but with one, e.g., the economic development goals of the host government. Quite consistently, we are now being pushed to measure our progress toward that goal. Is it not time to admit to the presence of two goals—ours and the host governments'—and dignify our hosts by letting them assess our contribution to <u>theirs</u> while we devote our resources to evaluating the progress being made toward <u>ours.</u>

Our 104s today say nothing about our goal. They speak exclusively about the host government's. Some are saying that the only reason we do this is to get the project approved in PC/W. I disagree. But I do believe it stems from a lack of thought about what our goal really is. It is time to remedy this, to reaffirm our ideals. The 104s should identify the objective, and show why the project is the best alternative. Of paramount importance in that decision is the host government's concern for and interest in that project.[2]

CHAPTER 16 STEINER'S PEACE CORPS PHILOSOPHY AND ITS ORIGINS

Fran Irwin *You have emphasized the most important thing was to work within the Afghan system, within the culture. To build relationships, to find out why the Afghans did the job the way they did.*

Bob Steiner *I think that's the one thing I tried to communicate to Volunteers. And I think most of you bought it. And I think it really was the hallmark of Peace Corps success versus AID, which often ignored what the Afghans did and why.*

Chip Steiner *I wasn't a volunteer but the thing I heard OVER AND OVER AND OVER AGAIN was the development of relationships between Afghans and PC volunteers resulting in REAL mutual respect, solutions to problems, acceptance of new ideas from every quarter and every nationality. Teams of aliens came together, although nobody called them that. Knitting real bonds across cultures. What seemed to be happening between Afghans and PCVs was no leap forward into a modern "western" world but a scaffold of trust and a deeply authentic appreciation of different ways, different approaches, different beliefs which all, astonishingly, were not so different in the end.*

Will Irwin *Where did you get the idea that building respectful relationships across cultures was the focus? Of course, Peace Corps goals call for learning across cultures, but why did Bob Steiner know that? How did Bob Steiner know that?*

Bob Steiner *Probably my folks.*

Fran Irwin *They spent much of their lives in Iran and they learned that by experience?*

Bob Steiner *They were in Iran from 1920 til 1939, some twenty years. Dad and Mother approached mission a lot differently than they were expected to.*

Dad was a teacher, not an evangelist. And there were divisions in the mission field between the educators and medical people on the one side, versus the evangelists. When I came back and was working in Washington, I went up to see Dad, who was dying with cancer. I got to talk to him. I had not really known my father very well, because I left when I was a teenager and didn't see him until I was career-bound. Anyway, I talked to him about the Iranians. I said, "How did you deal with the subject of Christianity?" He said, "You know, Bob, I found out that they liked their religion. Let 'em alone!" And that made a terribly deep impression. That was his philosophy, Mother's philosophy. So their job was to teach, in his case, economics and math, for twenty years in the college there. The doctors were busy treating people. So those two professions tended to disagree with the evangelists. Each approached the challenge differently.

But it was also my experience in the Embassy in Iran that influenced me. I was cultural officer from 1950 to 1952—at the time of Mossadegh.

Fran Irwin *The U.S. backed a coup to overthrow him in 1953?*

Bob Steiner *After I left. But the issue of Mossadegh, the beloved Iranian nationalist Prime Minister, was alive when I was there. He had nationalized the British-owned oil company. And the U.S. embassy, of course, opposed this move. All the Persians I knew were for him. So I think this is where I began to find out – these Iranians know what they want. And we were unwise to fight Mossadegh. But as a junior officer I didn't have much say. I started the Iran-America Society, a group of intellectuals who were very vocal about their disagreement with U.S. opposition to Mossadegh. I think that was part of my training process.*
Beyond my parents and my embassy experience, there was a third influence on my thinking—a fellow named Ed Wright—does that name ring a bell?

Fran Irwin *Yes.*

Sherry Steiner *Well, it would, because of your connections to Wooster.*

Fran Irwin *My aunts and my parents probably knew him and his family when he was in school there and certainly after he retired in the mid-sixties to Wooster. A cousin worked with him on education programs in northern Ohio about the Middle East over the next several decades.*

Edwin M. Wright was born in Iran in 1897 and grew up there. He attended high school and college in Wooster, Ohio, and graduated from McCormick Theological Seminary. He was a teacher and administrator at American high schools in Iran until 1937 when he returned to the United States and did graduate work at Columbia University, writing about the Medes and Persians. He served with U.S. Army Intelligence in Cairo during World War II and then for three decades in the State Department's Division of Middle East Affairs and taught at the Foreign Service Institute.[1] It was Ed Wright who served as interpreter for King Mohammed Zahir and Queen Homaira when they met President Kennedy.

Bob Steiner *Ed was the one who chaperoned me back from Iran, when I was sixteen. Ed Wright was a scholar, knew the Middle East, knew Turkish, Persian, Arabic, and Armenian, spoke all four languages, and, of course, English. He brought two of us back to the U. S. From Tehran to London cost $100 each. He would bargain every place we went.*

Fran Irwin *How did you travel?*

Bob Steiner *We went by train and car to Istanbul and then by passage on ships from Istanbul to Athens, and again from Athens to Brindisi on the heel of Italy. This was at the time of Mussolini, and we were offered a 50% discount for train travel if we visited Mussolini's Procreation Fair in Rome. So Ed Wright, being a good missionary, walked us into the fair, got our tickets punched, and walked us right back out. We said: "Well, we want to see this." He said: "No, this is very dull." So we did not learn how to procreate.*

Fran Irwin *Italy was trying to increase its population?*

Bob Steiner *Yes, definitely. Mussolini desperately needed men. So I want to write that trip up. It was a fantastic trip. We traveled on baggage racks in the train from Baghdad to Mosul to Turkey, to Istanbul. All along, he told us the history and who died here and who fought here and what happened there. It was <u>fascinating</u>, it was a graduate course in the history of the Middle East.*

Fran Irwin *And he had learned this . . .*

Bob Steiner *He was born there—in Tabriz—raised in Iran, and was very sympathetic to them. What a teacher!*

Fran Irwin *He brought you back to Wooster?*

Bob Steiner*: He brought us back to New York. And there my grandparents met us and we went to Uniontown, Pennsylvania. I was anchored there, it being Dad's home.*

Fran Irwin *My parents certainly credited their interest in the world to the missionaries they knew growing up in Wooster. Although it was a small Ohio town, they knew many people who had lived in other countries. The attitude they got was from the teachers and the doctors, who had very much a Peace Corps third purpose kind of educational effect when they came back to the U.S. When you came back . . . you'd been occasionally to the States?*

Bob Steiner *Yes, we came twice while I was in Iran. Once we went to the World's Fair in Chicago. But we always came to Uniontown, where my grandparents lived.*

Sherry Steiner *The family came when you were five, and then when you were twelve, just those two times.*

Fran Irwin *So when you came back, it must have been tremendous culture shock to be in the U.S.*

Bob Steiner *Yes. But at age five, or seven, or whatever it was, I was too young to know about culture shock. I do know that when we landed in Boston—we always traveled by ship in those days, wonderful—when we landed in Boston and got off and went in to tour the town, I said to Dad "Everybody talks English here!" Which I found kind of shocking.*

CHAPTER 17 PEACE CORPS TRAINING AND AMERICAN CULTURE

Will Irwin *Do you have any regrets, any disappointments, any "I wish I had tried this, done this, not done that," that you recall?*

Bob Steiner *I did feel that training did not adequately prepare Volunteers for the things that would really shock, the things that would really upset you when you came to Afghanistan. I didn't feel that training adequately got into these very tricky subjects. But, frankly, I don't know how you do this without immersing a person in another culture. I don't know how it can be done, so it was just a question of deciding how flexible a person would be, in terms of coping with a starkly different culture. I wish I had done a better job in defining the terms of reference for training. I didn't participate in this until I came and visited the training program. I do think that Peace Corps Washington needed to work with the field more, in my case, me [as PC Afghanistan director], in working on their program. But I don't know that I would have welcomed their intrusion. I was plenty busy without trying to run their training.*

Fran Irwin *The training was run by a totally different part of the Peace Corps?*

Bob Steiner *It was run by the staff in Washington. Particularly at the beginning there was no raw material to draw upon, few with real in-country experience. But later, I would have liked to have done more in terms of preparing the trainers. For instance, I think that the stress on preparing trainees to accept the Afghan as a person with the same intelligence you have was insufficiently emphasized in any training program. And it's hard, I think, for any American who's not been to Afghanistan, to really treat that subject effectively. That's a tough one when you've been raised to believe "everything American is great . . . if everybody would just copy us overseas, we would be a good fit." We are so proud of ourselves, in terms of our skills, our attitudes, everything that we do, that it's almost impossible to get any American to work hard on saying "Hey, we're not all that great. They may be just as smart." What American is going to say or think that? I believe that is a key part of preparing anybody for service in another country.*

Fran Irwin *Once you became regional director for North Africa, Near East, and South Asia for Peace Corps, were you able to influence training more?*

Bob Steiner *We tried a little more. But by that time they were doing training in-country. So that took care of that. But it did not take care of the attitude toward the host country nationals. I should have done more of that, but I didn't.*

Will Irwin *From your time as regional director, with more country programs under your supervision, could you get a perspective of the strengths of the Afghanistan*

program, or the circumstances that were special or differ-
ent from other programs?

Bob Steiner *I thought the Afghanistan program was*
better than any other program! Seriously, the other pro-
grams . . . not a one of them . . . prepared the Volunteer to
respect the host country national. Maybe fear him, maybe
puzzled by him, but always to "improve" him, technically,
and maybe even philosophically. And to change that ap-
proach is a tough one.

Will Irwin *You have to change the American culture.*

Bob Steiner *You do. Not going to happen overnight.*
But I think much more could have been done if I had tak-
en the time to try. The Peace Corps directors were prima
donnas. They—and myself included—didn't want anybody
from the outside telling them how to do things.

Fran Irwin *It would have been hard, especially at*
that time . . . ideally, it would have been more interactive,
perhaps. But it would have been hard to do that, when
communicating by exchanging written cables.

Bob Steiner *And when you go to visit them, you're*
there only a short time and you're dealing with a very sen-
sitive subject, a very delicate subject.

Fran Irwin *When you came to Afghanistan with*
Shriver . . . you were there with Shriver and later with
Jack Vaughn. . . . Those were important impressions for
them, and important for the program?

Bob Steiner *Washington was mostly busy wanting to meet the big shots, not so much the Volunteers . . . well, Vaughn did like to meet with the Volunteers. Shriver liked to meet with any Volunteer who was particularly unusual. You remember a Volunteer named Peter Fitzpatrick? He was assigned to the boondocks, outside of Jalalabad, up in one of those valleys. He was a colorful Irishman. I took Shriver out to visit him. He regaled him with stories of how the rats nibbled at his toes, which were the kind of colorful tales Shriver liked to hear. Shriver just ate this stuff up because he could relate these stories to the Congress and justify budgets.*

CHAPTER 18 CLOSE TO THE IDEAL PEACE CORPS PROGRAM

Bob Steiner *You know . . . the stage of Afghan development had a lot to do with the success of the Peace Corps then. We were there just at a time when the Afghans were interested in venturing a little more toward looking at the West. We were just lucky, just lucky.*

Fran Irwin *Yes, we were lucky—but when one looks back, the two of you were the right people at the right time in the 20th century. You had the background—the language and experience in the culture growing up. You were a good match for Peace Corps.*

Bob Steiner *That's right. And the embassy was . . .*

Sherry Steiner *He could communicate easily with them. . . .*

Bob Steiner *The ambassador and the deputy chief of mission, both of them . . . were very high on the Peace Corps. That helped a lot. If they had been reluctant, it would have been a different story. One important indication is that the ambassador instructed the CIA to stay away from our Volunteers in the field.*

The *Kabul Times* published an interview with Steiner[1] about what made for a successful Volunteer on the day before his departure in June 1966. It read:

"Few countries in the world have utilized the Peace Corps as effectively as Afghanistan," says Robert L. Steiner, who leaves Kabul Thursday after serving here almost four years as Director of the U.S. Peace Corps.

"Authorities here have been very helpful and as a result the Peace Corps has seen one of the most rewarding programs in the world develop in this country," he says.

"Although in the beginning it was looked on as a kind of junior technical assistance program, after two years people began to realize that our biggest contribution is an attitude toward work and a sense of responsibility toward a job."

About half of the Volunteers in Afghanistan teach English while others teach physical education, math and science, or serve as secretaries or nurses. In early June there were 220 Volunteers here but by July the number will be down to 180.

The number and skills of future Volunteers depend on the requests of the Afghan government. Right now one area of future expansion would appear to be agriculture. Some are already working in farm mechanics, surveying, and irrigation. Afghanistan also has the largest Peace Corps nursing project.

The success of a Volunteer depends on three factors, Steiner has found—a good volunteer, an ambitious Afghan supervisor, and a job to be done. Perhaps the most difficult kinds of jobs are those of rural development in which the Volunteer must use his own imagination to decide what to do.

The Peace Corps tries to stay away from jobs which require much equipment and financial support such as research or highway construction, Steiner explains. The important thing is person to person communication. Hopefully out of an exchange of ideas, new ways of solving problems will be found.

"The first six to eight months are usually the worst for the Volunteer just as they are for an Afghan who goes to another country," Steiner points out. It is in the second year that the Volunteer is most productive. To say that a Volunteer is doing a good job is the highest compliment an Afghan could pay us, he says.

Generally those in the provinces are happiest because they feel more useful and can see the impact they are making. About 70 Volunteers are now in over half the provinces.

About four per cent of Volunteers are sent home before their two-year term is over for failure to do their job. But the great majority of Volunteers leave feeling they have gained a lot from their experience.

Knowing the language is an important factor in helping the Volunteer enjoy himself and do a good job, Steiner believes. He learned Farsi as a child. He was born in Iran where his father was teaching in a college.

Steiner arrived in Kabul in August 1962 two weeks before the first group of nine Volunteers. He and his wife and four children leave Thursday morning having seen the eighth group of Volunteers begin work.

In connection with his job Steiner traveled around most of the country several times. His favorite city is Herat. He also enjoyed Bamian during a short vacation.

Steiner goes back to Washington to head the Division of Volunteer Support in Washington, D.C. Peace Corps headquarters. The Division is responsible for everything from handling baggage to deciding policies. [Instead he became the regional director for North Africa, Near East, and South Asia.]

The new Director, Walter Blass, arrived last week. He comes from a job as an economist for American Telephone and Telegraph.

The Steiners' farewell to the Peace Corps community came in the form of a letter[2] published in the Peace Corps Afghanistan newsletter after a party and a skit for them on June 10, 1966. "Practically the whole Peace Corps turned out – quite a few people," Will noted in a letter home. The Steiners wrote:

There are times when emotion ties the tongue and fogs the mind. Such a time was Roberta Auburn's farewell party. Your editor has now given us a second chance to give expression to our thoughts in leaving you, the Peace Corps in Afghanistan.

To have watched a program grow from its early timid days four years ago to its present solid strength with its diverse skills, approaches, and personalities cannot help but be exciting. Yet, it is gratitude, not excitement, that dominates our thoughts these last days; and that gratitude stems from the realization that you (past and present) have kept alive an ideal in which both of us strongly believe. The Peace Corps has come closer than most human institutions in representing that ideal; it took you to keep it alive.

Sherry and I have watched each and every one of you as you struggled with new hardships, different frustrations, real disappointments, the imperfections of those with whom you were associated (including us), and with your own individual inadequacies. And with very few exceptions, you made it. It worked.

The mark you leave is not only technical; it is equally, and more importantly of the spirit. You have lived, (not talked) an attitude, a philosophy, a concept that has enriched those who knew you, even if in no other way than that they can believe more intelligently that they are right and you are wrong. And you too have been enriched, whether you like it or not. This, we feel, is essentially what the Peace Corps is all about.

We are grateful, then, because you made it possible for our belief to live; we can brag about you and what you represent; you have permitted us an idol that cannot be easily toppled. So thanks for what you have done, for your inspiration, for keeping an ideal alive.

Good luck,
Bob and Sherry

Fran Irwin *So, overall, in Afghanistan and in Washington, you were involved with the Peace Corps for much of a decade.*

Bob Steiner *Yeah, I still am. (laughter)*

Sherry Steiner *They don't know it, but he is.*

Will Irwin *In how you have spent the rest of your life? Continuing to focus on how cultures engage.*

Bob Steiner *Oh, yes. Yes, those were interesting days. It was a generation in America that, I think, was pretty heady.*

Fran Irwin *It was a moment when both Afghanistan and the U.S. were open to new ideas like the Peace Corps— trying to work through the diversity of cultures to improve lives.*

Bob Steiner *That's right, and you know, what the Americans got from the experience—as well as what Afghanistan got—you cannot beat it. You cannot beat it. It was just magnificent.*

Most of the Volunteers in Group IV, who had come in October 1964, were about to leave the country, too. Len Oppenheim, in a letter to a friend dated February 16, 1966, provides an individual reflection on the experience of teaching in Kandahar. (see box). The completion-of-service conference reports provide a broader view.

Len Oppenheim
An experience I wouldn't trade for anything

I am in the Peace Corps, and as such I am supposed to live like my Afghan counterparts – which is impossible even in the best of situations. For one cannot become an Afghan mentally, nor become a member of the social system simply by living here, nor live in the Afghan manner without the first two mentioned items. Therefore, I am a low paid American classified by Afghans as a "foreigner" and by the other Americans who work for US agencies as "rather foreign."

I am a teacher. I teach more than my subject, English, and this means that everything I do and everything I say is an action which teaches the Afghan national something – you are never really alone and the things you do are watched. I try to do things that will deliver the most – act like an American, and yet speak the local language, which is not acting like an American. In other words, everything I do here should be to some advantage – ours or theirs.

The first few months are the hardest because they are so strange – everything new and unknown. The last few months are hardest because the world has opened up ever so slightly and inklings of knowledge have crept in, and so many things can be seen in the distance which need to be done, and yet will not be done since it is packing time, and time to think of home and the future. This is the heartbreak involved in the Peace Corps. You try, and you hope, and perhaps all you do is scratch around the surface. But if this scratching is kept up by successive and growing waves of Peace Corps, perhaps some cracks will appear, and maybe someday a mountain may have been moved – and I helped.

There are days when nothing goes right, literally, and days when the world couldn't be better. The day when a student, one of the most promising, is kicked out of school or just quits. The day that the students tell you that they like you, that they really appreciate your being here. The great days. . . .

I live in a huge home, six rooms or so, with lots of other rooms available, and gardens, and a full time servant. There is a small American community here in Kandahar other than Peace Corps (thirteen of us Peace Corps volunteers at the moment – highest ever) and they live the great American life. They make it possible for me to see a good movie every week (this week was the Beatles "Help"), attend a New Year's party, or Thanksgiving dinner, or just escape from my environment for a short time in their homes or in the AID staff house bar – illegal though it is for us Peace Corps, we are not kept out by the local American community.

There is the huge Afghan city of Kandahar extending on all sides of my home – impenetrable in so many ways. There are the other "foreigners" here, the Afghans from Kabul, or Kunduz, or Jalalabad. I am accepted by them in some form. There are my students – learning to be surveyors, an unknown profession in this country. The students come from all parts of the country. They live in a dormitory. They do not live in Kandahar and are not Kandahari. Among these students I have found a group of very good friends. We are all strangers here, and my home can be a place for them to stop at outside of their dormitory. To them, I live a life that is way above their highest expectations. And that on about $60 a month.

My electricity is sometimes – perhaps one full day out of five. My heat in winter is when I light the wood fire in the tin stove. My escape from summer heat is to retreat into the depths of my thick walled plastered mud home. My daily life includes vitamin pills, and perhaps a diodoquin pill or two for stomach disorders, or poly magma, or some other stopper, and the weekly malaria pills. And the immunizations that have to be renewed. And the colds and sore throats and drippy noses (wiped with short lengths of toilet paper) constantly appearing and disappearing because of the unheated school, or the sudden changes in temperature, or the exhaustion of the five mile bicycle ride to school (which on a day with both morning and afternoon classes makes twenty miles by bike just for work) – also add trips to the bazaar, or for mail, or visiting.

My life includes the wonderful opportunities that cannot be exploited to the fullest – the huge vacations with allowances, the chance to learn a language or at least try to cope with one other than English, the daily experiences that would never happen at home or anywhere else – occasions that are really exciting, the opportunity in many cases to have a position way beyond my background and previous experience – a position of authority and leadership unparalleled by any job I could have had at home.

There is the time – extra time which oftentimes can be frustrating, and not enough time which too can be frustrating.

There is my radio – a very necessary connection with the world – the news, perhaps some sports or important event or a drama or rock and roll (today's included music shows on BBC, VOA, Radio Australia, Pakistan, Afghanistan, Switzerland, Ceylon, and Germany so far). A radio – short wave – is the item I would recommend most highly to anyone going into the PC – portable of course. They should also bring some art works – favorite pictures etc., and certainly two or three favorite books. Culture cannot be escaped – and can be missed.

There is the cook book – helps you dream about good food, and gives you some possibilities – like the chocolate cake that I made last night – with a hole in the middle like a belly button. The stove didn't regulate too well, and the kerosene was unsteady. But it still tastes good.

And there is the dust storm which is raging outside my door, and partly inside my door, and the daily weather, and problems as in every other part of the world.

I have had a wonderful experience here – one I wouldn't trade for anything. . . .

And the friendships and impressions endure

Len's friendships lasted. He sponsored his next-door neigh-bors in Kandahar to come to the U.S. as refugees. A story Len related illustrates the lasting impressions Volunteers might make as they rode their bicycles. Visiting an Afghan refugee settlement in Pakistan in the 1980s, Len bought some chilled drinks for himself and his companion at a roadside bazaar.

"Just as I was about to pay for the drinks," Len recalls, "a man pushed his way into the center of the crowd and shouted 'Do not charge that man for those drinks! He is our guest. I know him.' I had never seen this fellow before, as far as I knew, and I asked him how he knew me. He said: 'When I was a little boy in Kandahar you were a teacher there. I used to see you riding your bicycle past my father's shop when you went to school. Now you are here with us again. You didn't forget us, and I haven't forgotten you.'"[3]

The Volunteers in Group IV met at a completion-of-service conference that was held in two sessions in late April and early May 1966 to share what they had learned and debate one more time just what the Peace Corps actually was or was intended to be. The sessions were conducted jointly by Leslie Hanscom, deputy in the Peace Corps evaluation office and a former editor at the *Saturday Evening Post* and *Newsweek*, and Robert Satin, who had been the Peace Corps Representative in the Dominican Republic when the U.S. marines invaded in 1965.[4] The first session was a mix of a few teachers, nine nurses, and another nine Volunteers in Kabul ranging from mechanics and secretaries to a graphic artist. The second session brought together teachers, who mostly had served in the provinces.

About the first session, Hanscom wrote "[a]lmost all seemed to take an interest in the problems and satisfactions of Volunteers different from their own, and all seemed united in their sense of identity as Volunteers. The latter quality was the most attractive thing about them. Although settled in jobs that in some cases were worlds away from the preferred image of the Volunteer life, they seemed to have held onto their idea of what they were and what they ought to expect of themselves."[5]

"[T]he secretaries were the group which expressed the most dissatisfaction. The placement and utilization of secretaries has tended to be a troubled matter in the Afghanistan program. In the offices to which they have been assigned, they have usually been relegated to the position of English language typist, or, worse, idle status symbols. Just as Madison Avenue executives prize British secretaries for the touch of class they add to the office, Afghans prize Peace Corps girls. Afghan officials also request them in the hope that the girls will live up to the Muslim image of Western women and turn out to be jolly playmates for chasing around the desk. Most of the girls found it reasonably easy to parry the boss's libido (he usually sulked for a couple of days and got over it), but a problem less easy to handle brought them persistent disappointment"[:] the secretaries' goal was to share knowledge about how to manage an office, but they seldom had Afghan counterparts with whom to work. Nevertheless, Volunteers agreed that the Peace Corps secretaries had helped change the attitude of Afghan men about hiring women in offices—the number has risen remarkably. "'If I've done nothing else,' said one girl, 'I've let the Afghans know that a woman is capable of thinking and standing by what she thinks.'"[6]

"Nurses, it was commonly agreed, had to withstand more on-the-job culture shock than any other group. Seeing all of their training and their ideals contradicted by the primitive conditions in an Afghan hospital was hard medicine to take. The lesson to be learned, the nurses reported, is that 'You can't create America here.' You must grasp that hospital patients in an underdeveloped country don't want or really <u>need</u> a daily bath. You have to accept the fact that linen cannot be changed every day in a hospital where the needed laundry facilities do not exist. You revise your standards to fit the actual realities." The hardest challenge was "not the poor hygiene and the lack of means, but the startling callousness of nurses and doctors . . . ." Nevertheless, they saw changes: "Afghan nurses, who formerly shrank from illness as something unclean, were now less reluctant to touch patients with their hands." Patients also were learning what kind of care they might expect. "By letting the patients know the kind of care to which they were entitled, they had encouraged the patients to demand their rights."[7]

One nurse wondered what her service "truly amounted to. What <u>was</u> the Peace Corps? Did it exist to serve the purposes of American politics or did it exist to serve humanity? There were many answers to this, but the typical one was as follows:

'If the Peace Corps were one Volunteer, you could ask that question; since it isn't, you can't. Each person has to settle that question for himself.' From another came this answer: 'Maybe it is politics to begin with, but it's politics of so much higher and cleaner a kind than the world has ever known that this in itself is a service to humanity. Try to answer that question, and you go round and round.'"8

"As careers go in the Peace Corps, theirs, collectively, should be considered a success," Hanscom concluded. "They considered it so, and there is no stronger criterion upon which an outsider can base a judgment. They were lucky in the country to which they were assigned—one of the most interesting on the Peace Corps map—and in the leadership they were given. Most of them had suffered from illness of one kind or another—since Afghanistan is also one of the least healthy of Peace Corps countries – but they had come through with morale high at the end."9

The second session, reported by Satin, involved 25 teachers of English, science, and social studies, most of them at the secondary level, who were "widely scattered over the country (the first Afghan group so programmed) and for some, it was the first time they had seen other members of Afghan IV since arrival in the country. Four PCVs served in Kabul, six others in large urban communities; seven in middle-sized towns; three in rural not-isolated communities; and five in rural isolated communities."10

Similar to earlier groups, over half the teachers checked frustration in the working situation as a concern. "[T]his frustration was based on a number of small annoyances such as: physical conditions of the schools; cheating by students; rote method of instruction; unskilled or non-existent counterparts; language barriers; lack of teaching equipment and books; and for some, overload of teaching assignment. PCV teachers, in spite of the above frustrations, had a universal feeling of contributing to the country's economic or social development. . . . Looking back, the PCVs could identify real changes in the society and cultural mores during their tour of service. PCV female teachers did teach in boys' schools – 'difficult and perhaps not a good assignment for non-married female PCVs'; some PCVs were, toward the end of their tour, invited to Afghan homes and would entertain Afghans in their own homes. The Peace Corps was fostering mutual understanding and accelerating attitude changes that were resulting in more freedom of action and choice for the Afghans."[11]

"The Afghan IV group broke the ice of governmental and cultural hostility and indifference to their presence. Their frustrations and feeling of accomplishment are intimately a part of the culture in which they are living. When asked 'What did they like most about the Peace Corps?' two-thirds of the PCVs replied, 'The chance to live in a different culture.' TEFL, in many areas, was the entering wedge into provincial Afghanistan and the PCVs in Group IV realized, with some satisfaction, that the way is now open for other PCVs to follow with diversified programs."[12]

"The country, its people and culture, seemed to be more compelling reasons for feelings of satisfaction with Peace Corps service than either the Peace Corps as an institution or the job," Satin wrote. "Good PCVs, in an exciting country, supported by a dedicated staff, come close to the ideal Peace Corps program. Afghan IV appears to be such a program."[13]

Bob Steiner *You may know the name Hanscom. He worked for Charlie Peters, the head of evaluation for Peace Corps. Leslie Hanscom came to Afghanistan and gave us* *one of the best evaluations of any country in the world.[14] But the thing that impressed him about Afghanistan was that the ideal, the original ideal of the Peace Corps, namely to get the youth of the two countries understanding each other, that ideal didn't get lost in Afghanistan. I think it was alive when I left. I am sure it was. And certainly was when it began.*

EPILOGUE

In *The Fort of Nine Towers*, Qais Akbar Omar shares his love of family and country and gives the reader his "load of griefs" from growing up in Afghanistan during decades of invasion, civil war, the Taliban, and then the arrival of the U.S. and NATO troops. He and his cousins grew up in the home his grandfather built in Kabul in the late 1960s that also housed his grandfather's six brothers and their families. Sixty apple trees grew between his grandfather's rooms on one side of the garden and those of his family on the other side. The trees were unusual because a cousin had brought small McIntosh shoots from America to graft onto Afghan apple trees. The home and the apple trees are gone now.

The Peace Corps Volunteers are gone, too. During their 17 years in the country, they offered their skills and culture for Afghans to graft as they chose into the stock of their own culture. And in sharing their lives and skills, Afghans gave the Volunteers a glimpse into Afghan culture that remains a part of those Volunteers decades later. In the sixties, "afghanistanism" was the term American journalists used for writing about something distant to avoid focusing on what was wrong at home. For us and many other Volunteers, Afghanistan will always be a place that once was home.

Afghanistan today is a very different country. Traffic jams, cell phones, a lively media, many more schools and universities—and weapons and waste from years of fighting. It is a youthful country of perhaps twice as many people as 50 years ago. Two-thirds of Afghans are under 25 and 60 percent are girls and women. In this extraordinary transitional moment, some Afghans and Americans are working in ways similar to the Peace Corps to find peaceful paths. Thinking long-term and small-scale, with Afghans in the lead, aware of the deep divides, seeking directions that respect the proud history and recognize the dreams of new generations, they are listening to and learning from each other.

One example is the School of Leadership, Afghanistan. SOLA (peace) is "about bringing peace through education." It is educating young Afghans in Kabul and obtaining scholarships, especially for women, to study in the U.S. and elsewhere. Former Volunteers are among those participating in activities such as mentoring, both virtually and face-to-face. A critical goal is to find leadership roles for women completing their education in building the government and economy of their country.

Another example is the Global Partnership for Afghanistan (GPFA) which works with men and women farmers to establish orchards, woodlots, nurseries, strawberry fields, and vineyards, providing technical and business training, high-quality plants, and links to markets. In an uncertain time, these farmers are looking to the future, relearning skills in grafting fruit trees and planting saplings expected to produce market-quality fruit in five years.

A Pashto saying "ka nakam se, bia pahlawan say" literally means "you will rise only if you fall." After decades of war, it is past time for peace in Afghanistan.

REFERENCES

Chapter I — A Moment of Openness

[1] Two sources on the history of Afghanistan are Amin Saikal, *Modern Afghanistan: A History of Struggle and Survival* (New York: L.B. Taurus Ltd., 2004, updated edition 2012) and Louis Dupree, *Afghanistan* (Princeton, NJ: Princeton University Press, 1973). See also, Peter R. Blood, ed., Afghanistan: A Country Study, Federal Research Division, Library of Congress, Washington, D.C., 1997.

[2] One statement of U.S. policy can be found in Revised United States Objectives in Afghanistan, Embassy Despatch No. 32, August 14, 1956, signed by Ambassador Sheldon T. Mills.

[3] The Faculties of Medicine and Law had been established in the 1930s. In 1957, the government had sent 26 Afghan students abroad to study. The number of educated was estimated at 7000 in 1962. Patrick J. Reardon, "Modernization and Reform: The Contemporary Endeavor," ed. George Grassmuck et al., *Afghanistan: Some New Approaches* (Ann Arbor: The University of Michigan, Center for Near Eastern and North African Studies, 1969), 170-71, citing Afghanistan Ministry of Planning, *Survey of Progress 1961-62*, Table 4, 50.

[4] Nasrine Gross points out that the women's movement in Afghanistan now has a history of at least 100 years. See her translation of her presentation to Afghan teacher trainers in Pictou, Nova Scotia, October 2012, "How Many Times is the First Time? Short Look at Social Change and History of the Women's Movement in Afghanistan." Personal communication. See also her presentation to the Middle East Studies Association in 2006, "Then and Now: Afghan Women Emerging and Disappearing," at www.kabultec.org. Also see Tamim Ansary's description of the rapid change in the roles of women in the early 1960s in *Games Without Rules* (New York:

Public Affairs, 2012), 157-158. "In the next five years, the status of Afghan women went through five centuries of evolution. Girls began attending the university. The graduates began working as teachers, nurses, and even doctors. Women started working in government offices, factories, and private commercial establishments. Ariana Airlines routinely employed women as flight attendants. Radio Kabul regularly exposed Afghan men to women's voices, singing or reading 'the news.' As transistor radios proliferated, people in towns and cities all over Afghanistan became accustomed to hearing the voices of women to whom they were not related, an unfamiliar experience for Afghan men."

[5] Nour M. Rahimi, ed., *The Kabul Times Annual 1967* (Kabul: Kabul Times Publishing Agency, 1967), 15.

[6] Rahimi, *The Kabul Times Annual 1967*, 6.

[7] "Remarks of Senator John F. Kennedy," October 14, 1960, http://www.peacecorps.gov/about/history/speech.

[8] John Coyne, To Preserve and to Learn—occasional essays about the history of Peace Corps. Early '60s Analysis of Youth Service. http://peacecorpswriters.org/pages/2003/0307/prntvrs307/pv307pchist.html. The book based on the feasibility study prepared for the Congress is Maury Albertson, with Andrew E. Rice and Pauline E. Birkey, *New Frontiers for American Youth: Perspective on the Peace Corps* (Washington, D.C.: Public Affairs Press, 1961).

[9] Roy Hoopes, "An Idea Whose Time Had Come," *The Peace Corps Reader* (Peace Corps, Washington, D.C., Office of Public Information, October 1966), 6-9, excerpted from Roy Hoopes, *Complete Peace Corps Guide* (New York: The Dial Press, Revised Edition, 1965). For a more complete history, see Charles G. Wetzel, "The Peace Corps in Our Past," *The Annals of the American Academy of Political and Social Science*, Volume 365, The Peace Corps, May 1966, 1-11. Also see Sargent Shriver, *Point of the Lance* (New York: Harper & Row, 1964), 6-7: "Let me emphasize that the politics of ideas is not party politics. The problems are too large and too important to be left to normal political methods. That is one reason why military terminology is used in the Peace *Corps* and the *War* on Poverty. To eliminate poverty at home, and to achieve peace in the world, we need total commitment, the large-scale mobilization, the institutional intervention, the unprecedented release of human energy, and the focusing of

intellect which have happened in our society only in war. We need what William James called 'the moral equivalent of war.'"

10 John F. Kennedy, "Speech of Senator John F. Kennedy, Cow Palace, San Francisco, CA," November 2, 1960. Online by Gerhard Peters and John T. Woolley, The American Presidency Project. http://www.presidency.uscb. edu/ws/?pid25928.

11 John F. Kennedy, "Inaugural Address," January 20, 1961. Online by Gerhard Peters and John Woolley, The American Presidency Project. http:// www.presidency.uscb.edu/ws/?pid8032.

12 John F. Kennedy, "Special Message to the Congress on the Peace Corps," March 1, 1961. Online by Gerhard Peters and John T. Woolley, The American Presidency Project. http://www.presidency.uscb.edu/ ws/?pid=8515. This message recommended the establishment of a permanent Peace Corps and set forth the reasons for doing so. Executive Order 10924, 26 Federal Register 1789 (March 1, 1961), established the Peace Corps on a "temporary pilot basis" in the Department of State, financed with funds available to the Secretary of State under the authority of the Mutual Security Act of 1954, as amended. Online at http://www.ourdocuments.gov/doc_large_image.php?flash=true&doc=92.   For   President Kennedy's remarks about signing the Executive Order, see http://www. jfklibrary.org/Asset-Viewer/2DfDYdjEA.

13 The Peace Corps Act, Pub.L. 87-293, title I, Sec. 2, Sept. 22, 1961, 75 Stat. 612.

14 Pauline Birkey-Kreutzer, *Peace Corps Pioneer* (Urbana, Illinois, 2003), 209, 212. Birkey also tells the story of serving as a key staff member for the West Pakistan program in 1962 and 1963. Also see John Coyne, Early '60s Analysis of Youth Service at http://peacecorpswriters.org/pages/2003/0307/prntvrs307/pv307pchist.html.

Chapter 3 — Getting to Kabul

1 Dupree, *Afghanistan*, 1-2. The Hindu Kush are "the westernmost extension of the Karakorum Mountains, and the Himalayas, which push from the Pamir Knot into central Afghanistan in a general northeast-southwesterly trend to within one hundred miles of the Iranian border. The ranges stretch about 600 miles . . . laterally, with the average north-south measurement being 150 miles . . . ." Dupree notes: "Almost all references in Western language sources define Hindu Kush as 'kills the Hindu,' a grim

reminder of the days when many Indians died in the high mountain passes of Afghanistan on their way to the slave markets of Muslim Central Asia. According to most Afghan scholars with whom I have talked, however, Hindu Kush is probably a corruption of *Hindu Koh*, name of the mountain range which, in pre-Muslim times, divided the area of dominant Hindu control to the south and southeast from the non-Hindu areas of the north, whose people were probably Zoroastrians and may have later developed into the modern Tajik."

[2] David Fleishhacker, *Lessons from Afghanistan* (DFPublications: 2001), 17-18.

[3] Nancy Hatch Wolfe, in collaboration with Ahmad Ali Kohzad, *An Historical Guide to Kabul* (Kabul: The Afghan Tourist Organization, 1965), 140-141. Her description of the trip to Istalif is found at 134-136.

Chapter 4 — A Cautious Start

[1] Peace Corps Program, Agreement Between the United States of America and Afghanistan, Effected by Exchange of Notes Signed at Kabul September 6 and 11, 1962. U.S. State Department, Treaties and Other International Acts Series, 5169, U.S. Government Printing Office, 1962. Deputy Chief of Mission William Brewer negotiated the agreement with the head of the economic section of Afghanistan's Foreign Ministry. http://adst.org/oral-history/country-reader-series/. To navigate to the interview with Brewer, click on "Afghanistan" under "Country Readers" on the left and then scroll down through the interviews in chronological order (very interesting reading) until William D. Brewer appears.

[2] Peace Corps, Washington, D.C., Director's Staff Meeting, 9:30 AM, Thursday, February 15, 1962, 2-4. Report on Afghanistan, Cleo Shook.

[3] Louis Dupree commented that Americans in Kabul were impressed that Peace Corps had sent a person to explore setting up a program who knew the language and country. Louis Dupree, "Moving Mountains in Afghanistan," ed. Robert B. Textor, *Cultural Frontiers of the Peace Corps*, (Cambridge, MA: M.I.T. Press, 1966), 107-108. ("Most of the material in this chapter appeared originally in "The Peace Corps in Afghanistan," an AUFS Report published by the American Universities Field Staff, Inc. (Copyright 1964)." Dupree, "Moving Mountains," 123.) Although Dupree identifies Shook as a former director of the Afghan Institute of Technology (AIT), Shook says in his memoir that he arrived

in Afghanistan in 1953 to teach electrical technology to 10th - 12th grade boys at the just recently established AIT and eventually headed the mechanical department. Later he worked for U.S. AID as deputy in the transportation advisory division and then director of a bus project. He left Afghanistan in 1960 after eight years. In 1961, he joined the newly-forming Peace Corps, leaving in 1962 to work at an engineering firm, then returning briefly to serve as director in Iran from March 1964 to January 1966. Cleo Shook, *While I Still Remember*, 2003. Shook died in 2010.

[4] Peace Corps, Washington, D.C., Presentation of FY 1963 Program to United States Congress, June 1, 1962, 65-66.

[5] Brent Ashabranner, *A Moment in History: The First Ten Years of the Peace Corps* (Garden City, NY: Doubleday & Company, 1971), 68-69.

[6] Charlie Peters, *Tilting at Windmills: An Autobiography* (New York: Addison-Wesley, 1988) 121, *quoted in* Scott Stossel, *Sarge: The Life and Times of Sargent Shriver* (Washington: Smithsonian Books, 2004) 214.

[7] Conversation with Pat Sullivan Meyers, September 12, 2013.

[8] "Afghanistan Project," undated.

Chapter 5 — The First Six Months on the Job

[1] Peace Corps, Washington, D.C., 4th Annual Peace Corps Report, 1965, 19.

[2] Dupree, "Moving Mountains," 108.

[3] Fleishhacker, *Lessons from Afghanistan*, 15.

[4] Fleishhacker, *Lessons from Afghanistan*, 16.

[5] "Keeper of the keys," *Peace Corps Volunteer*, November 1967, 16-18. Rosalind Pearson and Janet Bing working with Louis and Nancy Dupree designed these monologues for role playing by trainees on the challenge of dealing with storekeepers.

[6] Fleishhacker, *Lessons from Afghanistan*, 67-68.

[7] Memorandum to Robert Sargent Shriver, Jr., from Robert Steiner, Acting PC Representative, Kabul, "Report from Kabul, Afghanistan," February 21, 1963.

[8] Peace Corps, Washington, D.C., Thorburn Reid, Overseas Evaluation, Afghanistan, March 1963, 1, 3- 4.

Chapter 6 — Living on the Economy

[1] Peace Corps Afghanistan, Administrative Handbook, October 24, 1964, 18.

[2] Peace Corps Afghanistan, Administrative Handbook, 38.

[3] Robert L. Steiner, "Volunteers Gain Acceptance in Kabul," *Peace Corps Volunteer,* January 1964, 10.

[4] Sami Noor, emails to Bob Steiner, Nov. 20 and 21, 2011 (edited). Sami Noor worked part-time with Peace Corps 1962-1964 and then went to Vanderbilt University to get his MA in Economics. In 1973, he earned is PhD in economics from the University of Bonn. He is now Coordinator for Cooperation with Afghan Universities at the Institute of Development Research and Development Policy at the Ruhr University Bochum.

[5] Fleishhacker, *Lessons from Afghanistan,* 37.

[6] Peace Corps Afghanistan, Doug Bell, The Saw Dust Stove, no date but probably October 1964.

[7] Peace Corps, Washington, D.C., Reid, Overseas Evaluation, Afghanistan, March 1963, 6. The cost of shipping was a particular problem at this point since all shipping was through Iran. Steiner reported at a Washington staff meeting that ". . . it costs $300 to ship a jeep from the U.S. to Korramshar on the Persian Gulf and $1200 from there to Kabul." Peace Corps, Washington, D.C., Director's Staff Record, April 18, 1963, Report on Afghanistan – Bob Steiner.

[8] Fleishhacker, *Lessons from Afghanistan,* 78-79.

[9] Government of Afghanistan, Ministry of Press and Information, *Kabul Times,* Feb. 15, 1966.

[10] Peace Corps Afghanistan, Administrative Handbook, 17.

[11] Pat Weeks, "Romance on a Bicycle," Peace Corps Afghanistan Volunteer Newsletter, Vol. 1, No. 1, November 1964, 5-6.

[12] Cross-Cultural Studies Manual for Afghanistan Training Programs, prepared by Rosalind Pearson and Janet Bing, Dr. and Mrs. Louis Dupree, Consultants, 109-110.

[13] Peace Corps Afghanistan, Administrative Handbook, 11.

[14] Peace Corps Afghanistan, Doug and Pat Bell, memo on what to bring, November 9, 1963.

[15] Peace Corps Afghanistan, Current Kabul Prices of Household Items, September 1964.

Chapter 7 — A Program Ready to Grow

1 Dupree, "Moving Mountains," 116.

2 Peace Corps, Washington, D.C., Memorandum for the Director from Warren W. Wiggins, "Proposed Addition to the Peace Corps Program in Afghanistan," December 14, 1964. Ashabranner explains that the average figures per Peace Corps Volunteer for 1963, 1964, and 1965 decreased from $9,074 to $8,214 to $7,809 even as the number of Volunteers doubled because the size of Peace Corps Washington staff stayed the same. Ashabranner, *A Moment in History: The First Ten Years of the Peace Corps*, 136.

3 Peace Corps, Washington, D.C., Director's Staff Record, April 18, 1963, 1.

4 Peace Corps, Washington, D.C., 4th Annual Peace Corps Report, 20.

5 Peace Corps, Washington, D.C., Completion of Service Conference Report, Afghanistan I, conducted May 7-9, 1964, by Harold H. Morris, Jr., 1-2, 4.

Chapter 8 — Participating in the Afghan Community

1 Peace Corps Afghanistan, Administrative Handbook, 1.

2 Steiner, "Volunteers Gain Acceptance in Kabul," *Peace Corps Volunteer*, January 1964, 10.

3 Peace Corps, Washington, D.C., Completion of Service Conference Report, Afghanistan II, conducted December 10, 11, and 12, 1964, by David Schimmel, 5.

4 "Afghanistan", *Peace Corps Volunteer, April 1963*, 6.

5 Steiner, "Volunteers Gain Acceptance in Kabul," *Peace Corps Volunteer*, January 1964, 10.

6 Letter from Robert L. Steiner, Peace Corps Representative, to Miss Patricia Sullivan, Near East and South Asian Programs, Peace Corps, Washington, D.C., dated February 11, 1964.

7 "Anglo-American Jazz Quartet Brings Night Club Life to Khyber Restaurant," *Kabul Times*, Sept. 24, 1964, 3.

8 Faiz Khairzada, who organized the performance of Duke Ellington at a Kabul stadium in September 1963, described the experience on BBC Witness on Sept. 19, 2013. See www.bbc.co.uk/podcasts/series/witness.

[9] January 15, 1965, memo from Amembassy Kabul, to Department of State (Peace Corps) entitled "RGA [Royal Government of Afghanistan] Medal for Ex-PCV Jack White." The memo, sent over the signature of Harry M. Phelan, Counselor of Embassy for Economic Affairs, was drafted by Steiner. The quotation from Steiner and the previous paragraphs are based on the memo. Written in hand on the top of the memo: "Here's one we should certainly get some mileage out of. Sarge."

[10] Peace Corps, Washington, D.C., 4th Annual Peace Corps Report, June 30, 1965, 24.

[11] Ken Lampke, "Farsi songfest draws 3000," *The Peace Corps Volunteer*, November 1965, 15.

[12] "The Fantasticks," Peace Corps Afghanistan Volunteer Newsletter, May 1966, 7; Sheilah Kristiansen, "Fantasticks," Peace Corps Afghanistan Volunteer Newsletter, June 1966, 8.

[13] "Afghanistan," *Peace Corps Volunteer*, January 1964, 16.

[14] Dennis Egan, "Afghanistan, Then and Now: Reflections of a Peace Corps Volunteer," *Afghanistan Studies Journal*, Center for Afghanistan Studies, University of Nebraska at Omaha, Premiere Issue, Spring 1988, 101, 106.

[15] Chris Ballard, "The Wizard of Kabul," *Sports Illustrated*, July 22, 2013, 55-63.

[16] John Borel, "An Inconspicuous Approach," *Peace Corps Volunteer*, January 1964, 13.

[17] Steiner, "Volunteers Gain Acceptance in Kabul," *Peace Corps Volunteer*, January 1964, 10.

Chapter 9 — November 22, 1963 in Kabul

[1] Chronology, Grassmuck, et al., *Afghanistan: Some New Approaches*, 304.

[2] Dupree, "Moving Mountains," 119.

[3] Weisman, Steven R., ed., *Daniel Patrick Moynihan: A Portrait in Letters of a Young American Visionary* (New York: Public Affairs, 2010), 14.

Chapter 10 —A Reception in Paghman

[1] Wolfe, *An Historical Guide to Kabul*, 132-133.

[2] Dominic Medley and Jude Barrand, *The Survival Guide to Kabul* (Bucks, England: Bratt Travel Guides, 2003), 149-50.

[3] Dupree, "Moving Mountains," 123.

Chapter 11 — Going to the Provinces

[1] Rahimi, *The Kabul Times Annual*, 1967, 143.

[2] "Mr. Steiner Comments," Peace Corps Afghanistan Volunteer Newsletter, Vol. 1, No. 1, November 1964, 1.

[3] "The Brave Ones," Peace Corps Afghanistan Volunteer Newsletter, November 1964, 6.

[4] Peace Corps, Washington, D.C., 4th Annual Peace Corps Report, 20.

[5] Department of State Airgram No. TOPEC A-8 from Amembassy Kabul to Department of State (Peace Corps) dated January 19, 1965, "Material for Congressional Presentation," drafted by RS McClusky, approved by RLSteiner.

[6] Fleishhacker, *Lessons from Afghanistan*, 83-97.

[7] Peace Corps Afghanistan, Administrative Handbook, 19-20, and "Liaison Council," Peace Corps Afghanistan Volunteer Newsletter, Vol. 1, No. 9, Sept/Oct 1965, 1, 4.

[8] Dennis Aronson, Adventures in Afghanistan, presentation for Life-Long Learning, Fort Lewis College, Durango, CO, April 10, 2009.

[9] Leonard Oppenheim, quotations from letter written Nov. 14, 1964, shared in email dated May 20, 2013.

[10] Leonard Oppenheim, quotations from letter written March 6, 1965, shared in email dated July 22, 2013.

[11] David and Elizabeth McGaffey, Letters from a Vanished Country, Afghanistan 1964-1967, letters written December 20, 1964, and early January 1965.

[12] David and Elizabeth McGaffey, letter dated December 15, 1965.

[13] David and Elizabeth McGaffey, letter dated February 9, 1966.

[14] http://adst.org/oral-history/country-reader-series. Oral history interview with Charles Stewart Kennedy on behalf of the Association for Diplomatic Studies and Training, September 1995.

Chapter 12 — Using the Language

[1] Peace Corps Afghanistan, Administrative Handbook, 21.

[2] M. Ehsan Entezar, Farsi Reference Manual, March 1964 (David J. Burns, Coordinator Language Program, Experiment in International Living, Putney, Vermont).

[3] Peace Corps Afghanistan, Administrative Handbook, 21.

[4] Saul Helfenbein, Development is My Business: A Memoir. Draft, personal communication, May 2013, 14.

[5] David and Elizabeth McGaffey, letter dated December 15, 1965.

[6] David McGaffey, http://adst.org/oral-history/country-reader-series.

[7] "Group V Farsi Students," Peace Corps Afghanistan Volunteer Newsletter, December 1966, 5.

Chapter 13 — Challenges in the Second Two Years

[1] "For the Record," Peace Corps Afghanistan Volunteer Newsletter, Vol. 1, No. 7, May/June 1965, 1.

[2] Saif R. Samady, *Education and Afghan Society in the twentieth century*, UNESCO, 2001, 29.

[3] Peace Corps, Washington, D.C., 4th Annual Peace Corps Report, 21.

[4] Samady, *Education and Afghan Society in the twentieth century*, UNESCO, 2001. See chapters 1 and 2, especially pages 11, 17, 24 (Figure 2), and 41.

[5] Peace Corps, Washington, D.C., Completion of Service Conference Report, Afghanistan II, conducted December 10, 11, and 12, 1964, by David Schimmel, 1-4.

[6] "Dr. Morgan to return to U.S.," Peace Corps Afghanistan Volunteer Newsletter, December 1966, 4, 26.

[7] "Group VI Mid-term Conference," Peace Corps Afghanistan Volunteer Newsletter, September 1966, 4-5.

[8] Louis Dupree, "The Peace Corps in Afghanistan: The Impact of the Volunteers on the Country and of the Country on the Volunteers," American Universities Field Staff, Inc., South Asia Series, Vol. VIII, No. 4 (Afghanistan), October 1964, 829, 843.

9 "School to School," Peace Corps Afghanistan Volunteer Newsletter, July 1966, 2, 16; "John Barbee Joins PC Staff," Peace Corps Afghanistan Volunteer Newsletter, April 1967, 9.

10 "The Dammed Chan Chamast River," and Stuart Schmidt, "It Can't Possibly Work," Peace Corps Afghanistan Volunteer Newsletter, September 1966, 8-9.

11 Deborah Salter, "Around Afghanistan via the Kabul Museum," Peace Corps Afghanistan Volunteer Newsletter, September 1966, 8.

12 "Afghan Group 6H81/2 Arrives," Peace Corps Afghanistan Volunteer Newsletter, July 1966, 4.

13 In the summer of 1965, there were 178 Volunteers in Afghanistan. The 31 members of Group III who completed their service and departed in October were replaced by the three doctors and 25 nurses who arrived in June and December 1965. That brought the number of Volunteers to 175. The number 200 was passed in May 1966 when the 35 teachers in Group VIIIA combined with the 23 nurses and lab technicians in Group VIIIB brought the total in-country to 233. Group IV would soon depart, bringing the total back down to about 175. Of that total, 88 were English, math, science, or physical education teachers; 55 were medical personnel (nurses, laboratory technicians, and doctors); and 32 were in other fields (business education, rural development, secretarial, and accounting). About 100 were serving in Kabul and 75 in the provinces.

14 Robert L. Steiner, Letter to Pat and Ted Meyers, July 14, 1965.

15 Peace Corps Afghanistan, Administrative Handbook, 8-10; revised September 18, 1965, 8-10B; "Report on the Health Meeting," Peace Corps Afghanistan Volunteer Newsletter, December 1966, 5.

16 Peace Corps Afghanistan, Minutes of Liaison Council, July 1965.

17 Robert L. Steiner, "Usage more than reason," Peace Corps Afghanistan Volunteer Newsletter, Vol. 1, No. 8, July 1965, 3.

18 "To the Editors" from Margarete Silberberg, Peace Corps Afghanistan Volunteer Newsletter, Vol. 1, No. 9, Sept./Oct., 1965, 6.

19 "Liaison Council," Peace Corps Afghanistan Volunteer Newsletter, Vol. 1, No.9, Sept/Oct 1965, 4.

20 Leslie Hanscom, "The Magic of Caring," *The Peace Corps Reader* (Chicago, IL: Quadrangle Books, 1967), 111, 115.

[21] Dupree, "Moving Mountains," 121.

[22] Elizabeth Cobbs-Hoffman, *All You Need is Love: The Peace Corps and the Spirit of the 1960s* (Cambridge, MA: Harvard University Press, 1988), 262.

[23] Memoranda to All Volunteers and Staff from R.L.Steiner, 9 February 1966 (on Ashabranner memo) and March 12, 1966 on Peace Corps and Political Action.

[24] John Osborn, "Dissent: Peace Corps On The Line," and "Protest in Afghanistan, A Case Study,*" Peace Corps Volunteer*, March-April 1970, 6, 9, 13, 22. Letter to the *Volunteer* from Denise Behar, Mike McGrath, Norm Rosen, *Peace Corps Volunteer*, July-August 1970, 3-4.

[25] Dupree, *Afghanistan*, 590-97, and Reardon, "Modernization and Reform."

Chapter 14 — Forces at Work in Afghanistan in the Early 1960's

[1] Fleishhacker, *Lessons from Afghanistan*, 139-40.

Chapter 15 — Not under Economic Theory

[1] Peace Corps, Washington, D.C., 4th Annual Peace Corps Report, 21.

[2] R.L. Steiner, Regional Director, NANESA (North Africa, Near East, and South Asia), Memorandum for all NANESA Country Directors, Subject: Thoughts from an Itinerant Regional Director, Peace Corps, Washington, D.C., February 6, 1969.

Chapter 16 — Steiner's Peace Corps Philosophy and its Origins

[1] "Dr. Edwin Wright" and "An International Life," [Wooster, Ohio] *Daily Record*, Oct. 30, 1987, A4. Also, brochure for Edwin Milton Wright, Ninetieth Birthday Observance, January 10, 1987, Richfield, Ohio.

Chapter 18 — Close to the Ideal Peace Corps Program

[1] "Three Factors Govern Success of Volunteer," *Kabul Times*, June 15, 1966, 3.

[2] "To Say Goodbye," Peace Corps Afghanistan Volunteer Newsletter, June 1966, 12-13.

[3] Peace Corps Times, 30th Anniversary Edition, March 1, 1991, 5.

4 See chapter 6 in Stanley Meisler, *When the World Calls: The Inside Story of the Peace Corps and Its First Fifty Years* (Boston, MA: Beacon Press, 2011).

5 Peace Corps, Washington, D.C., Completion of Service Conference Report, Afghanistan IV-A, conducted April 28, 29, and 30, 1966, by Leslie Hanscom, Office of Evaluation & Research, and Robert Satin, Office of Planning and Program Review, (report authored by Leslie Hanscom), 4.

6 Completion of Service Conference Report, Afghanistan IV-A, 8-9.

7 Completion of Service Conference Report, Afghanistan IV-A, 11-12.

8 Completion of Service Conference Report, Afghanistan IV-A, 17

9 Completion of Service Conference Report, Afghanistan IV-A, 18.

10 Peace Corps, Washington, D.C., Completion of Service Conference Report, Afghanistan IV-B, conducted May 1, 2, and 3, 1966, by L. Robert Satin, Office of Planning & Program Review, and Leslie Hanscom, Office of Evaluation and Research, (report authored by L. Robert Satin), 3-4.

11 Completion of Service Conference Report, Afghanistan IV-B, 4.

12 Completion of Service Conference Report, Afghanistan IV-B, 9.

13 Completion of Service Conference Report, Afghanistan IV-B, 10-11.

14 "Hapgood and Bennett reprinted excerpts from Leslie Hanscom's evaluation of Afghanistan on pp. 120-22." Meisler, *When the World Calls*, 251. Meisler's reference is to David Hapgood and Meridan Bennett, *Agents of Change: A Close Look at the Peace Corps*, Boston: Little Brown and Company, 1968. We have not yet been able to locate a copy of this evaluation.

FIRST EIGHT GROUPS OF VOLUNTEERS IN AFGHANISTAN

Early Peace Corps Volunteers identified themselves as members of numbered groups. The following list provides an overview of the eight groups that served or began service in Afghanistan between September 1962 and June 1966. It identifies training sites; the numbers of Volunteers and dates of their arrival in Afghanistan and, for some, of departure; the nature of the jobs performed; and the locations of service.

A total of almost 300 Volunteers came during this period. Roughly 160 were teachers, mostly of English but also some in science, math, and physical education. About 70 worked in health programs as nurses, lab technicians and doctors. Close to another 70 provided a wide range of other skills from accounting to rural development. About half lived and worked in locations outside of Kabul during at least some of their time in Afghanistan.

We relied on PC Afghanistan newsletters, completion of service reports, the *Kabul Times*, and personal knowledge to prepare this summary. The numbers of Volunteers serving in different locations and jobs were constantly changing. Some Volunteers moved to the provinces after first working in Kabul. Some resigned early; others extended. The following list gives a sense of the numbers but should not be assumed "exact". We found numbers were sometimes inconsistent or did not add up, but they do provide a sense of scale.

We have found no list of Volunteer names by group, although a persistent search among Volunteers from each group might eventually uncover copies of these lists. Partial lists of the 1650 Volunteers who served in Afghanistan can be found in the 2009 Peace Corps Directory (about 600) and on the Peace Corps Wiki site. Friends of Afghanistan currently has about 450 members.

Group I Trained at Georgetown University in Washington, D.C. Nine volunteers arrived in September 1962 and completed their service in June of 1964. The five teachers, three nurses, and one mechanic all served in Kabul, although in their last months four taught in Kandahar and one in Mazar-i-Sharif. One extended to marry a member of Group III and another married a German she had met in Kabul.

Group II Trained at Georgetown University in Washington, D.C. Twenty-six Volunteers arrived in June 1963, and three terminated early. Most were English teachers though one taught physics and another physical education. Five were printers; four printers ended up working at the Government Press and one became an English teacher. Although most served in Kabul, at least two worked in Herat and two others in Bost. [PC/A newsletter, Vol. I, No. 1.]

Group III Trained at Experiment for International Living, Brattleboro, Vermont. Thirty-three arrived in January 1964, half teachers and half working in a variety of positions (secretaries, accountants) in government ministries. Eight served at least part of their time outside of Kabul. Thirty-one completed service in September or October 1965. [PC/A newsletter, Vol. I, No. 9.]

Group IV Trained at Experiment for International Living, Brattleboro, Vermont (most of the time at near-by Camp Arden). Fifty-six arrived in October 1964. The Group completed service in June 1966. Thirty-one were immediately stationed in the provinces—the first time that had happened. They included ten English and math teachers in Kandahar, six teachers (three English and three science) and two nurses in Lashkar Gah, two teachers in Farah, four English teachers in Mazar-i-Sharif, two teachers in Tegari, two teachers in Pul-i Khumri, and three English teachers in Jalalabad. Twenty-five of the group were in Kabul—nine nurses, two mechanics, three Ministry of Education, two Ministry of Press and Information, one Ministry of Justice, one Women's Welfare Institute, one Afghan Air Authority, one Kabul University, and five Ministry of Agriculture. [PC/A newsletter, Vol. I, No. 1.]

Group V Trained at the Experiment for International Living, Brattleboro, Vermont. Forty-eight arrived in May 1965. They completed their service in December 1966, although 12 extended for periods ranging from three weeks to a year. Twenty-nine were English teachers; 19 were assigned to Kabul, ten to the provinces (five to Herat, three to Charikar, two to Maimana). Nine were rural development workers, seven of whom were stationed in Kabul, two in Gulzar. Seven business education Volunteers were placed in commercial schools or ministries in Kabul. Two physical education teachers worked at Kabul University; one taught audio-visual techniques at the Ministry of Education. [PC/A newsletter, Vol. I, No. 6; *Kabul Times,* May 5, 1965.]

Group VI Trained at University of Texas at Austin. Forty-one arrived September 1965. They included 18 English teachers, eight math and science teachers, eight accountants, four lab technicians, three secretaries. Twenty-four were posted in Kabul, seven in Jalalabad, four in Kandahar, four in Mazar-i-Sharif, one in Tegari, and one in Jabul Seraj. [PC/A newsletter, Vol. I, No. 9.]

Group VIIA Three medical doctors started training at Duke University and the University of North Carolina in June 1965 along with doctors, and their wives and children, destined for other countries. They were posted to the Medical Faculty of Nangahar University in Jalalabad. **Group VIIB**, consisting of 24 nurses and one pharmacist, trained at Portland State University and arrived in Kabul in December 1965. Ten were stationed in Kabul, 14 in the provinces (five in Jalalabad, two in Kandahar, two in Mazar-i-Sharif, two in Maimana, and one each in Bost, Pul-i-Khumri, and Herat.) [PC/Afghanistan newsletters, December 1965, July 1966.]

Group VIIIA Thirty-five arrived in March 1966 ready for six more weeks of in-country training after the first six weeks at the University of Texas in Austin; 28 were English teachers, three were teacher-trainers, and four were secretaries. **Group VIIIB**, consisting of 19 nurses, three lab technicians, and an x-ray technician, arrived in May 1966, after completing their training in Austin. Seven of the nurses were assigned to Kabul and nine to the provinces. Two of the lab technicians worked in Kabul; the other lab technician and the x-ray technician worked in Jalalabad.

PEACE CORPS AFGHANISTAN
STAFF, 1962-1966

*T*his is a list of staff in Afghanistan roughly in order of hiring between 1962 and 1966. It is drawn primarily from Peace Corps Afghanistan newsletters, and includes staff who arrived within that time period though some served beyond it. Although it includes two training officers, the list does not include training staff or language teachers nor staff in Washington because we found no good source. With the exception of Group VIIIA, which had six weeks of training in-country, training during this period was entirely in the U.S.

Robert L. Steiner, Director, 1962-1966
Roberta Auburn, Administrative Officer, 1962-1967
Naik Mohammed, Janitor, 1962-1967
Mohammed Naim, Despatcher, 1962-1967
Sami Noor, Administrative Assistant, 1962-1964
Dr. Walter A. Morgan, 1963-1966
Robert S. McClusky, Deputy Director, 1963-1966
Habib Bahjat, Administrative Assistant, 1964-1965
Dr. James C. Chapman, 1964-1966
Laura Marthinson, Secretary, 1964-1965
Ava Boswau, Secretary, 1965-1966
Gloria E. Burgess, Secretary, 1965-1967
Helen C. Reardon, Secretary, 1965-1966

Jon A. Wicklund, Field Officer; Associate Director-Education, 1965-1967

Robert L. Pearson, Training Officer, 1965-1966, Desk Officer, 1966-1968

Dr. James deMaine, 1965-1968

Stanley G. Huskey, TEFL Contract Overseas Representative, 1965-1967

John W. Bing, Field Officer, 1965-1966, Training Officer, 1966-1968

Walter P. Blass, Director, 1966-1968

Dr. Samuel Chen, 1966-1968

Mike Edwards, Deputy Director, 1966-1967

Roscoe Morris, Associate Director for Education, 1966-1968

George O'Bannon, Associate Director for Health, 1966-1968

Mohammad Sadiq Sharifi, Assistant Administrator, 1966-1967

PEACE CORPS AFGHANISTAN PAMPHLET

In September 1964, shortly before the arrival of Group IV, Peace Corps Afghanistan prepared and distributed a pamphlet in Dari and English. The cover is on the previous page; the English text is reproduced below. The pamphlet also included pictures of King Mohammed Zahir, President Johnson, President Kennedy, and Sargent Shriver and a dozen of Volunteers at work.

The Peace Corps in Afghanistan

"My fellow Americans, ask not what your country can do for you – ask what you can do for your country. My fellow citizens of the world, ask not what America will do for you, but what together we can do for the freedom of man." (From his Inaugural Address, January 20, 1961.)

John F. Kennedy
late President of the United States

SERVING AFGHANISTAN

The United States Peace Corps in Afghanistan

In September, 1962, a group of nine Americans arrived in Kabul to begin two years of volunteer work in the fields of teaching, nursing and auto maintenance.

They have since completed their assignments and have returned to their homes. But other Volunteers have come to continue and expand the work they started.

They have come to participate in a new kind of international experiment . . . the work of the United States Peace Corps.

This pamphlet explains what the Peace Corps is and how its Volunteers are working with the people of Afghanistan.

September 1, 1964

The late President of the United States, John F. Kennedy, first suggested that the United States recruit young men and women, on a volunteer basis for work in foreign countries. In 1961, Congress established the Peace Corps and Mr. Sargent Shriver was appointed as director.

The Peace Corps has these objectives:

1. To help the people of other countries meet their needs for middle level skills;
2. To increase knowledge of the United States in other countries;
3. To increase American understanding of other countries.

Volunteers go only to those countries which request their assistance; the type of work and place of work is determined by the host government. The Volunteers receive no special privileges: no diplomatic immunities, commissary privileges or salaries. These Volunteers go abroad because of a <u>desire</u> to work for and with the people of other countries, not because of pay, privileges or other benefits. They go not as advisors, but as "doers" who work under the direction of their Afghan supervisors.

Today, there are approximately 8,000 Volunteers working in some 46 countries around the world. This number will be increased to 14,000 Volunteers by April 30, 1965. These people may be found in many countries of South America, Africa and Asia, including Afghanistan, Iran, India, Nepal and Pakistan.

**

Volunteers requested by the Royal Government of Afghanistan arrive in Kabul well-prepared for their work. Each group receives three months of training in the United States prior to departure. They study Farsi under Afghan instructors four or five hours a day, and also study the history, geography, government, economy and customs of Afghanistan. Special training and review in their particular fields of activity further prepare Volunteers for their jobs.

The size of each group is agreed upon by the Royal Government of Afghanistan and the Peace Corps prior to training. The number of prospective Volunteers entering training at one time might vary from 12 to 76 or more.

Fields in which these people are already involved or are scheduled to enter include the following: Teaching English as a Foreign Language, Physical Education, Public Administration, nursing, printing, mechanics, science teaching and rural development.

Until December of 1963, all Volunteers were living and working in Kabul. However, since then several Volunteers have served in provincial cities; some for two-month periods during winter school vacations in Kabul, and others on a permanent basis. They were placed in Kandahar, Mazar-i-Sharif, Herat, Bost, Puli-Khumri, Jalalabad, Farah and Tegari. Soon additional Volunteers will be permanently assigned to these and other provincial locations, the majority as English teachers.

**

In order that Volunteers may get to know and be known by the Afghan people, they try to live in much the same way as their Afghan friends and co-workers.

Volunteers work a six-day week, use bicycles and local buses as most of their Afghan colleagues do, and live in simple houses without elaborate Western furnishings. They buy all their food, clothing and other necessities in the bazaars.

Each Volunteer receives a living allowance from the Peace Corps which is sufficient for his food, clothes and personal needs. Under a new arrangement with the Royal Afghan Government, a part of this allowance is paid by the host country. The Volunteer agrees to use only his living allowance. He may not receive extra money from his family or friends in the United States; under no circumstances may he add to his income by taking any extra jobs for pay in Afghanistan.

**

Outside of their regular work, many Volunteers enjoy participating in the life of Afghanistan in various ways.

- Several American Folk Music concerts have been presented for the general public, and in schools.
- Volunteers have participated in programs for the benefit of charitable organizations (i.e., Boy Scouts).
- They have engaged in sports activities. Several have started volleyball teams or worked with basketball teams in their schools; and during the 1963 Jeshyn celebration, a Peace Corps basketball team played a match with Kabul University in Ghazi stadium.
- Most Volunteers have given special English classes for their co-workers, have started English clubs or libraries in their schools, or have tutored.
- Afghan students leaving for study in the United States have been entertained at parties to give them helpful information and advice about life abroad. Volunteers have given informal teas for their co-workers.
- On August 19, 1964, Peace Corps Volunteers and staff members were received by His Majesty King Zaher Shah and Queen Homaira at Tapa Garden in Paghman. His Majesty expressed happiness over the services rendered by the members of the Peace Corps and said their efforts are effective in promoting better relations between nations.

**

While in this country, a Volunteer is responsible for his over-all performance to the Peace Corps Director in Afghanistan; however, in his job he is *directly responsible* to his *Afghan* supervisor. The Volunteer is basically in Afghanistan to work for Afghans, under Afghan supervision on projects selected by the Royal Government of Afghanistan.

The Peace Corps office is located at Zargoonah Square in Shari Nau. The office telephone number is 21620.

**

This, then, is the United States Peace Corps in Afghanistan . . . seeking to serve Afghans and foster international understanding.

Hopefully, the work of the Peace Corps Volunteer will be of benefit not only to the Afghan people, but also to the people of the United States. He can serve, both in Afghanistan and in the United States, as a bridge of understanding . . . a personal link between two different cultures.

PART II

VOICES OF VOLUNTEERS

What did Volunteers write about their experience while they were in Afghanistan? Volunteers wrote many letters home. A few are quoted in Part I. This section reproduces three sets of pieces written by Volunteers for wider distribution. Together these stories provide a picture of the encounters of the early Volunteers with the people of Afghanistan.

The first is a collection of articles prepared for the *Peace Corps Volunteer* magazine by a few members of the first two groups after Peace Corps had been in Afghanistan about 15 months. The second reprints two articles from the *Kabul Times* page All About Women and another published in *WorldView*. The third includes contributions written to provide trainees a sense of life as a Volunteer in Afghanistan.

THE FIRST ENCOUNTERS

*T*his collection of articles appeared under the title *"AFGHANISTAN"* on pages 10 to 21 of the Peace Corps *Volunteer in January 1964.*

Material for this section on the Peace Corps in Afghanistan was compiled and organized by Volunteer Jon Wicklund (Minneapolis), an English teacher at Ibn-i-sina High School in Kabul. He holds a B.A. in humanities from the University of Minnesota.

Volunteers Gain Acceptance in Kabul
by Robert L. Steiner

Robert L. Steiner is Peace Corps Representative in Afghanistan. Born and reared in Iran, where his parents were American educational missionaries, he took his B.A. at the College of Wooster, Ohio, in 1942, and after World War II service as a Navy pilot, he earned a master's degree from Columbia University in international affairs. Steiner later went to Vermont and became a farmer, intending to use this new knowledge in agricultural work in the Middle East. He has been involved in student exchanges with the Middle East for many years.

Since the mid-1700's, no foreign power has either controlled or occupied Afghanistan for any length of time. If there is anything unique about the Peace Corps in Afghanistan, it can be traced to that fact. Foreigners are considered to be guests—and are expected to conduct themselves as guests. The Peace Corps Volunteer, whatever the literature said, was no exception.

Our first efforts to find low-cost housing met with almost universal opposition from the Afghans. As hosts, why should they be expected to help us find anything but the best? The first group of nine Volunteers who arrived in September, 1962, although well prepared, found the courteous but distant reserve of the Afghans a far cry from the open-armed welcome which would have eased the way. Whether English teachers, nurses, or the lone mechanic, the Volunteers went about their tasks patiently waiting to be accepted, yet careful not to abuse their assigned—but unwanted—role as guests. And the Afghans watched and studied and kept their distance. But gradually, there was a change. Some observers think that the coolness continued until after the arrival last June of the printers, the physical-education teacher, and the additional teachers of English of the second group of Volunteers to Afghanistan.

Sensing that the time had come to accelerate the pace set by the first group, the new Volunteers, after about three months of settling-in, have appealed to the Afghan's desire to learn more about cameras and art, social institutions, and informal, conversational English by accepting invitations to join groups meeting in the schools, the printing plant, or the Khyber Restaurant, a popular meeting place. Additionally, there is an increasing demand from the Afghans to hear Volunteer musicians perform; there are singers, guitar, and violin players in both groups.

Are the Volunteers in Afghanistan still treated only as foreign guests? We're not sure. We do know that the 35 here now are soon to be joined by 35 more (English teachers, secretaries, telephone operators, postal clerks, statisticians, accountants, and warehouse managers). But an important indication is the Afghan government's recent decision to permit some of the Volunteers to serve for the first time outside the capital city of Kabul. The lines separating the hosts from the Volunteer guests are being obscured.

A Teacher in Kabul
by Pat Higgins Weeks

Volunteer Pat Higgins Weeks (York, Neb.) came to the Peace Corps after two years as a child-welfare caseworker in Portland, Ore. In 1959 she received a B.A. in psychology-sociology from Tarkio (Mo.) College, where she was also editor of the college newspaper. In Afghanistan, she has been teaching at Aisha-Durrani, a junior high school for girls in Kabul. She was married last Dec. 2 to Volunteer Philip Weeks (Newport, N.C.), a printer working with the Afghan Ministry of Education Press.

In June, 1963, I was one of 18 new Peace Corps Volunteers receiving teaching assignments in Kabul. Nervously, we reviewed some of the principles of English teaching learned during training at Georgetown University in Washington, D.C. We were uneasy: along with most of my colleagues, I had never taught before. Teaching was a far cry from social work.

We were assigned to a variety of schools. Most of us were placed in girls' and boys' schools, teaching from grades 7 through 12. Four Volunteers were assigned to the University of Kabul, one to the Afghan Institute of Technology, and three to boarding schools here for boys who come from the provinces.

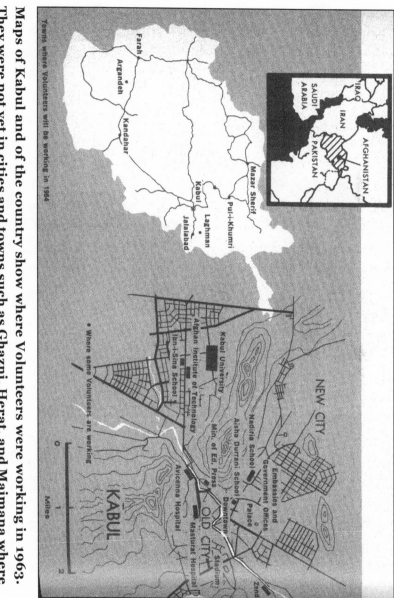

Maps of Kabul and of the country show where Volunteers were working in 1963. They were not yet in cities and towns such as Ghazni, Herat, and Maimana where they later served. (*Credit: January 1964 Peace Corps Volunteer*)

The school year begins in March and ends in December. Primary emphasis is placed upon grades. This leads to one of our major problems in teaching: it is hard to determine how much English a student knows. Whether the students are reciting orally or in taking tests, their altruism comes to the fore. They help each other, using clever and skilled methods.

Jill Rindelaub (Mankato, Minn.) was determined to cope with this problem. During one testing period, she tried to forestall any possibility of cheating. She placed white sheets of paper over the desks so her students couldn't write on the wood. She made three sets of tests and seated the students alternately. She looked to see that their scarves were tucked firmly under their chins so they couldn't whisper behind them. She checked for writing on their hands. She tried to anticipate every possible stratagem.

Certain that she had finally thought of everything, she began the tests. The period proceeded much more smoothly than usual. Flushed with victory, she gathered up the papers at the end of the period. She turned around to see the captain of the class performing her routine duty of erasing the board. Jill suddenly realized she had forgotten to remove the previous day's review from the board. In her own legible writing were most of the answers to the test, clearly visible to every class member.

We found teaching in Kabul to be a completely new experience. Approaching our assignments with a mixture of trepidation and excitement, we envisioned classes responding eagerly to our stimulating presentation of the English language. We dreamed of holding seminars as students brought forth their ideas in flawless English, learned in our classrooms. Perhaps we could even assign them some Shakespearean plays.

The rude awakening came quickly. Week after week we toiled over rudiments with few apparent results. We tried not to be discouraged with those who would never learn English, and grateful with the small minority who occasionally were able to assemble a sentence correctly. We had to curb our impatience with the necessity of starting from scratch with the advanced students.

Rote learning has been the standard technique of education in Afghan schools. Most of the students have a great fear of attempting anything beyond the rigid structures of the textbook. Progress was often imperceptible. But occasionally, a student would catch a spark and amaze me with her progress. Sometimes, after a disheartening period of standstill on a fruitless plateau, they would suddenly begin understanding and using the concepts with gratifying results.

We learned that all over the world teaching has many of the same problems: discipline, administrative frustration, scheduling difficulties, student motivation, and boredom. The redeeming factor in many cases was the students themselves. Never had I met such a group of appealing youngsters.

I was assigned to teach eighth-graders in a girls' school. The girls all dressed identically in black skirts, black blouses, black stockings, and white scarves. Some were strikingly beautiful with their raven-black hair, delicate features, and sparkling brown eyes. Their vitality, impishness, and warm friendliness won me over completely. I enjoyed being with them in the classroom or chatting in the school yard. Sometimes they would sing a song to please me, or bring me a little gift. Two girls once earned teacher's beaming thanks when they memorized two pages of English dialogue to recite during a recess.

As in all jobs, there are ups and downs. At one point I was feeling rather smug because the entire week had seemed successful. The students were studying with a new intensity. Some of the oft-repeated rules seemed, at last, to be sinking in. Oral sessions were progressing quite smoothly. The girls didn't seem to be relying so much on constant repetition but were timidly branching out into some creative thinking. Congratulating myself on my effective teaching methods, I began a review question-and-answer period.

"Is this a book?"

"No, she doesn't!" was the unison cry.

"Please turn back to the beginning of the book, Lesson One," I said wearily. We began anew.

An 'Inconspicuous Approach'
by John Borel

John Borel, 25, of Arcata, Cal., received a B.A. in journalism from the University of California in 1960. Before joining the Peace Corps, he worked as the editor of a weekly newspaper in Arcata. He is six feet two inches tall and weighs 200 pounds.

Among the goals I set for myself in Afghanistan was to go about my work efficiently and effectively . . . but inconspicuously.

Let's not blunder about and expose the shortcomings with the attributes, said I. To do the job conservatively would be the key to my success.

And with that in mind I went to work.

For instance, there are the Afghan English teachers who work beside me at Habibia College, a boys' secondary school with 2500 students.

We meet in the English Dept. office during class breaks. I'm so inconspicuous that sometimes they don't even notice me. This, I realize, must have its demerits, but it perturbs me not in the least.

As far as my students are concerned, too, I'm just another teacher. This status, of course, lets me in for the same pranks as other teachers. Each day, a little color comes my way, especially from one eighth-grader.

The other day, Sho-aib presented me with a limbless clay frog as I walked into the room. This brought down the house in hilarity.

Good enough. Get a good laugh at the beginning and work hard the rest of the period. To myself I thanked Sho-aib.

Another day found me hunting down a portable radio in class.

On yet another day, Sho-aib held up a police whistle and asked the word for it in English. Then he gave the thing a resounding toot. The classroom reverberated gayly. I could rationalize that *he* was being conspicuous, not I. So I didn't mind.

But these examples, you are thinking, don't prove much. Just a story. I could still be conspicuous, followed everywhere by mirthful eyes. Well, that may be; I don't know.

There was the time at Afghanistan's Independence Celebration. As is my wont, I stood in the midst of a wild, uncontrollable mob of several thousands who had come to see a parade.

I could have walked through a barrier to join an exclusive gallery of foreigners and favored Afghans. But I didn't. I stood it out with the throng. At that time, I did not know about the exclusive area because I couldn't see it. Nonetheless, my heart was in the right place.

Working my way to the front, I set myself for the parade. But no sooner had I consolidated my position than the militia started bruising back the crowd with their belts. Simultaneously, a group of horsemen behind us began an agitation. The crowd retaliated by pushing out in all directions.

No favoritism for me. I had to dodge with the best of Afghans, to whom this was all a big game. Finally, I retreated and went home, all in one piece and still a figure of equanimity.

The exquisite climax of my "inconspicuous approach" came a few days ago when a car struck a roommate and me late at night as we bicycled home from a dinner engagement.

Not only did the undaunted driver continue on his way as he would have for any other citizen, but two policemen who watched the action from a distance did nothing whatever to interfere with us or the driver. My roommate and I just picked up our bikes and limped home.

These chronicled events must be evidence enough that my policy has been an overwhelming success.

Nevertheless, you may understand that it was with some pleasure on Teacher's Holiday that I accepted a garland of flowers from my school principal and the applause of assembled teachers.

Nothing unique, really. But I was noticed at last.

The Amoebas Are Lovely
by Dorothy Luketich

Dorothy Luketich graduated from Michael Reese Hospital School of Nursing, Chicago, in 1947, and thereafter worked in several American hospitals. In January, 1957, she became head nurse of an obstetrical unit at George Washington University Hospital in Washington, D.C. In Kabul, she has been working on the obstetrical-gynecological unit at Masturat Hospital.

Being a Peace Corps nurse at Masturat Hospital here in Kabul is not the easiest nursing job available, but it may be the most interesting. Here we see many diseases and conditions rarely found in the U.S. In fact, one medical technician says that Kabul has the most beautiful amoebas in the world.

We also have some of the most fascinating patients. The Kuchis, for example, are Afghan nomads who wander through the mountains seeking eternal summer. Some of them, often in critical condition, travel for days on foot or by donkey or camel to reach medical facilities here in Kabul. They are a rugged people with an amazing capacity for fighting illness.

The women dress in bright-colored, embroidered costumes, their long, dark hair braided into hundreds of tiny pigtails, and their faces tattooed with tribal marks. Their coming into the hospital at all is a great step in local medical progress. A few years ago most women would not consider being examined by a male doctor, and as women doctors were few, not many Afghan women ever had any medical attention of any kind.

One of the problems in caring for the Kuchis is that they usually only speak Pushto, whereas we Volunteers speak Persian. Sometimes, before you can stop him, a patient gives you a long story, and you can't understand a word of it. Fortunately, some other patient generally can translate.

We have had many minor frustrations, but, after a while we adjusted to working with a minimum of equipment, and hardly missing the fancy gadgets and sterile brightness of the hospitals at home. Nowadays, when we get something that we always used to take for granted—such as towels or soap—we feel as though it's Christmas.

Afghan nurses are a delight to work with. They love to joke and delight in teasing me about the names the patients call me. Loosely translated, the names come out as "Madame Sir," "Miss America," and "Foreign Lady."

It's a gratifying type of nursing: walking into a ward full of patients who respond with genuine delight to your presence; having an Afghan nurse do—without being reminded—something you taught her; and seeing a mother carry out of the hospital a healthy premature baby after losing three earlier.

These are a few of the things that can cheer us up and give us a feeling of progress when our morale is low.

Office Aide Must Know Her Posies
by Roberta Auburn

Roberta Auburn, Peace Corps secretary in Afghanistan, has been work-
ing at her job for a year. She is the wife of an employee of the U.S. Agency
for International Development. Before going to Kabul, she lived for four
years in Turkey and, before that, seven years in Taiwan.

As Peace Corps secretary in Afghanistan, I am the principal administrative helper to the Peace Corps Representative.
But that is only the beginning: I also minister to the many
and varied wants of 35 Volunteers, all of them in Kabul, the
capital.

A morning's barrage of questions may sound something
like this:

"Has the mail come?"

"Where are the candles you promised for my physical-education project?"

"Where's my passport? I know I gave it to you."

"When is the mail due?"

"Where can I buy a tambourine?"

"How do you spell 'Srinagar'?"

"Where's the mail?"

"How much did we pay for the last curtain fabric, and how
many meters do we need for a room?"

"Is my leave money at the embassy?"

"I've just arrived from Tehran (the questioner will
look like as though he has walked all the way); where can I
stay—cheaply?"

"May I borrow a bicycle?"

"Where can I get an American flag?"

"Is there any mail?"

I began working a little over a year ago in the then small-est Peace Corps program in the world. I was employed half time to do routine stenographic work connected with the Volunteers—all nine of them. I worked in a spare room at the rear of the American Embassy; two buildings separated me from the office of my boss. Until a few months ago, when we moved into our present quarters, we seldom saw each other.

As we anticipated the arrival last June of the second group of Volunteers—26 of them—my job took on a Jill-of-all-trades aspect. Accompanied by an able Afghan assistant, I combed the markets of Kabul, commonly and collectively referred to as "the bazaar." Furniture design, tailoring, and carpentry became our specialties, low-cost equipment our forte. We learned that the unseasoned wood used by most cabinetmakers soon cracks, that Afghanistan's beautiful carpets are priced far beyond our resources, that most dishes are imported from the Soviet Union, that the brilliant blue pottery of the nearby village of Istalif is colored by pure, powdered turquoise mined in the area, that the cotton cloth manufactured locally is varied, serviceable, and abundant.

I have had to solve some problems of communication. I have acquired little Persian, the most widely used language of Afghanistan (Pushto is considered to be the official language), but I have acquired the knack of demonstration. Modern detergents, cleaning powders, and bleaches are all available in the bazaar, but these household aids are unfamiliar to many Afghans. The bleach particularly delighted the turbaned *baccha* (literally, *boy*) we employed to clean our new quarters. At first he and I could not understand each other, but I told him what I wanted him to do—in sign language—and we got along fine.

With 35 Volunteers in Kabul, my "secretarial" duties multiplied. I now worked full time. Those Volunteers in need may receive limited first-aid treatment, small loans, message service, help with visas, and possibly a dash of personal advice. Visitors who occupy our office guest room may be served breakfast.

"I suppose you're a florist, too?" an unsuspecting acquaintance inquired facetiously. "No," I said, "but I did have one experience with flowers, though."

During Jeshyn, Afghanistan's big national holiday, celebrating independence, the Peace Corps basketball team played a team from the University of Kabul. Local custom dictates that members of the two teams exchange flowers before the game. We wanted to observe protocol, and arranging the matter fell to me. Cut flowers are plentiful in Kabul during the summer, so getting them was no problem. But getting our players to carry them was.

"You're kidding!" they said. "What are they really for?"

I'm sure no one believed my story that tradition required flowers until the players and the bouquets met on the court.

Peddling chickens doesn't require much skill, but it is another field in which I now have had some experience.

We heard about some choice broilers an enterprising young Afghan was raising, and we arranged for him to sell them to the Volunteers. The Volunteers responded with their customary enthusiasm, and on delivery day, much of our floor space was devoted to weighing, wrapping, and selling chickens—at 30 afghanis (about $.60) per pound.

At the close of the day, we were sold out; merchants and customers were equally satisfied. So was I until asked: "Are there any other businesses you'd like to get into?"

The Bride Stayed Home
by Paul Gardner

Paul Gardner of Oakland, Cal., received a B.A. in sociology from San Francisco State College in 1962. Last year he taught at Neue Kabul, a boys' junior high school outside Kabul. Next year, he will be teaching in Farah, a city in southern Afghanistan.

It was about one in the afternoon. The fall air was chilly, and the woods were tinted with color. As I was making ready for the four-mile trip back to Kabul, one of my ninth-grade English students hurried up to me from the village schoolhouse. He told me there was to be a wedding that night, and I was invited. All the other teachers who were going were to meet at the school-house at 3 p.m. and, along with a guide, journey eight or nine miles to the scene of the wedding in another village.

Two hours later, equipped with camera and overcoat, I was ready for both my colleagues and the guide. Seasoned by previous engagements of this sort, I knew that I had not been left behind. I was right; 90 minutes later everyone turned up, and we set out on our bicycles over a trail through the pictur-esque Kabul Valley. By this time the sun was nearly down, and reflections of purple, red, and black lined the towering rims of the canyon. Beside us ran the Kabul River; extending from it were multitudes of neatly formed *juies* (canals) irrigating the year's final crop of this narrow but fertile valley.

When we reached Lallandar, our destination, darkness had fallen. I could barely see the outline of a maze of walls sur-rounding mulberry orchards and the main buildings. From far off came the sound of drums and flutes. I was told that the procession led by dancing drummers had just begun, but we would not be able to watch at that time since they were going to the bride's family compound, reserved for women.

Once inside the village walls, our hosts—the father and brothers of one of my students—met us and ushered us to a room on the upper floor of the bridegroom's family dwelling. Below us in the open area of the compound were at least 500 men and boys gathered around an Afghan orchestra composed of a singer, two tambor players, an accordionist, and a drummer. For two hours we sat on quilted mats and talked quietly while listening to the music. Periodically, a boy came into the room and offered us a *challow* (water pipe) and *naswar* (chewing tobacco).

Around 9, in came three of my students, all residents of Lallandar. One carried a bundle of white sheets, and the others armfuls of Afghan bread. They placed the sheets on the floor in front of us and put a piece of bread, each the size of a large pizza, in front of each guest. Soon the boys returned bearing platters heaped with *pallow* (rice doused with oil and mixed with cubed meat and potatoes). Around each platter four of us sat cross-legged, eating with our fingers, Afghan-fashion, and sipping black tea. The platters were replenished twice before we were full and ready to join in the festivities outside.

In the open compound, we were seated prominently on cushions bordering a 20 x 20 foot blanket-covered square. Moments later, a man dressed as a woman walked into the arena. He wore a long, thin blue veil, a black sweater, and a full red skirt over his baggy white pants. His feet were bare, and about his ankles were dozens of small bells. On his wrists and arms were gold and silver bracelets. His cheeks and lips were heavily painted with rouge, and all over his face were pasted tiny pieces of red, blue, green, and white foil. In time, four other dancers, all dressed like the first, joined in and performed together in the square. Each danced his own routine, but all followed the rhythm of the music with bells, hips, arms, and heads. It was as if five cobras had been hypnotized in the atmosphere created by the musicians.

All but one of the dancers were village amateurs. The professional, the second to enter the dance area and the last to leave, was hired for the three-day event at the equivalent of

$10 plus tips. He was very graceful—perhaps good enough to impersonate the most graceful dancers of Bali or Siam.

The beginning of the wedding ceremony was signified by the entrance of the dancing drummers. These men, each carrying drums the size of rain barrels, skipped, twisted, and twirled their way into the middle of the compound. With sticks they beat out four or five interwoven rhythms at a time. The men were turbaned and dressed in knee-length white shirts and baggy white pants; all wore red sashes.

After they had danced for a half-hour or so, the father of the groom joined them. Above his head he carried a large platter heaped with candy, cookies, and colored paper. At this time bags of candy were passed out to all guests sitting near the dance square. The bridegroom, dressed in white and carrying an umbrella made of colored strips of crepe paper, then joined his father. He was smiling broadly, and as he danced, he shook hands and exchanged greetings with nearby friends. Men began dumping candy on his turban, and he would pick the sweets off by the handful and throw them into the crowd. All those present with firearms began discharging them into the air as people laughed and cheered.

Within 10 minutes several plump pillows and a beautiful rug were placed in the center of the square. An elderly man, perhaps a mullah—a holy teacher—sat down with the bridegroom and his father for several minutes. When they stood up, it was obvious that the marriage had been completed. At once the female impersonators re-entered the square, guns went off, and candy and cookies flew through the air.

As I rose to go to my sleeping quarters for the night, I noticed that all along the high walls of the compound and on top of the surrounding buildings, women and girls, all veiled, peered down at all the merriment. How strange it seemed to me that the bride was not present for her own wedding.

Thoroughly exhausted by this time, I soon fell asleep to the music of the Afghan orchestra while my colleagues prayed together in silence.

Printers Make Progress
by Richard David and Marshall French

Volunteers Richard David (Syracuse, N.Y.) and Marshall French (Silver Spring, Md.) are both printers assigned to the Afghan Ministry of Education Press. David is a graphic-arts graduate of Smith Technical and Industrial High School in Syracuse. He went to Belgium in 1957 as an American Field Service exchange student. He has worked as a typesetter and pressman. French attended Indiana University at Bloomington, Ind., then served for 18 months with the U.S. Army in France as a medical supply clerk. On return, he worked for five years as a printer-compositor for a Washington, D.C., publishing company.

As we bicycle through the streets of Kabul to work, we can see the mountainous terrain which has contributed to the isolation of Afghanistan for so many years. Afghan people have the traditional independence of mountain inhabitants the world over, and cling to their ancient way of life.

This independence is especially reflected where we work, the Ministry of Education Press. There are six Volunteer printers working here to help improve the quality and number of textbooks produced. The Press publishes books in Persian, Pushto, and English. Afghanistan is a bilingual country, with English taught as a third language. While Afghanistan lacks skilled technicians in many fields of modern printing, it has craftsmen in hand-bookbinding whose skills would be hard to find in America. Their patience and craftsmanship are a pleasure to observe.

At first, we Volunteers encountered suspicion; there was a definite lack of purpose at the Press. Most of the workers have little formal education, and do not feel the importance of their jobs. We hope we can instill a sense of pride and a feeling of responsibility among the workers, along with technical knowledge. At first, many of our ideas and methods were politely refused or forgotten, but gradually we have seen a few slight signs of progress. Now, more ideas are taking root in the plant. None of us was really accepted until our colleagues realized that the knowledge we had could be put to use for Afghan benefit.

We have the same hours as our Afghan co-workers, 8 a.m. to 4 p.m. Each Volunteer is in a separate department and we try to demonstrate co-ordination between departments. In the past, each department has worked independently and the lack of over-all co-ordination is critical. If we can get each department to consider the others' problems, it will be a step forward. Until then the work load will continue in erratic cycles.

One of our more serious problems is the delay in getting supplies. After a requisition is initiated by a department foreman, it requires many official signatures. The order of signing is rigid, and if someone is sick or absent, the requisition form stops until he returns. These delays are a hindrance to production, for the press can't run without ink, and adequate reserves of supplies are not kept in individual departments. After about three weeks, a requisition is approved, and presented to the storekeeper. Three witnesses are rounded up to witness the opening of the door. Following the removal of supplies, the three guardians sign a slip of paper, which is pasted around the padlock.

We have been working at the Press for more than six months now, and can see some progress in both technical skill and mental attitude of our Afghan colleagues. We all hope it will continue at the same pace.

Books, Buzkashi, and a Shanzdah Piece

The following material was prepared by a number of Volunteer authors. They describe street scenes, reactions to Kabul, reflections on life.

A German, whose home I visited when I first came to Kabul, had an enormous library. But with the exception of *The Scarlet Letter*, his collection was devoid of American literature. When I mentioned this omission, he told me that he didn't enjoy our writing because most of the good writers discussed only what made the American an American, and not a man.

Keeping this comment in mind, I began teaching a literature course at the Afghan Institute of Technology. I looked forward to the reactions of a group of exceptionally bright students to a book of American short stories.

The first one was "The Tell-Tale Heart." My students had mixed reactions. Although they seemed fascinated by the method in which the corpse was disposed of, the brighter students only asked at the end of the class, "But why, teacher?"

The next two stories, "The Gift of the Magi" and "The Great Stone Face," went over better. Both were staffed with basically good, kind people—an important factor, it seemed, to each member of the class.

The last story, Jack London's "To Build a Fire," caused a general ferment among the group. Although I finally convinced them that the temperature in parts of Alaska did fall to 50 below, they couldn't accept London's premise that the dog was smarter than the man. Even the fact that the man froze to death while the dog ran back to warmth and safety of the camp didn't help. An Afghan would have had to write the story differently.

I told an Afghan teacher about the class's comments and, in the ensuing conversation, asked him if he had read any

American novels. He said that he had read a few but that the only American writer whom he liked or thought he understood was Hemingway. When I asked him why, he replied that Hemingway's characters know how to live and, what was even more important, how to die.

**

One day as I was loading up my bicycle with groceries after shopping, a little boy shuffled up to me in his bare feet and said, "*Paysae, paysae* (money, money)." I gave him a stock answer: "I don't have any money." He looked at me a minute. "Don't you have even a *shanzdah* piece?" he said, mentioning the smallest Afghan coin. No, I said. So he rummaged around in his pockets, came up with a grimy *shanzdah* piece, and proferred it to me, saying, "Then I'll give you some money."

**

Buzkashi is the national sport of Afghanistan, yet few Afghans have even seen it. It is generally played in the northern provinces and comes to Kabul only once a year, on the king's birthday.

The game is played by two teams on a field 500 meters long by 400 meters wide. Each team has 15 horsemen. Each team tries to pick up the "buz," a 150-pound beheaded calf, and move it to its scoring circles.

In ancient times, the game was played by as many as a thousand men and occasionally ended in deaths among both players and spectators. Rules and safety regulations have changed the game drastically since then. Trenches, to stop the charging horses, have been built between the field and spectators, and the game has been modified to demonstrate the endurance and horsemanship of the players.

The location of the field is almost as spectacular as the game itself. It is played on a plateau overlooking the city. Rising from the field abruptly is an enormous, barren hill which forms a natural grandstand. Into it crowds what seems like the whole population of Kabul, 400,000 persons.

When the game finishes at dusk, and the king's party leaves, the hill clears; for miles, all you can see are thousands of moving black shadows set against the purple mountains as they move slowly into the city below.

**

A year ago, when the fall winds were beginning to bring mountain snows to Kabul, I first went into the corner shop to buy a pair of warm stockings.

"Please," the boy said to me in Persian, "I want to learn English."

It began with "This is a book," and as the winter snows turned to rain and the rain into clear spring streams, we talked and we read. We talked about the hardships of military school, about the evils of money, about selling his store, about the traumas of having and losing a sweetheart, and about America.

And the other day, when once again fall winds were blowing down the streets of Kabul, he said, "This book is a good friend to me. When I speak to it, it speaks to me. But when

I don't speak to it, it is quiet. And you are a good friend, too, because you make the book speak to me."

**

My husband and I went to see two other Peace Corps Volunteers one day. They live in a second-floor apartment over a crowded street in the bazaar. Because of a huge dog which lives in the same building, we are in the habit of yelling up to our friends from the street instead of going inside.

While I was in the store below the apartment, I heard the following conversation, in Persian, which was shouted between my husband and Ata, the boy who works for our friends. The rest of the crowded street had also turned to listen.

"Are Dave and Frank there?"

"No, *sayb*. How are you?"

"Fine, thank you. How are you?"

"Fine, thank you."

"Where are Dave and Frank?"

"I don't know. Where is *xanom sayb* (your wife)?"

"She is in the store selling herself."

At that, the shopkeeper doubled up in laughter. I looked out the window and saw everybody in the street laughing. My husband, who had meant to say "She is in the store buying something," only then suffered the shock of his mistake.

**

. . . And Where Royalty Walks the Streets
The brush glided through my hair,
Soft and silver-white—symbol of being a grandmother.

Relaxed, I smiled and watched
Two ladies enter, greet and kiss my hairdresser,
Then sit down.

One was young and dark
And spoke her language . . . so it echoed
All the glory of her ancient Aryana.

She spoke of my hair, its beauty, its color,
And I replied
That some day her hair, too, would become silver-white
    like mine.
She laughed and her friend laughed with her.
They talked again, and then the hairdresser told me,
"This is the king's daughter, and this her sister."

About the Country

The completely landlocked Kingdom of Afghanistan is
bounded by the Soviet Union, Iran, China, and lands of the
Indian subcontinent. The country has an area of 250,966
square miles (about the size of Texas) and a population estimated at 13.8 million (almost double that of Texas), of whom
about 50 per cent are Pashtuns, 30 per cent Tajiks, and the
rest Uzbeks and Hazaras. Kabul, with a population of about
400,000, is the capital. Rising above it is the Hindu Kush, a

chain of mountains 14-16,000 feet high and reaching higher than 25,000 as the chain approaches the western Himalayas.

Some 100 miles southeast of Kabul is the historic Khyber Pass, connecting Afghanistan with West Pakistan. The pass, an important military point from the days of Alexander the Great to those of Kipling, is 33 miles long and only 10 feet wide at its narrowest point.

The official language of Afghanistan is Pushto, although the most widely used tongue is Farsi (Persian). *[The Constitution adopted in late 1964 stated that Pushto and Dari shall be the official languages.]* Except for a few Hindu or Jewish people, all Afghans are Muslim. Main exports of the country are Karakul lambskins, dried fruits, and carpets; leading imports are machinery and consumer goods.

The area that is now Afghanistan became part of the Persian Empire in the 500s B.C., and was seized by Alexander the Great about 330 B.C. Tribes from Central Asia conquered it in the 100s B.C., and for the next 1300 years the region was ruled variously by Persians, Indians, Parthians, Hindus, Arabs, and Turks. After the hordes of Genghis Khan swept over the area about 1220, Mongol leaders ruled Afghanistan until the 1700s. The Persians conquered Afghanistan again in 1727, but a successful revolt in 1747 by the Afghans gave them control over their land.

In the 19th century Britain, seeking to protect India from Russian encroachment, twice invaded Afghanistan, forcing it in 1880 to surrender control of its foreign relations. Britain returned control of foreign affairs to the Afghan government in 1921, and the country's first constitution went into effect in 1923. Afghanistan was neutral in World War II, and became a member of the United Nations in 1946.

THREE WINDOWS INTO WOMEN'S LIVES

*T*hese three pieces provide pictures of women's lives in three different parts of Afghanistan in the mid-1960s: the first on a farm in Kunar on the eastern border; the second in the "hamam" (baths) of Herat, once a leading cultural center in the west; and the third in the girls' schools in the capital city of Kabul.

In 1965 and 1966, the Kabul Times started special weekly pages on education, women, culture, and business, an initiative in which Peace Corps Volunteers participated. The articles about a visit to Kunar province and about the Kabul schools were published January 10, 1966, on the page called All About Women. The piece about the baths of Herat was published in The National Peace Corps Association's magazine WorldView in 2001.

The Story of a Pair of Hands During One Woman's Day

The Story of a Pair of Hands by a staff reporter for the Kabul Times catches the rhythm of a day in the life of women in rural Afghanistan. It came out of several days that a Peace Corps Volunteer teaching in Kabul spent at the home of the family of a fellow teacher. They lived on the Kunar River near Chawki in a mountain valley up against the Pakistani border.

In a mud-walled compound, she found women of all generations who laughed as they showed their guest their skills—churning butter, making bread, feeding the chickens and milking water buffalo, carrying water, washing and sewing clothes, arranging bedding—all while caring for children and pausing to pray. Even as they worked, they plied her with questions about her family and the tasks women did in her country. She told them about the sometimes different tasks—but similar hard work—done by women's hands in the home where she grew up in the United States.

This is the story of a pair of hands – slender, capable hands.

Early in the morning, before the sun rises, they take the milk they got from the water buffalo and boiled the night before and put it in a large bowl. Then they set up the tripod, adjust the leather strap between it and the wooden stick with the round wooden block at the end of it and begin churning. After an hour or so, the butter swims to the top and is gently raked off and put in a smaller bowl where it is shaken gently. The hands then pull the butter together, shape it into a firm square lump, and place it on a saucer ready for breakfast.

Add a few sticks to the fire and set the big water kettle on it. Put some fat in the round pot, set it on the fire. When the fat gets hot, the hands make a ball of the water and wheat flour dough they've mixed, slap it back and forth from hand to hand until it's round and flat, then place it in the fat. It cooks in three or four minutes – nane-roghani – two, three, four, five laid on the square cloth. Has someone boiled the milk? They lift the kettle, rinse out cups and teapots, then fill the teapots – hot milk, two black tea, one green tea. Nan wrapped up, butter, sugar, cups and teapots on the tray? Breakfast is ready to be served.

They take a little nan and butter, put it into baby's mouth, but baby's busy helping herself. Some black tea for baby while the hands rinse out cups and teapots. Is some of that water still warm? The hands wipe clean baby's face, pour some water on her hands and wash them.

The household all up and out? The hands fold up quilts, mattresses, and stack them on the charpai in the corner, sweep out the room and straighten the rugs. Then go through the rooms collecting clothing, open the trunk to get baby a clean set of clothes. They take baby out in the sunny part of the courtyard, change her clothes, then set an old kerosene can full of water on the fire.

The pile of dirty clothes, a big bar of brown soap and the pan-like wooden bowl ready, the hands begin washing. First, some clothes, a little hot water, now the soap. Flap! Squish! They rub the soap back and forth over the clothes, squeeze them out, turn them over and begin again. Flap! Squish! Squish! They push them under the water, ring them out and pour out the water. The clothes back in the bowl, a little more hot water, again the soap, back and forth, kneading the clothes. The soapy water turned out, more hot water as they rinse the clothes, ring them out and put them aside to be hung up to dry. The fire's low so they get some more corncobs from the roof, then begin again. Finished, they stop to put back on their rings – three gold rings on each thumb.

Almost time for lunch. They mix water and wheat flour in one bowl, water and corn flour in another, then build a fire in the bottom of the bee-hive shaped mud oven. The oven hot, they sprinkle in some water to dampen the fire. Once again the hands slap the round ball of dough from one to the other till it's round and flat, then stick it to the side of the oven. Six or seven of wheat flour, eight or ten more of corn flour, they cook in two or three minutes and are peeled off the sides.

Chopped finely, the spinach simmers on the fire while the eggs, swimming in butter, cook over a low fire. The hands put the spinach in a bowl, the eggs in another, wrap up the bread and bring in lunch. Then they return to put the water kettle on the fire and get the cups and teapots ready for tea.

Dishes washed, the hands bring out the sewing machine and a half-finished dress. Back and forth they push the material as flowers and intricate designs appear on the bodice, the cuffs and the hem of the dress, stopping only to take hold of the cup of tea or put a piece of brown sugar in baby's mouth.

Late afternoon settles down, dress and sewing machine are put away. The hands take a small bowl, set it under the animal and slowly squeeze the milk from the long teats of the water buffalo.

More fires are made. The hands set the milk on one fire, a pot of rice on another. They take long stalks of corn and dump them in the trough to feed the three water buffalos and the calf. A little water, they wash, then check on the rice. They put some roghan in a pot and cook several pieces of boneless meat. Everything done? They pile the rice on a large platter, put the meat in a bowl, take the bundle of nan that this time other hands have cooked, and bring in dinner. They prepare the tea and after dinner wash up the dishes.

It is quite dark now and having lit the lanterns, the hands lie idle for an hour or so by a cup of tea. Then, stir themselves, bring out mattresses, blankets, pillows to make the many charpai beds.

They put baby in her square wooden bed that hangs by ropes from the ceiling and rock her till she goes to sleep. They pause then for the fifth and last time that day, in prayer and rest. The day's work is finally over.

This is the story of a pair of hands – slender, capable hands.

A Woman's Place

Betsy Thomas Amin-Arsala wrote this piece, drawing on her experience as a Volunteer in Herat in the mid-1960s, a decade or so after she returned to the United States. It was published under the title "The Baths of Herat: Purdah's hidden place of freedom" in the Fall 2001 issue of <u>WorldView</u> magazine (Volume 14, Number 4). We appreciate the permission of the National Peace Corps Association to reprint it.

We pedal our bikes down the bazaar street of Herat, slowly because we are searching for the entrance to the public bath, the *hamam*. The language here uses Arabic script of which we have mastered only alphabet recognition and a few simple phrases such as "I am happy" or "Roses are very beautiful." So I ask my friend, "Do you think they write 'hamam' above the door or something more complicated that we could never read?"

Finally we realize we have gone too far; the women hurrying by in their floor-length veils turn and giggle at us. None of them seems to be entering the doorway that might be the hamam. A man approaches in the native costume – mid-thigh shirt, voluminous trousers, a shawl draped dramatically over his shoulder and a multi-meter length of cloth wound around his head as a turban.

When I call out, he stops and looks us over.

"Excuse me, brother," I say, using the Muslim polite but warm greeting, "but could you tell us where the entrance to the hamam can be found?"

He continues to look at us and replies,

"The men's hamam or the women's?"

I am dumbfounded and search his face for laughter or sarcasm. There is none. He is perfectly serious. Shirin Jan covers a chortle with a cough.

"Brother," I say, "am I a man or a woman?"

He looks again with an open face and replies, "I don't know." In exact translation his reply is "What news of this do I have?"

I turn and look at my friend. My Peace Corps housemate whom I have dubbed Shirin Jan, a common local nickname which means "Dear Sweet" and the most logical correlate to her American nickname of "Sugar." She is wearing what we call a shirtwaist dress, well below the knee with full skirt to accommodate the bike riding. The roll-up sleeves come to her elbow. I am in an almost identical outfit. Our heads are uncovered and of course we have bicycles that are definitely male trappings in this world. I say in English and out loud, "This guy is really serious. He can't tell what sex we are. We are neuter. Maybe we should proceed to the men's hamam. It might be more interesting than the women's." We both laugh and ask for directions to the women's bath.

As it turns out, we had been passing back and forth in front of it for almost half an hour. It is virtually invisible to the uninformed and untrained. The doorway is very small and low and reminds me of something to do with Alice in Wonderland. Shirin Jan and I look at each other, take a deep breath, bend over and walk in.

Immediate and total darkness is suddenly all around us. My eyes cannot adjust; a flurry of swishing in the background is accompanied by a few squawks, giggles and shouts of "Who is it? Who are these?" Gradually we can see more, a table near the door where a beautiful woman in a white head veil takes entrance money. We introduce ourselves, not by name but by profession. Teacher here is a highly respected and understood member of the community. It has been our ticket to acceptance more than once. We explain that we live in the city and had heard about the public bath and have found it difficult and expensive to fire up the water boiler in our house for bathing. For half a penny we can come here, all the hot water necessary.

Her name, she tells us, is Hadjirah. She is pleased to meet us, having heard all over Herat about the Americans who have come to teach in the local schools and hospitals. She brings us tea and some round hard off-white cookie-looking things. I pick one and start to put it in my mouth. The large crowd of women, which has gathered out of the darkness exclaims as one "No, No." They laugh hysterically.

Hadjirah explains that this little cake has something to do with bathing. She will show us later when we enter the bathing room.

The tea is good and hot, and is making me perspire. I feel uncomfortable with clothes on and suddenly realize how humid this place is. The land to which we have come is high and dry in the mountains of Asia, and humidity is unheard of. In only several months our feet have become dry and cracked and we have not yet learned what to do about that. The humidity, therefore, feels strange and good although it is interfering with my breathing. Maybe this is claustrophobia, I think to myself.

Shirin Jan is being led through a doorway. I follow them into a room which opens up huge and wide before us. The ceiling is a large dome with a small window at the very top through which the only light in the room enters. All around the walls are small square openings – like windows but with darkness on the other side. Some women, wearing two-meter strips of silk tied like sarongs, are dipping steaming water out of these windows with large silver cups. The cups are etched with beautiful designs but they are more like beer mugs than anything else we can think of.

We are led to an alcove where everyone's clothing is hanging up. I suddenly realize that these women do not bathe nude; and we do not have sarongs. We pictured public bathing in a large pool – somewhat like the Japanese family hot tub. Shirin Jan says "Oh God." Both Shirin Jan and I have dark hair and dark eyes that makes us appealing to the people of this country. "Black eyes" is the stuff of much poetry here. We exaggeratedly open and close our eyes at each other.

The problem, as is often the case here in Afghanistan, is to what degree can we be different with a positive effect and when does being different diminish our credibility. We agree that bathing nude would be one thing, but with what is now approaching 30 women staring at us, we would just be embarrassed.

When I tell Hadjirah that we need someone to show us how to bathe in this place, in the appropriate manner, we are inundated with sarongs, buckets, those gorgeous beer mugs, rough, mitt-like washcloths and several baskets of those little round cakes, which finally get a name, *rui shereh*, which means facewashers. Another large and low bowl is brought filled with a reddish-brown liquid for washing hair.

Our new friends show us how to bring buckets of hot water, to squat on the floor and take turns pouring the warmth over each other. Using newfound condiments, we scrub and rub and wash.

Hadjirah calls out, "Madar-e-Halim, Madar-e-Halim!" and an old and winkled lady approaches our group. Some of the teenagers who have been constantly giggling for the past half-hour now laugh out loud. They huddle together pointing first at us and then at this old woman. I feel apprehensive. Hadjirah gives some instructions and before I realize what has happened, Mader-e-Halim is rubbing me down – arms and then legs as far as she can reach considering that the borrowed sarong accomplishes its purpose of protecting a great portion of my body. I almost faint from mortification. How many years has it been since anyone – who was only my mother in any case – has given me a bath?

At one point Shirin Jan and I take out razors and begin shaving our legs. This causes an eruption of murmuring and exclamations and a question from Hadjirah, who asks how it is that we are old enough to be teachers and are apparently unmarried. We stumble through our standard answer for this oft-repeated question and hope that it does not lead to the usual birth control questions. As teachers, we should know, but as virgins, which in Afghanistan refers to all women who are not married, we should be ignorant of these things.

We discover that the questions about marriage arose because we are removing all the wrong body hair. As correct provincial Muslims, the married ladies of the hamam remove certain body hair including that of the private regions with either a homemade honey and lemon juice wax or by pulling each hair out one at a time with a looped sewing thread. Hadjirah and her sisters have somehow managed to notice that we have not done this despite the fact that we are both in our early 20's.

In the process of bathing and washing our hair in this hamam, we find ourselves cleaner than ever in our lives. The hairwashing mud has produced a squeaky-clean, shiny and unbelievably full-bodied hair. The mineral content of the water here is heavy; and we have already noticed the incredible build-up within our teapot. We think this is a partial explanation for the very good dental health, except in women who have had too many babies and no calcium supplements. The effect of these minerals on our hair in combination with the local soapstone is marvelous. Thinking the hamam was over, we head toward the dressing alcove.

Hadjirah comes forward and exclaims, "Oh, no. No dressing. Now we must have lunch." We turn to see large platters of rice, bowls of stew and vegetables on a table near the main door. The aroma is tantalizing. All of us, still in our sarongs, sit cross-legged on mud berms covered with brightly colored cotton rugs and take plates of food.

When we leave this hidden place where women enjoy the pleasure of each other's company, the warmth and humidity, the food and tea, we have realized that this is no mere place of bathing. Once a week these women gather here; they spend hours together, not just the half-hour it would take for a bath. Because of purdah, such places of relative freedom are not many. Most other relaxation takes place within the home among family. It is only here in hamam that gossip is exchanged, news of tragedy and happiness passed from family to family. In the hamam, women can scrutinize each other and each other's progeny. The inevitable arranged marriages between unintroduced couples are not without prior peeking into the physical attractions of the intended brides.

Later that night, Shirin Jan and I sit together drinking tea. The light from our kerosene lantern flickers on the wall and we hear the call to prayer from the mosque across the street. But for the dust of the street that powders our toes, we remain squeaky clean. Together and alone we mull over our day, the feeling of being so different from those around us, and yet feeling some new kind of sisterhood with those we found in the dark, humid hiding place behind the inscrutable door.

"Another pregnant woman died at the hospital today," Shirin Jan tells me. "Again the same reason: she had waited too long." A large tear pops out of her black eye and rolls down the half-Tlingit-Indian cheek. I am struck by the picture we make: two Americans – one from Alaska and one from New York – huddled in the weak light to drink Indian tea from a Russian teapot and to mourn the death of yet another Afghan girl whom we never knew existed until the day of her death. Still slightly stunned from exposing ourselves to so many women, feeling too young and yet too old at the same time, we seem to know too much about some things and nothing about others. This nighttime peace belies the thoughts that crowd our minds. We have found the woman's place and we decide to make it our custom to return each week to the hamam of Herat.

Girls' Schools Graduate 142 Students

This Kabul Times article provides a picture of secondary education for girls in Kabul by reporting on graduation at five girls' high schools in 1965. (Schools in much of Afghanistan had vacation in the winter when it was cold, while in the warmer areas of the country vacation was in the summer.) The article focuses particularly on the first 12th grade class to graduate from the Vocational school run by the Women's Welfare Institute. Peace Corps Volunteers were teaching at many of these schools in the mid-sixties.

Out of 275 students in five girls' high schools in Kabul, 142 have passed the final examination which ended on December 24, 1965. 54 students stand for the second chance examination and the other 47 have reported either sick or absent.

This year for the first time the Vocational school of the Women's Welfare Institute succeeded in graduating the first group of its twelfth grade students. Upgraded to a high school in 1963, the school has now 800 students enrolled and the graduates of the 12th grade of this school will be assigned to social work.

The Vocational school of the Women's Welfare Institute at the beginning was established as an adult education course but later because of women's need for further education, this course was expanded first to a middle school and finally to a high school.

The aim of the establishing of this school was to provide an opportunity to study for those women who, for some reason or other, had been unable to enter the regular schools.

The Ministry of Education has been trying for the last few years not only to make women literate but also to train them in home economics and equip them with such knowledge as to enable them to work as social workers.

In the curriculum, therefore, such subjects as home economics, cooking, first aid, anatomy, and the training of children are included. Students spend two days a week in the various hospitals helping patients and learning the practical handling of patients. They have also taken part in instructing the midwives in the rural development projects.

Now, the Vocational High School of the Women's Institute, with the graduation of 20 prospective social workers, has taken a great step towards social progress.

The curriculum of the school has been arranged so that students at the 11th grade can select either office work or psychology, although at present the school only has graduates in the field of office work.

At the end of March of this year the school plans to establish training centres on the outskirts of Kabul to train people in first aid.

The social workers who are and will be graduated from Vocational school of the Women's Institute will help and guide pregnant women and help mothers in postnatal care and feeding of children as well as in sanitation to women villagers.

The graduates of the Vocational school of the Women's Institute can enter the Colleges of Letters, Education and Economics for further studies. They may also enter other colleges if they wish by taking the competitive entrance examination.

Distributing the report cards to the graduate students, Mrs. Kubra Omar, the Principal of the Vocational School of the Women's Institute, expressed pleasure that the students, despite their family responsibilities, were able to obtain an education successfully.

Mrs. Saleha Farouq Etemadi, the President of the Women's Institute, said that it is hoped that in the near future a number of the graduates may be sent abroad for further study under scholarship programs of friendly countries.

Malalai School, the oldest girls' school in the country, had its 15th batch of graduates this year. The Malalai school, which has 2240 students and 83 teachers, distributed report cards to graduates on December 28, 1965. Of 25 twelfth grade students, 15 passed the final examination. Six students stand for the second chance, three failed and one reported sick. French is taught as a foreign language in the Malalai High School.

Zarghuna Girls High School graduated 49 students out of 85. The rest of the students either stand for the second chance or failed. English is taught as a second language in the school.

Rabia Balkhi is another large girls' school in Kabul with 2,600 students enrolled in it. In 1960 this school graduated its first graduates and last December out of 112 students 54 passed the final examination of the twelfth grade. 26 failed, 28 students stand for the second chance and the rest reported sick.

The vocational girls school of Bilquis had its fourth group of graduates. The school is from 7th class and 400 students are enrolled in it. Cooking, raising children, home economics and economics are included in the curriculum of the school. In the final examination at the end of last December, 28 passed, 3 failed and two others stand for the second chance.

MISTER, WHERE YOU GO?

During the winter of 1966-67, Judy Bowsman and Janet Walback prepared a collection of pieces by Peace Corps Volunteers in Afghanistan to give trainees an idea what to expect. The contributions from 16 Volunteers who had been serving in Afghanistan for between 5 and 30 months include one Volunteer's request to resign early and another's to extend service for a third year. The blue pamphlet was published in the spring of 1967 as GSA PC 67-6147 with the picture of a small boy rolling a hoop on an Afghan street framed by a mirror. The title comes from the following poem written by a ninth grade student in Maimana. It won a poetry contest covering grades nine through twelve.

Hello Mister, How Are You?
Where you go?
Are you there?
Mister where you are?
Let me where.
I have a good.
Quickly Quickly.
How are you?
You eat tea?
Come here.
You carry me?

You eat tea Mister.
Come Come.
It is near not far.

Lunch of nan, kebabs, and tea. *(Credit: Frances Hopkins)*

Climb aboard!
by Judy Bowsman and Janet Walback

This brochure is especially designed to give a prospective PCV a closer look at the actual working and thinking of the

Volunteers in Afghanistan. Since all the material was written, compiled and edited by Volunteers only, we feel we are presenting a unique view of the PCV in Afghanistan. We have gathered material from personal interviews and written reports, comments about job situations and personal reactions. Additional material included is a letter from a PCV who terminated early, and on the other side, a PCV who extended for one year. It is to your advantage to consider both the positive and negative conclusions drawn by the Volunteers.

Some of the Volunteers indicated that there are three general areas of particular difficulty for them. One is in justifying one's presence in the host country. A second is justifying one's existence as an English teacher. A third is grasping the meaning of being a foreigner, e.g., What can one do that will exist on a continuing basis? Or, should one undertake a project just for the sake of saying, "I did thus and so. . . ."

Another realm of importance for you – priority is often given to a Volunteer with a special interest field in which he is capable. Many Volunteers who were trained for TEFL found a niche once they got here that gives them more self-satisfaction and broadens the field of the Peace Corps.

For example, one female Volunteer with a background in social work is involved in a children's orphanage in Kabul, working full time. Another TEFL trainee who had worked for an airlines in the States found a job teaching technical airlines procedures at the local airlines office. Still another Volunteer works at the local tourist bureau and also teaches a class in hotel management.

If your acceptance in the Peace Corps is not dependent upon a special skill, and if TEFL is not for you, can you pursue another line? In plain words, what will make you happy? That is, of course, a vital question and demands your attention and thought before you enter two years of voluntary service.

"A capital: the toughest place to excel"

- by Frances Hopkins

The following paragraphs were excerpted for Mister, where you go? from an article that appeared in the Peace Corps Volunteer in September 1966.

A capital city may be the most difficult place for a Peace Corps Volunteer to work out his role, but it also offers an exciting opportunity to be at the nerve center of change.

First of all, the city Volunteer misses the traditional "image." The provincial Volunteers tell of hiking 33 miles over the Farah Desert when a truck broke down, or having their wood delivered by a temperamental camel.

The Kabul Volunteer does not even have the satisfaction of overcoming really difficult living conditions. He may well pedal against the dusty wind to his mud house with a leaking roof and ten cockroaches to kill every night before going to bed but he has access to cheese from Denmark or a tape recorder from West Germany if he wants to spend his living allowance that way. The Volunteer does face a higher rate of bicycle thefts and a better chance of catching amoebic dysentery in the city.

Why then, are half of the Volunteers in Afghanistan in Kabul?

It is in the capital that change is most rapid and if the Peace Corps wants to take part in the action some Volunteers must be stationed in the city.

Some theorize that a large number of Volunteers in one place means there is an opportunity to exhibit a sense of social action and show the value of organization. However, in general, it has been primarily through individual projects that Volunteers have found their niche in the city.

A nurse is making home visits with a midwife in an effort to cut the infant mortality rate. A mechanic is putting together seed-cleaning machinery that has been in storage for years to help increase the yield of wheat. A commercial artist is helping to get an advertising agency off the ground. Others are coaching girls in volleyball, designing plans for the university's student union, teaching students how to manage the hotels needed to increase tourism.

It has been the Volunteers who have gotten involved in working with the people of Afghanistan in one of these many facets of development who have found Kabul a rewarding place to be a Volunteer.

Girls riding on a ferris wheel in Kabul. *(Appeared in Mister, where you go? Photographer unknown)*

Ivan Lee Weir
Age: 25
Bemidji, Minnesota
Faculty of Engineering, Kabul University
English Teacher
11 months-in-country

Kabul University is perhaps the most turbulent place in Afghanistan. It represents the perennial struggle between the new and the old, the young and the aged, the ignorant and the wise, progress and the status quo, poverty and riches, etc. Usually it is a quiet, silent struggle, but the fuse is always burning. The PCV finds himself as anybody's match.

A typical day is rather uninteresting. I ride my bicycle five miles to work, and if I don't get run over by a taxi or kicked by a donkey, I get there on time to teach my classes of aspiring engineers how to read, write, and speak English as a first language because unfortunately for them most of the world's engineering literature is in English, and there is neither world nor time enough to translate it into Dari, their native language. So for two hours we drill in sentence patterns, talk about simple experiments, and struggle to learn something without merely memorizing.

But the atypical days! The days of wine and roses! Those are the days when a man with a turkey under each arm runs over you and your bike in the middle of a crowded bazaar; when a bus runs you into a juie; when you learn that you have just been deposed from your job; when there are two hundred soldiers marching just outside your window where you teach, to remind your students that the world is at peace. I love those days.

Teaching English isn't easy. The Middle-Eastern student has twenty centuries of rote learning and memorization behind him. He has learned that grades can be bought. He believes that the ends justify the means. His language, and that of his classmates, is different from yours, and it is yours which is strange, idiotic sounding, and stupid. Concepts such as germ theory, vectors, magnetism, and cause and effect are not within his mental experience. In fact, he has none of the mechanization of the West, nor any of the tradition of contemplation of the East; he only has twenty centuries of doing things like his father did, and that's been a workable solution for a long time now.

And naturally, to make things more relevant, the Peace Corps has taken these problems into cognizance, and during training one learns how to teach English as a foreign language, based on the American way of learning. Of course, morphemes, free-morphemes, phonemes, and structural pattern method doesn't work here, but that's because it's a backward country. And so, Walter Mitty, Peace Corps Volunteer, develops a new theory of language . . . and we're back to a typical day.

But the rewards are worth it. They are when two little barefoot boys are happy in the middle of winter because you are going to spend two afghanis for a kite for them; or when one of your students attempts to explain his country to you in English; or when the Dean of the Faculty invites you into his office for tea but not to talk business; or when your favorite rug seller questions you about John F. Kennedy and you happen to have a Kennedy half-dollar in your pocket. As Camus said, one must conclude that all is well.

Dennis "Bones" Hamilton
Age: 24
Seattle, Washington
Music Teacher
17 months-in-country

After seventeen months overseas, I would venture to say that the biggest job frustration Volunteers are apt to find in Afghanistan is the lack of successful completion of a given project.

Trained as a TEFLer, I wandered into the Afghan educational system at the end of a school year. I was to finish up several different classes on different levels of English. Most of these classes had gone through three teachers already that year. I immediately hit my head against several brick walls: communications, discipline, study habits (lack of), and a whole realm of cultural differences. The most valuable experience with my students the first two months was participating in an English Club started by a previous PCV. We usually ended up singing simple folk songs in English and Farsi. Also a few field trips with the students were most beneficial, probably more for me than the students. Inside the classroom chaos reigned – mentally and sometimes physically. "I am a book!" gets a little boring after a week. Discouragement set in when I found only one-third of the students even had a chance to go to the University. Most of them would be sent out as teachers to the provinces. There they would teach everything under the sun except English. They might never really use this language in any real situation in their life. What was and still is the real purpose of propagating our language except to those who are interested, motivated and have the need to learn it has never been fully answered.

As my outside interests lay in music and I was able to get a minor in it the last two years of college, I fell into a job at Kabul Radio Music School for a winter project. Then the real fun began! The school had a Russian teacher for three months some time before. He left no notes and no one really knew what he had taught except "do, re, mi." (Afghan music is rarely based on the major scales anyway.) So I brashly set up an introductory course in harmony and counterpoint for the students with advanced standing. I soon found out that many were tone-deaf, others had little or no interest in music. Still later I found my students were being paid ten afs (fifteen cents at the time) to attend my classes. I raised the roof! It took a year before certain necessary changes were made. Some of these included: entrance exams, practice rooms, unlocked doors, music paper, ability to flunk a student and not vice-versa, and, light bulbs for classrooms.

Some of these things seem trivial, I'm sure. But after you've been here a while you will change a lot of your values and the willing acquisition of even a light bulb will seem like something.

The city schools again opened in the spring and thanks to a benevolent director I was able to continue to teach music rather than English. I began to teach part time at a Teacher Training Academy run by UNESCO. The equipment is great, funds are available, the students are wonderful . . . but there were and still are definite hang-ups:

a. What do 250 students (10th, 11th, and 12th grade levels at ages sixteen to twenty-four) want to learn Western music for? Their tradition says music is not so good, at best neutral and maybe even bad. People (musicians) associated with this art are definitely lower class. There is a musicians' ghetto in Kabul. Its name – "the Home of the Asses."

b. The few students in each class who were inclined toward music were smothered and held back by others who couldn't have cared less.

c. The UN staff questioned many basic necessities. A change of administration brought the PCV status at the school to an all-time low.

d. My counterparts had to double as personnel in other departments.

e. The Afghan principal and teachers (both UN and Afghan) warned me not to flunk anyone as the Ministry of Education was watching very carefully and did not think highly of the idea of music training. Of course I did anyway, so my name is mud, but those who passed deserved it.

f. On the planning books of the Academy, a UN expert has his salary and equipment provided for. Yet, a PCV was supposed to fill the job and the funds were shared with the Art Department. Every request of mine was questioned by an agriculture expert in the Delhi office who must have thought I was money mad. So I ended up spending thirty dollars for local instruments.

But all was not negative. We were able to do the following:

a. We had the first woman's music class in the country (35 girls, ages nineteen to twenty-four), all teachers from Kabul schools. They started half way through the school year on a program for a higher teaching degree. They were delightful and after a week of uncontrollable giggling, we got down to study and even caught up with the other classes.

b. The music courses at the Academy inevitably turned into music appreciation classes, as the students could not be selected or divided in any way. However, by not deluding ourselves that we were manufacturing musicians, we were able to have a lot of fun with Afghan and simple Western melodies.

c. An excellent Afghan counterpart and some others aided in many ways both in and out of the classroom.

d. A work book was printed and plans for a musical text drawn up.

e. The Radio School moved under the auspices of the Ministry of Culture. A more liberal attitude has helped administratively. Students are there because they are interested in music – not money or their own self-glorification.

f. Because of my temper, I have been fired three times but recently was asked to stay an additional year at one school and to teach the teacher educators at another.

g. Outside activities have included: musical activities with combos, dance bands, choruses, folk-singing groups, shows and performances at the best and worst places in Kabul. Entertaining everyone from Afghan royalty to fellow PCV's, the international community, working with German and English Volunteers – all in all, meeting a wider scope of people of all nationalities, interests, and positions than I ever dreamed possible. All because of a secondary interest which I brought with me to Afghanistan.

Again I would say to a Peace Corps Trainee. Your life may be very structured right now. In six months you may have nothing or everything to do. Evaluate what is the most important long before the end of your term! And be sure and finish it to the best of your abilities. The biggest aid to this is your-self, your ability to communicate, and your own desire and fire. Some will have a hundred irons in the fire, others seem-ingly none. If sitting in a tea house two or three hours a day is what is most important when you are out in the sticks, then do it! That's where a lot of projects get started, with some peo-ple-to-people talking and some down-to-earth thinking and planning. Although we run the staff over the coals regularly, I still believe basically they are here to help us. And they will inevitably admit that you as an individual are the Peace Corps and will continue to make it what it is and can be by your abil-ity to look beyond the day to day frustrations to some positive, attainable goal in the not too distant future.

Judith Bowsman
Age: 24
Denver, Colorado
English Teacher
11 months-in-country

Teaching at a girls' school has been quite stimulating, considering my almost-horror when I was first assigned to teach there. However, in a country which separates the boys and girls from school age to marriage, and where girls are free only to speak to males in their family circle, you can un-derstand that I was happy to avoid problems that might arise in teaching boys – especially since I conduct an informal classroom. Of course, there are single, female Volunteers who have been quite successful at teaching boys – but they were able, to my observation, to be strict disciplinarians at first – I'm not, and I cannot pretend to be. Also, married women Volunteers seem to have no problems since marriage is a more natural state.

But things appear to be loosening up. The University is co-ed and, of course, both boys and girls attend the same classes. That's also where the process seems to stop. There is not one social activity outside of school which brings co-eds together and a girl is socially unacceptable if she is seen talking with a male. Certainly, all of this is important to grasp in terms of understanding the society – and to avoid blundering and embarrassing people and self.

Rabia Balkhi High School has about 3,000 girls attending. Each girl is required to take thirteen subjects – among these are three languages: Dari, Pushtu and English. Sometimes it is difficult to convince the girls that speaking or commanding English is the most important of their thirteen subjects. Perhaps that's because I'm not convinced either. Teaching reading skills is, to my way of thinking, much more valuable for 11th and 12th grades, because few girls will ever leave the country but they do have access to a lot of reading material in English. Many of the girls will go to the University and are sometimes required to read in English because nothing is available in Dari. It is tragic that their background in language does not prepare them for any kind of advanced study – in fact, education in general does not stress studying and learning but has accidentally, perhaps, promoted the "getting a passing grade" attitude because of the thirteen-subject load.

The girls were aware of some points of needed change in their society and often confronted me with these nagging problems in an apologetic way, seeking to see if these were hurting me in any way. I had to play it cool and admit the problems but make a positive, reassuring statement that affairs were getting better; that I was happy to be in Afghanistan and happy to be teaching them. So you see, if one related to his students, one must also be responsible to keep those students from picking at themselves with certain guilt feelings and apprehensions about things out of their control – trying to keep their teacher and friend from feeling the repercussion of things that they see as injustices.

One fact that comes across clearly is that of being a foreigner. In working with the school staff, I can initiate new programs and start new paths. However, these are for me hollow moments, because of the superficiality of achieving something on the merits of being a foreigner – and guilt feelings that your Afghan counterparts would have gotten a definite "no" were they to have presented the same innovations.

As the only PCV working in this school, I was regarded as somewhat of a novelty. Frankly, I feel that as far as teaching a great deal of English to many girls was concerned, I probably was unsuccessful. As far as instigating permanent programs such as in sports or the English Club or the newspaper, this too was probably unsuccessful except on a temporary basis. This of course leads to unsettled feelings of having done nothing. But since people are my source of joy and sorrow much of the time, I think the bits and pieces of the girls and myself which were exchanged will have a more lasting effect on them and me – and this, then, is my satisfaction.

. . . . a situation where strength was imparted . . . . .

The weather was cool but the middle-aged man was hot and sweaty from his efforts. We gave him money. As he wiped his brow, he talked with a big smile on his face about this and that . . . as we prepared to leave he again mopped his brow and with a broad, quizzical grin on his face he said, "I just don't know why I'm so tired – at one time I never got tired."

And still smiling amusedly at himself, he crawled away.

David and Kathie Miller
Ages: 24 and 26
New Jersey, Indiana
English Teachers
5 months-in-country

TEFL can be a very monotonous subject to teach unless you know <u>how</u> to teach and <u>what</u> to teach. "How" can be mastered in training, both through study and practice. The "what" is a little more difficult to gain in 12 weeks. In our opinion, vague recollections of high school grammar are not enough. A good TEFL teacher should know a good deal about the structure of the English language and understand it well enough to be able to teach it effectively. It is said that some people have the personality for teaching and others do not. All of us know from experience that this is true, and also that there are many different kinds of successful "teaching personalities." Each person has to develop his own classroom manner suitable to his own personality quirks. <u>But</u> a classroom manner is not substitute for mastery of the subject matter.

Outside the classroom is the Afghanistan of the majority of the people. This is the hardest to get to know and the hardest to understand and appreciate. Women in chaderi – lots of them – and jowalis – men of all ages carrying impossible loads on their backs – are the two things we find the hardest to accept. There is no doubt that Afghanistan is still very underdeveloped and that Islam permeates every aspect of life. These two facts often make it hard for an American – especially a PCV – to accept the fact that his effect will be <u>very</u>, <u>very</u> small indeed.

Kathie's regular job is at the Afghan Institute of Technology and David's work is at Kabul University. But, as so-called extra-curricular activities, Kathie is working with the American Field Service program here helping in the selection of Afghan students to go to the U.S. for a year of high school and in the selection of Afghan families for American teenagers spending a summer in Kabul. Dave is the editor of the Peace Corps newsletter in Afghanistan.

Both of us greatly enjoy teaching and find our personal satisfaction in our jobs – teaching English.

Leona Ruggiero
Age: 26
Waterbury, Connecticut
Kabul Nurse
9 months-in-country

My work in general is concerned with pre-natal clinics, home deliveries, and post-natal home visits.

The clinic is staffed by ten Afghan midwives, one secretary, a charge midwife and an assistant. My position is as a PCV staff nurse working within the standards set up by the hospital. The girls are technically highly qualified and have adapted their knowledge of midwifery to practical situations. They have limited knowledge of English, therefore a high percentage of our communication is in Farsi. I probably can justifiably say we have attained a certain rapport (not without effort on both sides) and share the problems and conflicts that arise in every working situation.

Post-natal home visiting follows deliveries, which are under the guidance of the clinics. Each case is usually visited five consecutive times and the patient is discharged on the recommendation of the midwife. The clinic midwives are assigned on a rotating basis on a two-month tour of duty. The "home-visiting team" includes drivers, midwives, an older man who acts as protector, pathfinder and porter (he carries our equipment), and myself. There are also periodic observations of students who accompany us. Each day proves interesting and my job has allowed me within boundaries of Afghan life which are usually not open to foreigners. Our visits are far from ideal and are adapted, quite naturally, as we enter into each specific home.

Job frustrations are unique to each individual and what one may consider an absolutely absurd situation, another may find humorous. Frustrations are personal and degrees vary according to personality, insight, desire, how goal-oriented one is, and how people-oriented. Job frustrations exist in all situations and will be exaggerated in this case because of cultural differences, gaps in communication, and being estranged from the formalities.

I will relate a few of my experiences which will probably tell more about me, rather than situations that another will encounter.

The working day starts at nine o'clock. The midwife and I may wait until twelve noon before starting on the visits. (Any reason given for the delay may sound trivial after waiting for three hours.) So by noon we are hungry, tired and harassed – and at last – embark upon our visits. We may get lost, the car may break down, our driver may cross words with people who cannot see their way clear to move because of the vehicle; at any rate, each episode detracts from the time spent in the home and what has started as an eight-hour working day may be reduced into five hours. The end result is still exhaustion.

Initially, I had started conferences and English classes for the clinic mid-wives. When I reached a point where I really felt we had a swinging program my head nurse became fearful that I was, without a doubt, a usurper. Never once did she have an unkind word to say in connection with my name; however, unless I was dreaming, life became progressively more miserable for myself and the people associated with me. (A gentle hint – my home visits were discontinued for a period.) I quickly grasped the situation and discontinued going to work – my main goal was to get my home visits back, talks with the staff and a "smile" at work, I was reinstated, so to speak. The people involved were aware of the existing situation, however. But even now I will be questioned to why I discontinued my program – this hurts!

I have found it difficult to be a foreigner and although help is needed, a natural pride prevents help from being welcomed freely.

Technical skill, language training and personality are necessary facts. Rationally speaking, one cannot be expected to possess all in equality. One should look within and decide which of these is most unique to their specific situation. After seeing one's way through this matter, one is able to see his or her role more clearly. Consider the "whole" as important – be alert to the "part" that complements both one's self and the people one will be associated with. In my case, language ability is extremely important (while in the States I had hoped this unnecessary as I was a poor student), but nevertheless personality has proved an asset – technical skills rate disapprovingly low!

Certainly cultural differences will affect your job and personal relationships. Perfect understanding and empathy is not feasible. However, a striving for this is essential. Take into account that personal setbacks, depressions, disagreements, inability to understand specific situations are normal and should be considered in this light. I guess the striving is the important thing – although it leaves me totally "unnerved" at times! Re-evaluation of personal reactions, etc., outside the given situation is probably helpful in attaining understanding of the what, why and wherefore of a situation, good or bad.

Daily living is difficult (however, I have found this true since the age of reason) and is affected by physical and mental well-being. Tiredness, the cold of the winter, the heat of the summer, lack of running water, no letter from home, and vacation time has approached and much to your dismay you have purchased too many expensive candy bars.

These seemingly "petty" things also affect your counterparts and if you simultaneously hit a bad day – look out! In order to get through some days the quality most useful is an everlasting sense of humor! But if one's long-term goals, ideas, dreams and aspirations can meet and shake hands with the hum-drum of everyday life – terrific!

Relating situations where I feel communication was reached – dare I? Flowers from a little Afghan boy; looking into the eyes of a wise and stately grandmother who's saying, "I know the scoop, kid. Keep up the good work. We realize you care and we do, too!"; a Christmas gift from your counterparts; a smile of gratitude from a young mother – I'm people-oriented, and not job. Had the latter been the case, my satisfaction would not be!

I'm stationed in Kabul where life can be filled with as many or as few outside activities as one so desires. My social life centers around my friends, both Afghan and American, reading, painting when the desire is acute, wandering about deriving pleasure or pain in my immediate surroundings. I don't have the gall to evaluate what I give – but what I digest is, again, a different story.

I care for the people. They are warm, sincere, quick-witted. I love the children with their tremendously large, black eyes and "runny" noses. They always remind me of Keane's paintings – come to life in the streets of Kabul. I have a great respect for the older generation who have known and survived a difficult life with grace and dignity. I empathize with the educated set who have insight into the problems of their developing country and whose hands are tied.

Rod Norrish
Age: 23
Rock Falls, Wisconsin
Medical Technician
9 months-in-country

My job consists of full-time work in the community blood bank located in the Public Health Institute. I am the only American Peace Corps Volunteer working in the blood bank. Another PCV works part-time in the same building, but in a different department, teaching English.

The job involves direct contact with Afghans. My status within the structure of the blood bank is not well defined but it is definitely not one of authority. Because of this lack of authority, I find it difficult to promote any permanent change. In my estimation, change has to begin from an authoritative position near the administrative head rather than at the various tangents that branch off from it.

In highly technical areas such as this one, two of the key factors in a successful operation are equipment that can be utilized and conscientious personnel. A PCV can be of some use in promoting a conscientious atmosphere throughout the laboratory, but if there is a definite lack of equipment available with which to operate conscientiously and with reliability, the changes are not permanent. An authoritative position is probably the only position from which laboratory equipment can be visualized.

To illustrate this point, I'll relate one of my experiences in the blood bank. When I came to the blood bank, I found the glassware that was being used filthy. (In a blood bank more mistakes are made because of incorrectly cleaned glassware than any other reason.) At that it seemed relatively easy to get things clean. All that was needed was a little soap, a little hot water, and some distilled water. I found that all the warm (not hot) water had to be carried in from another part of the building, the distilled water likewise. I depleted the yearly allotted supply of soap in a very short time and found that even when all the supplies were available, they weren't used unless I happened to be present.

It is difficult to get blood and serum stained test tubes clean without a little soap. The department that distilled the water for all of the laboratories throughout the building started refusing to give us distilled water. We were using about four times as much as before, which meant that the stills had to be kept going a couple hours longer each day. This involved a little more work on their part which they did not like, so they refused to cooperate. Needless to say, without a little authority to get a little soap and distilled water, I really doubt that the glassware will be clean in the near future.

When one tries to decide which is the greatest asset or of greatest importance to the PCV on the job, technical skills, language, or personality, it is almost impossible to make a choice. I can only say that in a technical field, technical skills and language seem to rank a little higher than personality, but each is very dependent on the other.

In my case, I feel the Afghan culture inhibits many technical advances. An "enshala" (if God wills) attitude in the laboratory does not promote accurate or reliable results. One of the best ways to combat this attitude is to instill a meaningful purpose for doing the job. This needs to be done during the training process of the laboratory worker. I find myself working toward this area.

During the last school year, I started teaching a couple of English classes to students in the technical areas connected with public health. These classes started out as an extra-curricular activity, but have developed into a full time job. Besides the English classes I taught a hematology class. This is a technical course taught with the aid of a translator. I have become so interested in this class that I hope to expand into other classes of this type next year. These are a real source of satisfaction and visible accomplishment.

So much for the job situation.

One of the enjoyments of being in this part of the world is the market system. I found it a lot of fun bargaining with the local shopkeepers. He robs you every time, but it's still fun. I've learned to really enjoy most Afghan food. I eat lunch with the Afghans every day and have become quite fond of their various rice dishes.

It's difficult to specify what trainees destined for Afghanistan should know before getting here. Much depends on their prospective jobs. I think they should know about the value system that goes along with the Moslem religion. People in technical areas should know that they will have to make their own jobs. The job situation may appear quite structured, but in order to promote change the individual will likely have to define his own work.

One thing which trainees do not need is a vast number of generalizations. I'd favor giving qualified specific details and let the individual fill in with his own ideas after he has gotten here.

Volunteer Stuart Schmidt at the kiln that he and Volunteer Farrell Walback built with their students in a Kabul Teacher Training College ceramics program in September 1966. (*Credit: Hugh Tilson*)

Stuart M. Schmidt
Age: 23
Milwaukee, Wisconsin
Manual Arts Teacher
21 months-in-country

I live in Kabul, although I work with the provincial training schools. To two of the schools I commute by plane. While in Kabul I work with two other PCV's and an AID advisor on curriculum and texts for use in the Practical Arts course. In the provincial schools, I work with the Afghan teacher and also give demonstration classes.

In the course of a day's work I have learned to expect the unexpected. At one new campus under construction, I spent five hours organizing classes and distributing textbooks which were to have been distributed eight weeks prior. Why the delay? Lack of communication between the teacher, principal, headmaster, and storekeeper, all of whom must concur in order for the books to be released. Just when I got everything straightened out, the teachers had a meeting and decided to have a ten-day holiday because of the construction noise.

The most important element in my job is being able to communicate with my Afghan co-workers. Without language ability one is a complete outsider. So much of their way of life is reflected in the language. Before one can teach one must sell oneself in order to gain the student's confidence. Often it is necessary to motivate the students and this can only be done in the framework of their culture.

A Volunteer should know himself, his capabilities and his limitations and come to the field prepared to learn. Only after he has learned the culture, i.e., the language and customs, can he effectively work with the host country nationals and make a genuine contribution. Most PCV's who fail in their task do so because of a lack of one or more of these personality traits. They give up because they can't see any progress being made or because they become discouraged about the people they are trying to help or because they can't bring themselves to tackle their problem from another angle.

I have found that it is impossible to transfer values or concepts per se from our culture and expect Afghans to understand them. Take this statement, "All students are equal." To one of my co-workers this means that all students have equal ability. Students aren't more or less able but rather more or less lazy. As a donkey must be beaten to make him go, so must a student be beaten to make him study. Our concepts of equal are different. It is most difficult to communicate abstract ideas. Often values must be modified to fit into the existing system.

True, there are numerous frustrations and disappointments but these serve to magnify the successes and personal satisfaction. For me they are two-fold. Each day allows me to make a new discovery about the people and the land. After nearly two years, I feel that I have barely scratched the surface. The greatest satisfaction is when I am explaining a new idea to a student and suddenly his eyes glow and he says, "Now, I understand."

Frances Hopkins
Age: 25
Lakewood, Ohio
Journalist
30 months-in-country

I have been involved in all facets of putting out the government's daily four-page English newspaper in Kabul for 28 months. Perhaps it is indicative of how much I like my job, the people, and the place that I have never counted how much time remained. Nevertheless, I still do not know what the role of Peace Corps Volunteer should be. What I should be doing is a decision I remake frequently.

Is one supposed to be a drone doing exactly what one is asked, be it typing a letter or editing a story, without asking any questions? Or should one be a gadfly always harping on some point like the need for standard spelling or a different proof-reading system but never doing anything to make it possible? Or how about the lovely term from chemistry – the catalyst? Maybe a Volunteer should provide the missing ingredient, whether it is enthusiasm, organizational ability, or a minor technical skill, that makes other members of the staff better able to perform their jobs.

Perhaps one should not worry about such roles at all. Isn't it possible just to become a member of the staff and perform a job for two years? One of the most difficult things about being a Volunteer is that becoming a member of the staff just like anyone else is not quite possible. The trust that is so essential in any job may be established but still the decisions can never really be yours; the responsibility must really always belong to someone else. The goal is to enable the staff to do the job on its own – to work oneself out of a job.

Assuming that a Volunteer's role is different in some way from that of other staff members, just how does one combine doing with teaching? Having observed three Fulbright journalism professors, two Colombo Plan advisors, and several Volunteers try their hand at helping the *Times,* I know there is no one right approach. I have discovered that an attitude of only offering advice not accompanied by sustained efforts to put it into action and an interest in learning about Afghanistan is equally as disastrous as a major concern with what one can get out of his stay here for himself, monetarily or otherwise.

Certainly, a Volunteer must offer some technical skill. I have found ten years' experience on high school and college papers and one summer of formal publishing training adequate in most cases. Advisors with 25 years of experience become extremely frustrated; I am satisfied to have transferred a little knowledge in such areas as layout and headline writing.

Certainly, language is important. It obviously helps in communicating. It shows one is interested in learning as well as teaching. It enables one to edit more intelligently. For example, one knows why a translator uses "capital" only to refer to Kabul and not to a provincial center. In Dari the word for capital means "at the foot of the throne" and therefore is not appropriate for provincial centers.

Sometimes one is just a drone or a gadfly. On good days one may indeed be a catalyst. But through it all perhaps the most important thing a Volunteer can offer is a "constant caring." That involves in my case being at the press 8 to 10 hours a day six days a week and frequently interviewing, editing, writing, or talking to staff members outside those hours.

Sometimes it is difficult to care. Concepts of time and responsibility are different. When one has worked with other staff members to meet a deadline, it is disappointing to hear that it has been decided that changes must now be made that could have been made a month before. January doesn't really end until the middle of February, they say. Learning to accept the status of journalism in Afghanistan is not easy either. The importance of printing facts, attributed to sources, is not recognized. Printing a story mentioning that Mrs. Gandhi was hit by a stone during an election rally is considered injurious to relations with India. Printing the name of a hospital where someone died is considered injurious to that hospital. Writing an obituary before a person dies is considered a sign of disrespect for that person. The line between understanding that there are reasons for such policies and suggesting that there may be even better reasons for printing the facts, difficult as they sometimes are to determine, is a particularly hard one to draw.

But many days caring is fun. The members of the staff are worth caring about, and the *Times* is changing. We no longer work in a room heated by a bukhari fed by USIS bulletins and Pravda indiscriminately. The new press has central heat. A good, growing staff has enlarged the paper from tabloid to New York Times size and introduced special features on culture, women, business, and students. The first edition of a yearbook is almost out. A stylebook may be completed within a month.

And on the days when there are misunderstandings and failures, a look out the window helps. A man plays an accordion as he rides his bicycle. A woman in purple chadri clutches two bulbous pink balloons. A kite spirals like a graph recording the fluctuating afghani exchange rate. A file of fifty-five camels free from their loads lopes by in front of the snow-covered mountains.

Vicki McNatt
Age: 26
Atlanta, Georgia
Business Education Teacher
11 months-in-country

At the time I was invited to enter training, I was working as a sales training supervisor for an airline. The invitation I received to enter Peace Corps training for Afghanistan said that I would be trained to be a TEFL teacher – and so it was. For six weeks in the States I learned the techniques of "Teaching English as a Foreign Language." When I arrived in Afghanistan for six more weeks of training, preparations were being made to place me with Ariana Afghan Airlines, a job that I had indicated during Stateside training I would like.

The airline office was a pleasant surprise. The employees there were receiving higher salaries than most other office employees in the country, and they were eager to learn. English is a necessity since all transactions of the airline must be in English. Thus my TEFL training has come in handy. I teach English about two hours every day and such related courses as "Telephone Techniques" using the English language. In addition, I write training courses concerning the technical aspects of reservations. I usually review this course with my excellent counterpart who speaks English and Farsi and is invaluable. In my spare time, I help with special projects or just busy myself with routine work such as writing tickets. A recent project has been helping the newly created "Outside Sales Office" with ways to increase business – becoming as efficient as your competitors.

Farsi is not very important to my job performance but I have fun with it and it brings me closer to my fellow workers. Most know some English and like to practice it with me in social conversation. But, they get great pleasure out of teaching and helping me with Farsi. We sit around in our spare time at the office and discuss proverbs of both languages. It's really fun to learn a catchy phrase and use it. They say when Afghan humor starts seeming funny to you, it's time to leave the country. I must really be getting in bad shape, as it's amazing how much funnier their jokes seem to me than a few months ago.

The absolutely most difficult part of being a PCV is that you are on your own. To be a good PCV demands an enormous amount of initiative. You have to decide what should be done and then kick yourself into doing it. Nobody is going to make you work hard or go to work every day. If you can't get the enthusiasm by yourself, the Peace Corps is not for you. At times everybody gets discouraged but for people working in offices it is a tremendous problem. There is absolutely no structure. Sometimes I get to thinking "None of the Afghans work hard, so why should I?" You just have to have the will to go on, hopeless as it may seem. The psychiatrist in training said, "You have to become less goal-directed to be happy in Afghanistan." I disagree, because if you are not highly goal-directed, you won't accomplish anything. What you need is a high tolerance for goal frustration.

I like my job most of the time and appreciate the fact that Peace Corps staff in Afghanistan has gone out of its way to find jobs suited to the qualifications of the Volunteer.

As for Ariana Afghan Airlines, a lot of things they do would be improper in the States. If this wasn't so, I wouldn't be needed. When I get disgusted, I stop and consider the progress this country has made in the last few years. In terms of environment and culture, Ariana does quite well. Things just take time. I won't revolutionize anything in two years, but maybe I'll help a little.

Grant Farr
Age: 22
Auburn, Washington
Math/Science Teacher
5 months-in-country

I am a Peace Corps Volunteer working as a math teacher at a UNESCO staffed and financed school. Working with UNESCO, I believe, gives me an opportunity to view the Peace Corps from a slightly different point of view. Being a Volunteer I have a view of the Peace Corps from within but by working closely with the UNESCO staff I also have an opportunity to catch a glimpse of what the Peace Corps looks like from the outside and also to see what makes it unique.

The fact, then, that the Peace Corps has something unique to offer, is what I find particularly interesting. To find what this unique thing is we must first examine the function of UNESCO and like agencies. The main function of these agencies is to supply technical and monetary assistance. The U.N. school I work at is a training academy for teachers and the United Nations staff operates as experts giving technical aid and education. Other U.N. projects are involved in other work and agencies like USAID or the Asia Foundation have projects of their own, but in the long run they all boil down to the same thing: technical and monetary assistance.

What, then, does the Peace Corps do that is different than this? What makes it unique is that the Peace Corps is also concerned with the attitudinal change that comes with technical change. What the U.N. and many other agencies fail to realize is that going with the physical change that they hope to implement is a subtle but present social and cultural change. The Peace Corps does or should realize that this change is taking place and account for it in its decisions and actions.

I remember in my training we came to a consensus that the Peace Corps should not be an agent of social change. Most of us agreed that it is ethically wrong for one culture to impose its values on another culture. In theory I still agree with this but I now realize that giving technical assistance implies changing social values. Simply by being in Afghanistan we are examples of a different culture and whether we like it or not we are always being observed and copied. It is our duty, then, to be conscious that this is going on.

There are many examples of this attitudinal change and many Volunteers find that some of their most rewarding experiences come in this area. Teaching math is a good example. The trouble Afghans have in mathematics is not so much that they don't have the technical skill but more that they are unable to think in a mathematical or scientific way. Mathematical reasoning simply makes no sense to them. The problem, then, is attitude. Therefore, to train an Afghan in mathematics involves implementing a change in his way of thinking and his way of looking at life.

Another example is the role of women in Afghan society. The mere presence of Peace Corps girls who operate at basically the same level as men cannot help but change the role of

Afghan women, even though the change may be slight. One might say that the Peace Corps has no right to change the role of women, since, after all, it can be argued that cultural values are arbitrary and we have no right to say that our values are better than another culture's values. This, however, is to avoid the issue, since the mere presence of Peace Corps girls is a suggestion of a different way for women to act and therefore a suggestion for cultural change. This should be realized and not passed over lightly. Not that our behavior should be necessarily different because we can only be ourselves.

This, then, is what I see the Peace Corps working for. The Peace Corps has what one may call a special sensitivity to people that I find lacking in other agencies. As well as being an agency for technical assistance, the Peace Corps is aware of the social change involved and this awareness makes it unique.

Jack Coyle
Age: 25
Danbury, Connecticut
English Teacher and Arts & Crafts Teacher
21 months-in-country

There is an equation that has wandered unchecked in my person which still, after completing two years of service in the north part of this country, remains an enigma that I ponder in darkness. It is not an obstacle, but I've often wondered if the awareness was shared to any extent by my fellow Volunteers. I don't aspire to the image of Sir Lawrence, for isolation appalls me, and for that matter the filth in which I am often required to grovel does not "turn me on" in any way. Thereby evolves the equation: an agent of the swish western world, by the execution of free will, chooses to spend a considerable amount of time in the clime of the opposite extreme. And this equals what? As a point of reference, permit me to call it you and I, the Volunteer.

From the beginning you and I are subject to change as sensitive souls whose motives, if not very altruistic for the most part, then revolve about a genuine desire at self-improvement; undoubtedly there are motives as noble as these. The Volunteer in Afghanistan finds himself in a unique situation. The irregularity of Afghan terrain is perhaps significant of a popular temperament as unpredictable as a Kabul taxi cab. These people are capable of extending the most genuine hospitality and at the same time avail every opportunity for you to discover that East is East and West is West. They are capable of thieving you of material and emotion until you are pathetic, but won't leave until they have you laughing at what they've done.

Different Volunteers have different approaches to their work and varying structures for the execution of their ideals. It would be difficult to tie them all together in a way that would have everyone nodding yes. I would be interested in the forces at work on the free agent. Perhaps I can best deliver my intention by presenting some excerpts from a log maintained at random which hopefully will demonstrate most specifically the forces at large. Admittedly, the tone to the following is provincial.

--- The room is about ten square feet and presently there are forty-seven sweaty Afghans and three sweaty Americans in it. They are burning camel dung for fuel but the stove pipe leaks and our eyes are barely working with the stifling smelly heat and smoke. It is 99 degrees inside and -10 degrees below zero just outside, the door with no light for reading except some inadequate rays sneaking through a hole in the mud wall. We pass the time watching the rats run here and there six feet above us and then when we eat our ration of bread we spend time picking sand out of our teeth. The rest of the time everybody just looks at one another and hopes for the sound of a lorry coming off the pass. We've been here seven days now and if we ever get out of here, the hell with the Peace Corps.

--- The entire town gathered in a field and stayed on their knees for two hours as they prayed for rain. As they stretched before my eyes I suddenly realized an entire town could pray.

--- The first time John went to the bazaar someone shot at him with a Czech air rifle. He was examining the hole in the awning under which he had to stoop in order to talk with the shopkeeper.

--- I was once asked if I had ever taken any hashish. In all honesty I had to say "yes." It happened on a famous Afghan bus and the possibility of it ever occurring never failed to disconcert me. An Afghan, whom you couldn't consider out of order in any way, spit carelessly from the top of the bus and the second hand hashish came to settle upon my lips. As I remember, it smelled like fish, second hand of course.

--- The middle-aged koochi gingerly received the offered cigarette, bit off the filter and swallowed it, then lit up and smoked the remainder.

--- Quodsya was one of my eighteen year old, married seventh graders and a good student. One day she was having her difficulties during an English exam because my location in the room never afforded her the chance to assist her best friend, a few desks away. There is no more blatant co-op than an Afghan classroom at test time. Finally she ventured a move and I quickly swooped to intercept the evidence in mid-air. Such a case demanded instant firmness and Quodsya was reprimanded on the spot for betraying her teacher and classmates on a theme well drilled during the year. The upshot of it was that all thirty-two girls burst into violent tears which I was at a loss to remedy. I had attacked the emotional nucleus of the Afghan female and it ran out of control. The exam was cancelled that day and I've wondered ever since to just what extent their cooperation can be carried.

--- The fathers and brothers and sons are standing at a distance with hate and tears in their eyes. The tension is noticed everywhere. The men from the bus are standing in single file outside the tents of the nomad women, their sweaty palms nervously clenched about a fifty Af. Note. It is quiet here amidst the green dunes of spring and when the passengers are finished they walk through a mild drizzle toward the bus in silence. Do you understand poverty? It is very undignified.

--- There were two camels that men had introduced, then pitted against one another. For thirty minutes they leaned against one another in a noiseless, almost motionless test of strength. Suddenly the larger one fell on the smaller and the neck of the latter folded like a piece of loose leaf paper. In another minute it was over and almost everybody was entertained, everyone except the answer to our question, you and I. Possibly from this point we were a little less like you and I.

I haven't answered my own question, "What is the Volunteer?" It's much easier to delineate the atmosphere to which we're exposed. Maybe in Afghanistan we could say that the Volunteer is the agent at the mercy of the forces at large.

Betsy Thomas
Age: 23
Rye, New York
English Teacher
17 months-in-country

Thoughts of a city like Herat can keep one awake at night. At one time in its history Herat was a cultural center rivalled by few others. It was an oasis radiating philosophical contemplation, poetic expression, and creativity and imagination. Two of the greatest Sufi poets – Jami and Ansari – are buried in Herat. But today American Peace Corps Volunteers, as the only foreign influence, have the task of rekindling that same creativity and imagination that gave Herat its historical recognition. Volunteers everywhere work with people and therefore with minds; and it is the minds of Afghanistan that have suffered most from Mongol invasion, resultant poverty and isolation. The minds, the people, know the need for survival in a society of pressures. To survive they protect themselves, overly so, and the result is isolation and stagnancy.

Herat has always been halfway between Tehran and Kabul and until the 20th century its periods of allegiance to one or the other have never allowed a complete dependence on or security from the other. Only now are communications allowing the cooperation with the rest of Afghanistan necessary for progress, the utilization of the wealth hidden behind Herat's mud walls. The Iranian influence, however, is still strongly apparent in religion, music, dancing, and ideals of beauty. Herat still has several artists who produce the miniatures for which Persia was so famous.

Volunteers in Herat, teachers and nurses, face the frustrations and the rewards PCV's all expect. But we have learned that these problems are not ours alone. For us they are obstacles to our work – leading to anger and a feeling of impotence. But for the Afghans the problems of frozen attitudes, superstition and the constant fear of change mean heart-breaking delays in the process of modernization which they see as their only salvation. Our investment is minor in comparison to theirs and so must our disappointment be.

So in Herat we have jobs – bringing us a day of enjoyment, then a day of boredom and futility. We have friends – ones who discuss Islam, the changing politics and their own folk customs. But students are not yet free to visit their own friends, much less PCV's. Progress is indeed a direct function of the outlook of government officials. And no innovation is guaranteed existence. A library opened up by the one official may be closed by another – as a symbol of new authority.

Herat is in a pioneer stage. Natural beauty mingles wonderfully with ruins from better times. Roads are unpaved, dust flies high, water is bad and electricity is weak enough to guarantee several nights a week of romantic lantern light. Women who venture into public notice are few, and gossip is their reward. But they are there. They are contributing and Herat feels the need for their participation. They are pioneers, just as is a student who defends her PCV friend to hostile and suspicious classmates. In Herat we are indeed deeply involved with a culture foreign to our own. We are learning more than can be imagined. If we feel we are accomplishing little, it is because our time there is so short, because we are young and impatient, and because there is so much to be done.

Marylee Minehart
Age: 25
Fort Washington, Pennsylvania
Nurse
12 months-in-country

Thinking back on this year's work in Mazar, I can honestly say it that it has been one of the most rewarding, interesting, and challenging years of my life. The nursing school Helene and I started gives the appearance of being successful. Our ideas are accepted by the hospital staff and there also seems to be a desire on their part to improve the condition of the hospital.

It is difficult to explain how we gained the confidence, support and acceptance of the hospital staff in Mazar. We were the first foreigners sent to help improve this hospital and in some ways this was to our advantage. We did not have to continue programs already started – instead we could initiate our own.

In many respects it seemed like they accepted us without any effort on our part. When I think back upon our initial introduction to the situation, I know there was a strong effort put forth by both the Afghans and us. It was a two-sided game – neither team won or lost, both teams learned and gained through mistakes and understanding.

We arrived in Mazar at the end of December – and the middle of Ramazan – not exactly the best time of year for accomplishing anything. We were fortunate in one way. The Director of Health, Dr. Bashar Dost, had arrived only two months before us. Because he was in a new position, the fact that the weather was cold and he was fasting from sunrise to sunset did not curb his interest and enthusiasm for improving the conditions of the hospital, and our arrival perpetuated his desire for improvement. Although he was impetuous, sometimes to the point where it became exasperating to us, we gradually established a workable relationship with him.

The frustrating times occurred when we would go to see him in his little office to talk about a specific problem. It is no exaggeration that at the same time we were talking about obtaining some type of equipment or a discipline problem, ten other people were crowded into the room asking him to sign this or that, the telephone ringing in the middle of the conversation – and more people waiting outside to see him about something else. This is not an atypical situation. Coming from a society where appointments are made, conferences held at an exact time and a person expects to have the attention of the man with whom he is discussing plans or problems, it becomes extremely frustrating to compete with ten other people to get one problem solved.

It is hard to give "helpful hints" on establishing relationships with Afghans. Each person is different and affects other people differently. We found that by moving ahead slowly, being alert to feelings and responding to the emotional setting, we could achieve positive results.

Helene and I at first were extremely friendly and rather passive in our attitudes about the hospital. It is hard to believe that for the first month we spent numerous hours just trying to keep warm. The rest of the hospital staff was doing the same thing. Thus it was an excellent opportunity to become acquainted with the midwives, nanas and bachas. We almost ignored the hospital – instead we just talked about Afghan foods, our families, the weather, and numerous other subjects far removed from the problems of the hospital.

We could not help but notice the lack of care and attention the patients received, the apathetic attitude of the personnel, and the poor physical conditions of the hospital. These things were boldly apparent.

Here again we were fortunate. In Dr. Bashar Dost's impetuous way, we acquired fifteen young girls for the auxiliary nurse training program. It was through them and their needs that we acquired minimum amounts of necessary equipment. For example, syringes, needles, thermometers, disinfectant and cleaning materials like basins and rags. The students became our excuse for getting this equipment out from behind closed doors and being used in the hospital. Dr. Bashar Dost was kind enough to trust us with using this equipment and gave us "carte blanche" in dealing with the storehouse keeper and the pharmacist. These two people almost hold the key to success in themselves. If a Volunteer nurse cannot acquire the authority in dealing with the "holder of the keys," an extremely frustrating situation is created.

There were days when we felt completely defeated. I remember so vividly a cold day in March. We arrived at the hospital, our students were gathered around a dying patient who had been carried outside to die in the cold. The students just stood and watched, showed no emotion, and accepted the patient's death and the placement of the patient outside as a matter of fact.

As time passed, more patients have died, but strangely enough there have been occasional tears in the eyes of our students, and several times we have seen our students hold the hand of a patient in pain and offering comforting and assuring words to patients. These are not everyday events, but when it happens and we see it, every frustration, every curse word we uttered, every tear we shed for our own situation was quickly forgotten and a feeling of joy and accomplishment was felt.

It was easy to like and be liked by our students, but it was another thing to gain their respect. At first this friendly passive attitude we took was delightful. The students enjoyed us, we were no problem to the personnel, but we were also not getting very much accomplished in the way of setting up a daily routine or improving the physical conditions of the hospital. An attitude of indifference became more apparent in our students and the staff to the point of annoyance for us. It was then we decided to take action.

Our "charming" smiles were forgotten, we yelled, screamed and scolded everyone we saw, including doctors, midwives, nanas and students. It was sudden on our part, but it produced fantastic results. The Afghans became acutely aware of the fact that we were not here for the sheer joy of entertaining them. If they continued to want our help, we demanded cooperation – and we got it.

Periodically it is not a bad idea to arouse the people and remind them that you are here to help, not do all the work, not to take all the responsibility and that it is their hospital, not yours. We found this was best done after establishing a workable relationship with the people involved.

To be flexible, adjustable, observant and sensitive are the ways one can be happy working in Afghanistan. Just forget about time and let each day be a surprise. Think only of tomorrow, not the far future. These are things any Peace Corps Volunteer might hear over and over again in training, and although at the time they seem irrelevant, when you are in-country they are most helpful.

A letter of resignation

Mr. Walter Blass, Director
Peace Corps, Afghanistan
Kabul, Afghanistan

Dear Mr. Blass:

I hereby submit my resignation from Peace Corps, Afghanistan.

My reasons are as follows:

I entered Peace Corps service with the expectation of teaching and of working closely with the people here towards the improvement of hospital conditions and nursing care. I was assigned to a hospital that does not want us to teach and wishes only to use us as staff. We expected to be working with and through counterparts, thus facilitating some kind of permanent effect on the nurses and the type of care they give. We work alone. Nearly every suggestion of change we have proposed has been blocked, if not openly opposed or criticized.

I also entered service with a great deal of enthusiasm and felt that I had something creative to offer my job situation. My enthusiasm has appreciably decreased, and I feel I lack the creativity at the present time to plan a decent conference or lesson. I don't like these changes in myself.

I feel that imperative to a positive working situation is a deep sense of responsibility to the job and to one's fellow workers – and also in the context of my work, to one's patients. This factor, to my mind, must not be based merely on a self-imposed commitment to keep a promise, or to fill a slot for two years, but on a feeling of deep personal involvement in one's work, and a love of that involvement. It must be based on a desire to fulfill the needs of those people and that job, not a decision to "sit tight," or "stick it out."

To remain in this situation would be to betray this conviction.

I still have a deep love of my work and faith in my ability to do a good job. I don't blame Peace Corps for my inability to evidence this in my work here. I have seen Volunteers become embittered in their attitudes towards Peace Corps and themselves as Volunteers. I would prefer to leave with a faith in the ideals and goals of the Peace Corps, even if it is not a structure within which I function well. I want to leave feeling I have done a positive thing, which I do, and feeling that I have grown and benefitted from my work in the Peace Corps.

I have learned a great deal about Afghanistan and the Middle Eastern culture, and what it means to work and live in another country. Also, I understand a little better how changes come about, and what is involved in the process. I think I have profited in numerous ways from the time I have spent here, and from my work.

The Peace Corps staff has been extremely kind and helpful in assisting me in making my decision and in their interest before the decision was made.

Sincerely,

A letter requesting extension of service

September 25, 1966
Maimana, Afghanistan

Mr. Walter Blass
Peace Corps Director
Kabul, Afghanistan

Dear Mr. Blass:

Several months ago, while John Bing was visiting Maimana, I spoke with him concerning the possibilities and procedures for extending my Peace Corps service in Maimana for one more school year. John explained to me the necessity of forwarding two letters to you – one from myself officially requesting extension and enumerating my reasons for this; and the second from a supervisor requesting that my service be retained for the set period. In regard to this second point, Mr. Mohammad Ausee, the Director of Education in Fariab Province, has sent such a request to the Ministry of Education in Kabul, and they at the Ministry will forward it to your office.

I, myself, would like to use this letter to present my personal request for a one-year extension of service, from December '66 to December '67 to be serviced in Maimana, teaching English at Abu Faid Jausjani College.

My reasons are these:

First, comparing my job performance of both years of service I have, and I think correctly, seen an almost profound difference in the effects of my teaching <u>this</u> year as compared to my first year. I believe this change to be a definite improvement, and would like to give two years of <u>good</u> teaching to Maimana – as I originally agreed to when I entered the Peace Corps.

Second, I have found myself very favorably disposed for a career in TEFL, and would like to gain another year of experience in this field, picking up experience in teaching basic reading and handwriting. In several discussions this summer with Stan Huskey, I have decided to eventually do graduate work in TEFL and to use teaching experience here as a possible source of topic for a paper or thesis, with further advice from Mr. Huskey.

Third, it is just recently that I have been able to engage in an outside project in which I have been interested for some time, namely the Boy Scouts. I would like to put in some real time with these boys next year, as I am already the assistant Boy Scout "Teacher."

Fourth, I personally love Maimana very much and think it offers excellent, almost unparalleled opportunities for Peace Corps work. I am very happy here.

There, Sir, are my reasons for my request of extension of service for one year. They are as sincere and honest as I am confident that I can give an ever better <u>third</u> year of service to Afghanistan and the Peace Corps.

Thank you, Sir, for your consideration. I am yours sincerely,

John J. Wall, Jr.

THE SOURCES

In-person conversations Italicized dialogue in the text, which has been extensively reorganized and edited for clarity and accuracy, comes from these conversations.

Interview with Robert L. and Margaret (Bob and Sherry) Steiner, Lancaster, Pennsylvania, December 2 and 3, 2011. Follow-up editing session, Lancaster, Pennsylvania, September 6 and 7, 2012.

Pat Sullivan Meyers, PC desk officer for Afghanistan, September 12, 2013.

Emails Italicized contributions in the text also come from the following emails, which have also been edited for clarity and accuracy.

Betsy Thomas Amin-Arsala, member of PC/A Group VI, April 2 and May 15, 2013.

Dennis Aronson, member of PC/A Group III, June 21, 27, 28, and July 25, 2013.

Robert S. McClusky, PC/A deputy director, July 22, 23 and 24, 2013.

David McGaffey, member of PC/A Group IV, September 13, 2013.

Sami Noor, PC/A staff member, responses to questions from Bob Steiner, November 20 and 21, 2011.

Leonard Oppenheim, member of PC/A Group IV, May 20, 2013, which attaches his letter of Nov. 7, 14, 1964; July 22, which attaches his letter of March 6, 1965.

Rosalind Pace, member of PC/A Group I, November 4, 2011.

Bob Pearson, member of PC/A Group I and later desk and training officer, January 27, October 18, 2012.

Chip Steiner, email comments on transcript and attached memories. February 7 and 23, 2012.

Jon Wicklund, member of PC/A Group II, January 12 and 14, 2013.

Peace Corps Afghanistan 1962-1966 This section lists material, mostly prepared by PC Afghanistan or PC Washington or otherwise produced by former Volunteers and staff which we used in documenting this period. Those obtained from the National Archives are listed separately below. Also see later section on additional memoirs by Volunteers who served in Afghanistan primarily during other time periods. We are sure this and the later section are incomplete and look forward to learning that there is more material available.

Afghan IV: A Peace Corps Experience. DVD using slide show originally prepared by David Lemery for 25th reunion. Distributed at 2010 Group IV reunion thanks to Len Oppenheim.

Afghanistan, *Peace Corps Volunteer,* Vol. 1, No. 4, April 1963, 6-7.

Afghanistan, Jon Wicklund, ed. *Peace Corps Volunteer,* Vol. 2, No. 3, January 1964, 10-21.

Afghanistan, Peace Corps Program. Agreement effected by exchange of notes. Signed at Kabul September 6 and 11, 1962, Entered into force September 11, 1962. 13 UST 2100 (1962).

Betsy Thomas Amin-Arsala, "The Baths of Herat: Purdah's hidden place of freedom," *WorldView,* Vol. 14, No. 4, Fall 2001, 38-42.

Dennis Aronson, Adventures in Afghanistan, PowerPoint presentation for Life-Long Learning, Fort Lewis College, Durango, Colorado, April 20, 2009.

Brent Ashabranner, *A Moment in History: The First Ten Years of the Peace Corps* (New York: Doubleday, 1971).

Judy Bowsman and Janet Walback, *Mister, where you go?* Reproduced in Part II of this book, this collection presents reflections by Volunteers aimed at explaining to trainees what it was like to serve in Afghanistan. GSA PC 67-6147. 52 pages.

Louis Dupree, "Moving Mountains in Afghanistan," chapter 6, pp. 107-124, in Robert B. Textor, ed., *Cultural Frontiers of the Peace Corps,* Cambridge, MA: The M.I.T. Press, 1966, pp. 107-124. The chapter (and the rest of the book) can be downloaded at www.stanford.edu/~rbtextor/Cultural_Frontiers_of_the_ Peace_Corps.pdf. The quotations from Dupree in the text of this piece are from "Moving Mountains," much of which also appeared earlier in a paper about the Peace Corps: Louis Dupree, "The Peace Corps in Afghanistan: The Impact of the Volunteers on the Country and of the Country on the Volunteers," American Universities Field Staff, October 1964. This version is also now available online through the Peace Corps Digital Library.

David Fleishhacker tells the story of the first group of Volunteers in *Lessons from Afghanistan*, DFPublications, 2001. 153 pages. The italicized Fleishhacker quotes come from this book. In telling the story of the first Volunteers, he catches the nuances of cultural tensions between Americans and Afghans. On page 4 he writes: "I felt a need to explain Afghanistan to Americans and, as I sat down and started to do that, I found myself explaining America to myself. . . . This book is about a country I love, what it once was like, and what we need to understand in order to help it revive."

Leslie Hanscom, "The Magic of Caring," *The Peace Corps Reader,* September 1967, pp.11-15. Describes the work of Peace Corps nurses in Afghanistan. Hanscom joined the Peace Corps Division of Evaluation in 1965 and became its director in the fall of 1966. He conducted the completion of service conference for Group IV in April/May 1966.

Saul Helfenbein, A Memoir of Development. Personal communication of a draft including PC/Afghanistan experience in Group VIII which was followed by a career in health development, May 2013.

Roy Hoopes, "An Idea Whose Time Had Come," *The Peace Corps Reader*, October 1966, pp. 6-9. It was Hoopes who connected Steiner with Shriver. This piece is excerpted from Hoopes' *Complete Peace Corps Guide,* 1965 Revised Edition, first published by Dial Press in 1961.

Frances Hopkins, "A Capital: the toughest place to excel," *Peace Corps Volunteer*, September 1966, pp. 11-13. A piece on serving as a Volunteer in Kabul in a special issue of the Peace Corps magazine on The Peace Corps in the City.

Letters from Peace Corps Nurses, 1967. This recruiting booklet now available through the Peace Corps Digital Library includes letters by a dozen nurses describing their work in almost that many countries. One is from Margarete V. Silberberg writing about her experience in Afghanistan between 1964 and 1966. http://collection.peacecorps.gov/cdm/singleitem/collection/p9009coll13/id/24/rec/1.

Robert S. McClusky, Peace Corps Afghanistan. Recorded transcript of presentation made at Kendal at Oberlin, Oberlin, Ohio, February 18, 2010.

David and Elizabeth McGaffey, *Letters From a Vanished Country: Afghanistan 1964-1967.* Their letters from Farah. Also see oral history interview with David McGaffey by Charles Stewart Kennedy for the Association for Diplomatic Studies and Training, September 1995, at http://adst.org/oral-history/country-reader-series.

Stanley Meisler, *When the World Calls: The Inside Story of the Peace Corps and its First Fifty Years.* Boston: Beacon Press, 2011. Meisler was deputy director under Charlie Peters of the Peace Corps Office of Evaluation and Research. He quotes Hanscom on Peace Corps nurses in Afghanistan in a chapter titled "Does the Peace Corps Do Any Good?"

Peace Corps Afghanistan Volunteer Newsletters, Vol. 1, No. 1, Nov. 1964; No. 6, April 1965; No. 7, May-June 1965; No. 8, July 1965; No. 9, Sept.-Oct. 1965; December 1965 (no volume or issue numbers starting with this edition); May 1966, June 1966. Also, minutes of Liaison Committee (July 28, 1965). Assorted memoranda from PC/Afghanistan staff in February and March 1966.

Peace Corps Afghanistan, Handbook, Kabul, 1964-1965. 38 pages.

Peace Corps, 4th Annual Peace Corps Report, June 30, 1965. The third chapter, "Four Years: Past and Present," uses Afghanistan as an example. See pp. 19-25.

Rosalind Pearson and Janet Bing, Cross-Cultural Studies Manual for Afghanistan Training Programs. Dr. and Mrs. Louis Dupree, consultants. Washington, D.C., 1967. The Peace Corps Evaluation Division sponsored development of such manuals by returned PC Volunteers and anthropologists to get at areas of cultural conflict in different countries.

John Steiner, "Bob Steiner, First Afghanistan Country Director," *Afghan Connections,* Friends of Afghanistan, September 2011.

James Tobin, JFK at the Union: The unknown story of the Peace Corps speech, January 15, 2008. http://michigantoday. umich.edu/2008/jan/jfk.php.

See also the Peace Corps Digital Library, http://collection. peacecorps.gov., On that site, click on "Browse All," then click on any collection listed on the left-hand side of the page that you do not wish to include in your search. Then enter "Afghanistan" (or "Kabul" or other entry) in the search box. For example, a search for "Afghanistan" in the collections of Congressional and legislative materials; historical papers and articles; newsletters; press briefings; speeches, essays, and letters; staff stories; and Volunteer stories on August 2, 2013, produced 74 results. For this project, for example, we first identified some articles in the *Peace Corps Volunteer* from 1963-1970 in this library, and also found the Peace Corps fiscal year presentations to Congress. As the guidance for using the digital library says, it is a work in progress— and additional items of interest appeared during the time we were working on this project. However, it does not purport to be a comprehensive archive of Peace Corps historical material.

Peace Corps records related to Afghanistan in the National Archives

Friends of Afghanistan website: For information on Peace Corps Afghanistan History Project prepared by Steve Nadler, go to http://afghanconnections.org and click on link under Member Projects on the left. In his "Memo Research 409," Nadler lists the documents he made copies of during his visit to the National Archives II (8601 Adelphi Road, College Park, Maryland) in April 2010, based on entering "Peace Corps Afghanistan" in the Archives search engine, http://arcweb.Archives.gov.

Will Irwin visited the National Archives in January 2013 to check some sources listed by Stanley Meisler in *When the World Calls: The Inside Story of the Peace Corps and its First*

Fifty Years. He found that the records of the Peace Corps files are listed in Record Group 490. Some of the "MLR" numbers listed in the binder for Record Group 490 have changed. For example, the MLR Number for "Close of Service Conference Reports, compiled 1963-1979" has changed from "A1 23" to "P 63", but Archives' consultants are very helpful in finding the new listings and in assisting in the filling out of Reference Service Slips requesting particular files. The descriptions of the contents of particular files are not always accurate; for example, P 63 contains close of service conference reports only through 1966 (Group IV).

The documents located are:

Peace Corps Director's Staff Meeting, 9:30 AM, Thursday, February 15, 1962. 5 pages. Cleo Shook, who had taught and then worked with technical assistance programs in Kabul in the 1950s and was in early 1962 working with Peace Corps Washington, reported on his trip to Afghanistan to discuss a possible program there.

Memorandum to Robert Sargent Shriver, Director, from Robert Steiner, Acting PC Representative, Report from Kabul, Afghanistan, February 21, 1963. 2 pages. Steiner describes the change in six months in PCVs and the Afghan view of them.

Overseas Evaluation, Afghanistan, March 1963, 30 pages, by Thorburn Reid. A report after the first six months.

Afghanistan I Completion of Service Conference Report, conducted on May 7, 8, and 9, 1964, by Dr. Harold H. Morris, Jr., Consultant.

Afghanistan II Completion of Service Conference Report, conducted on December 10, 11, and 12, 1964, by David Schimmel, PE&R. Includes an Addendum, PC/Washington Follow-up, by Warren Kinsman, DVS.

Afghanistan III Completion of Service Conference Report, conducted on September 2-4, 1965, by Sidney L. Werkman, M.D., PC/W, and Lee Bomberger, PC/Nepal. Report submitted by Sidney L. Werkman, M.D.

Afghanistan IV-A Completion of Service Conference Report, conducted on April 28-30, 1966, by Leslie Hanscom, PC/ Washington, Office of Evaluation and Research, and Robert Satin, PC/Washington, Office of Programming and Planning Review. Report submitted by Leslie Hanscom; this report covered 23 PCVs who were in a wide variety of occupations.

Afghanistan IV-B Completion of Service Conference Report, conducted on May 1-3, 1966, by L. R. Satin, PC/Washington, Office of Planning and Program Review, and Leslie Hanscom, PC/ Washington, Office of Evaluation and Research. Report submitted by L. R. Satin; this report covered 25 PCVs who were teachers.

Memorandum for all NANESA Country Directors from R.L. Steiner, Regional Director, NANESA, Thoughts from an Itinerant Regional Director. February 6, 1969. 6 pages. Besides discussing the goals of Peace Corps and ways to measure them, this memo also says that PC/Washington is reviewing all its regulations to end paternalism whenever possible including areas such as leave policy, petty cash disbursements, and training as well as considering more bi-nationalism in staffing.

Edwin Wright In writing about Ed Wright, Steiner's mentor, we used a brochure: Edwin Milton Wright, Ninetieth Birthday Observance, January 12, 1897, organized by the Northeast Ohio Committee on Middle East Understanding, at Richfield Holiday Inn, Richfield, Ohio, January 10, 1987. Also see Grace Schantz, "He's Helped to Write History During his 90 Years." *The* [Wooster] *Daily Record,* Jan. 17, 1987, B1.

Afghanistan in the 1960s To check our memory of Afghanistan in the early 1960s, we relied on:

Afghanistan: Some New Approaches, George Grassmuck, Ludwig Adamec, with Frances Irwin, editors, University of Michigan Center for Near Eastern and North African Studies, 1969. This collection includes contributions from two writers, Dunning Wilson and Patrick Reardon, who had served as Peace Corps Volunteers, as well as a chronology that covers the period.

Louis Dupree, *Afghanistan*. Princeton, NJ: Princeton University Press, 1973. An anthropologist who started working in Afghanistan in 1959, Dupree often participated in Peace Corps training.

The *Kabul Times,* published by the Afghan Government Press of the Ministry of Information and Culture, for the years 1964-1967. Also the source for two articles reproduced in Part II.

The Kabul Times Annual 1967, Nour M. Rahimi, ed., Kabul, Afghanistan: Kabul Times Publishing Agency, 1967.

Nancy Hatch Wolfe in collaboration with Ahmad Ali Kohzad, *An Historical Guide to Kabul*. Kabul, Afghan Tourist Organization, 1965.

These more recent publications expanded our understanding of Afghanistan in the 1960s:

Thomas Barfield, *Afghanistan: A Cultural and Political History*. Princeton, NJ: Princeton University Press, 2010.

Afghanistan: A Country Study, Peter R. Blood, ed., Federal Research Division, Library of Congress, Washington, D.C. 1997.

Ehsan M. Entezar, *Afghanistan: Understanding Afghan Culture 101*. Xlibris, 2007. Entezar also wrote the first text for teaching Dari for Peace Corps Afghanistan. In this later volume, he outlines the differences between Afghan and American cultures.

Barnett R. Rubin, *The Fragmentation of Afghanistan: State Formation & Collapse in the International System*. Yale University, 1995. Particularly Part I on the "Old Regime: State, Society, and Politics."

Amin Saikal, *Modern Afghanistan: A History of Struggle and Survival*. I. B. Tauris, London, 2012 revised. Saikal relies on Ravan Farhadi as a source and mentor. A colleague, Kirill Nourzhanov, helped Saikal through his knowledge of Russian sources.

Saif R. Samady, *Education and Afghan Society in the twentieth century*. United Nations Educational, Scientific and Cultural Organization, Education Sector, Paris, November 2001. Available at www.unesco.org. See also "Changing Profile of Education in Afghanistan," a paper by Samady published in 2013 and available at www.eslus.com/articles/Ed-Afghanistan.

Astri Suhrke, *When More is Less: The International Project in Afghanistan.* New York: Columbia University Press, 2011. In writing about the future, she includes a brief analysis of the 1960s.

Shaista Wahab and Barry Youngerman, *A Brief History of Afghanistan.* Infobase Publishing, 2007.

Two online archives are also a source of materials about Afghanistan:

The Afghanistan Digital Library, Preserving and Creating Access to Unique Afghan Records, is being developed by the University of Arizona Libraries in collaboration with the Afghanistan Center at Kabul University. See www.afghandata.org. This includes a digital record of the *Kabul Times*, although some copies are missing.

The Arthur Paul Collection at the Criss Library, University of Nebraska at Omaha, is an important source of documents about Afghanistan. See http://world.unomaha.edu/cas/projects collection.

Afghanistan in more recent years We found these books provided insight into more recent years:

Akbar Ahmed, *The Thistle and the Drone.* Washington, D.C.: Brookings Institution Press, 2013.

Sarah Chayes, *The Punishment of Virtue: Inside Afghanistan after the Taliban.* New York: Penguin Press, 2006.

Nancy Hatch Dupree, *Afghanistan over a Cup of Tea: 46 Chronicles.* Markus Hakansson, ed., Swedish Committee for Afghanistan, 2007.

Ashraf Ghani and Clare Lockhart, *Fixing Failed States: A Framework for Rebuilding a Fractured World*. Oxford and New York: Oxford University Press, 2008.

Qais Akbar Omar, *A Fort of Nine Towers: An Afghan Family Story*. New York: Farrar, Strauss and Giroux, 2013.

Stories about Peace Corps Afghanistan More stories about Peace Corps Afghanistan are being published. This section lists those we found which primarily cover later periods. Two sources are the Friends of Afghanistan newsletter *Afghan Connections* and Peace Corps Worldwide at www.peacecorpsworldwide.org, which covers Peace Corps history and all programs around the world. We are struck by both the continuities and the changes in watching and reading stories about all periods of Peace Corps Afghanistan.

Chris Ballard, "The Wizard of Kabul," *Sports Illustrated,* July 22, 2013, 55-63. A story about Tom Gouttierre and his experience coaching basketball in Afghanistan when he and his wife Marylu served as members of Group V and later in the nine years they spent in Afghanistan. Since 1974, Gouttierre has been the director of the Center for Afghanistan Studies at the University of Nebraska Omaha.

Walter P. Blass, Glimpses of Afghanistan: A Country Director looks back on the 1960's http://peacecorpsonline.org/messages/messages/2629/2016140.html. Blass followed Steiner as director.

Beryl Brinkman, "Women of the Hazarajat," *WorldView,* Vol. 14, No. 4, Fall 2001, 20-22.

Janet Colberg, "Absence of Smiles: How a baby girl entered Afghanistan," *WorldView*, Vol. 14, No. 4, Fall 2001, 35-36.

Dennis Egan, "Songs of Love: Everyone waited for the speeches to end," *WorldView*, Vol. 14, No. 4, Fall 2001, 45-46.

Maggie Eccles and Lynne Lafroth for Afghan 15, "Taking Out Smallpox," in ed. Jane Albritton, *Even the Smallest Crab Has Teeth: 50 Years of Amazing Peace Corps Stories*, Volume Four: Asia and the Pacific (Palo Alto: Travelers' Tales, 2011), 120-130.

Natalie Firnhaber, "Rules of the Chadri," *WorldView*, Vol. 14, No. 4, Fall 2001, 18-19.

Susan Fox, *Little Women of Baghlan: The Story of a Nursing School for Girls in Afghanistan, the Peace Corps, and Life Before the Taliban*, A Peace Corps Writers Book, 2013. Based on the experience of Joanne Carter Bowling from 1968-70.

Eloise Hanner, *Letters from Afghanistan*, Wellesley, MA: Branden Books, 2003. These are letters to her mother beginning in 1971.

Thomas Gouttierre, "Roses and Clay: Witness to the misfortunes of poets and warriors," *WorldView*, Vol. 14, No. 4, Fall 2001, 27-30.

Frank Light, "Back to School," in ed. Jane Albritton, *Even the Smallest Crab Has Teeth: 50 Years of Amazing Peace Corps Stories*, Volume Four: Asia and the Pacific (Palo Alto: Travelers' Tales, 2011), 15-24.

Ed Madinger, "The Power Class," *WorldView,* Vol. 14, No. 4, Fall 2001, 19-20.

Janice Minott, *Letters from Kabul 1966-1968.* www.trafford.com.

David Moats, "Just a Bend in the Road: Dealing with the uluswal, the mamur and the wakil," *WorldView,* Vol. 14, No. 4, Fall 2001, 54-58.

Ruth Kesselring Royal and Beryl A. Brinkman, *Never Gonna Cease My Wanderin': Letters Between Friends,* A Peace Corps Writers Book, 2012. Pages 194-236 cover Beryl Brinkman's service in Afghanistan from 1967-1969.

John Sumser, *A Land Without Time: A Peace Corps Volunteer in Afghanistan.* Chicago: Academy Chicago Publishers, 2006. Sumser served in the last years that Peace Corps was in Afghanistan. He tells about teaching in Laghman, Tashkurgan, and Kabul and being caught up in the coup in 1978.

John D. Tobias, "Snapshots from the Graveyard of Empires," in ed. Jane Albritton, *Even the Smallest Crab Has Teeth: 50 Years of Amazing Peace Corps Stories,* Volume Four: Asia and the Pacific (Palo Alto: Travelers' Tales, 2011), 241-246.

Jill Vickers, Jody Bergedick, and Katherine Wheatley, *Once in Afghanistan,* a documentary by Dirt Road Documentaries, 2008. Available through www.dirtroaddocumentaries.com. It tells the story of the women who served in Peace Corps as vaccinators in a World Health Organization Program in 1969. Vickers has posted later insights in a blog also called *Once in Afghanistan* at www.peacecorpsworldwide.org.

Bill Witt, "The Goldsmith of Kandahar," *WorldView*, Vol. 14, No. 4, Fall 2001, 22-25.

Bill Witt, "Boy in a Mulberry Tree: What a shepherd remembers, others only read," *WorldView*, Vol. 14, No. 4, Fall 2001, 31-32.

ABOUT THE AUTHORS

Fran and Will Irwin *(Credit: Nancy Walker)*

Fran and Will met as Peace Corps Volunteers in Kabul in March 1966. After returning to the U.S. from Afghanistan in 1967, Fran worked for the Cleveland *Plain Dealer*. They married in 1968 as Will started law school at the University of Michigan, where he had gotten his AB in American Culture. Fran, with a BA in history from the College of Wooster and an MA from the Fletcher School of Law and Diplomacy, worked in the university's international programs office and co-edited a book on Afghanistan as Will finished his law degree. After a year in Germany as Will researched water law, they moved to Vermont, where Will worked for the Vermont Water Resources Board and Fran with the Vermont Natural Resources Council – and where their daughter was born. In 1973, they moved to Washington, D.C., where Fran has worked for four decades in environmental policy at The Conservation Foundation, the World Wildlife Fund, and the World Resources Institute. After five years with the Environmental Law Institute, Will served as an administrative judge for the U.S. Department of the Interior from 1978-2006, deciding appeals involving surface coal mining, public lands, and natural resources. Fran and Will live in Bethesda, Maryland, and water their roots in Ohio and Iowa.

Made in the USA
Lexington, KY
24 August 2014